The Life, Voyages, and Exploits of Admiral Sir Francis Drake

With Numerous Original Letters from Him and the Lord High Admiral to the Queen and Great Officers of State

By John Barrow

PANTIANOS
CLASSICS

Published by Pantianos Classics

ISBN-13: 978-1-78987-509-6

First published in 1843

Sir Francis Drake, as depicted by Antoine Maurin, 1793-1860

From the Wellcome Library, no. 2606i

Contents

Preface

AMONG the number of distinguished characters which the reign of Queen Elizabeth produced, the name of SIR FRANCIS DRAKE must always hold a prominent place. Born of humble parents, and thrown upon the world, in early youth, as a common seaman, by honest industry, by perseverance and resolution in overcoming difficulties, and by unflinching courage, he rose in gradual succession to the highest rank in the Naval Service, and to the honour of knighthood bestowed by the Sovereign; "an honour," says Johnson, "in that illustrious reign, not made cheap by prostitution, nor ever bestowed without uncommon merit." It will not be denied that the Life of such a man must supply matters of great interest, of curiosity, and of profitable example.

But the little volume, that is now presented to the public, may perhaps by some be deemed a work of supererogation, as most of the events of his public life have been carefully collected and described by contemporary historians, and remodelled by others of more recent date. Be it so; yet I may be permitted to say, that much still remained to be discovered and told; in point of fact, in all the scenes, the acts, and adventures of this extraordinary man, the first Englishman that circumnavigated the globe, or, as one of his historians says, the first "who ploughed a furrow round the world," we have nothing, or next to nothing, published of his own writing, not even a common sea-journal, with the exception of a few sentences in his third voyage, revised by himself; yet how much is discovered of the real character of a man from his epistolary correspondence! The difficulty was, where to look for it? Obviously in the public depositories of the records of the kingdom, and accordingly to these I made application.

In the first instance, I received a most ready permission, by the kindness of Sir James Graham, to have free access to the State Paper Office, where I was well assured there would be found something to my purpose; and also in the numerous collections of manuscripts in the British Museum. From these sources I calculated on receiving much additional and unpublished information; and by the obliging assistance of Sir Henry Ellis, in the latter, and of Messrs. Lechmere and Lemon, in the former, (as also from Mr. Thorpe, who obligingly took the trouble to collate my copies with the almost illegible manuscripts,) so far from being disappointed, I have obtained numbers of autograph letters, not only of Sir Francis Drake, but also of the Lord High Admiral, the Earl of Effingham, more particularly those relating to the Spanish Armada, miscalled "the Invincible;" together with many other documents connected with the public transactions of Sir Francis Drake.

My next application was to Sir Francis Palgrave, who says there is nothing at the Tower, so early as the reign of Elizabeth, among the Admiralty Papers, but thinks there may be something in the Rolls'-House relating to payments, but observes that the search would be laborious, as there are no indexes.

From the Bodleian Library the answer was, nothing new to interest a biographer of the gallant Sir Francis Drake.

In the Ashmolean Museum there are a few notices, but only such as have already appeared in print.

At the Magdalen College, Cambridge, there are numerous and voluminous documents collected or composed by Mr. Pepys, chiefly relating to naval matters, but little or nothing has been found concerning Drake.

To Mr. Bolton Corney, a private gentleman of great literary acquirements and research, I am highly indebted for the loan of several valuable and rare tracts, besides detached notes of information on points connected with my subject, for which I am desirous of thus publicly acknowledging my sincere thanks, more especially for the ready and willing manner in which they were communicated.

There is still, however, a remarkable deficiency of materials, of a private or domestic nature; and as the family may be considered extinct, or at least only continued in the female line, there is but little hope that any such are likely hereafter to be forthcoming.

I have not however failed to apply to every quarter wherein any information was in the least likely to be procured. To Sir Thos. Trayton Fuller Eliott Drake, Bart., the nephew (I believe) of the late Lord Heathfield, to whose property he has succeeded, with a patent from the King to take the names of Eliott and Drake, after that of Fuller, and to bear the arms of Drake, I made application. His reply was that he had nothing whatever but some relics that were given to Drake by Queen Elizabeth, an account of which has been published.

As Sir Francis Drake was much in communication with the Lord Treasurer Burleigh, and had frequent correspondence with him, I applied through a friend of the Marquis of Salisbury to have access to the Burleigh Papers, at Hatfield House, or to know what was the nature or extent of the documents relating to Drake. The reply was that it would be a long time before the catalogue was finished, and that his Lordship must decline to let any person have unlimited access to the papers, but as soon as they are completely arranged, his Lordship would let me know how far he could contribute to my object.

My next application was to the Marquis of Exeter, who was supposed as likely to be in possession of documents connected with Drake or his family; his reply was that he had sent all his papers to Lord Salisbury. Thus then these memorials, whatever they may be, are and have been closed up for two centuries and a half, since the death of this extraordinary man, as it were in a *mare clausum, in* or *out* of which he, when living, never suffered himself to be confined or excluded.

In transcribing the autograph letters of the Lord High Admiral and of Sir Francis Drake, I have as much as possible rigidly adhered to the phraseology and the spelling, which can scarcely be called systematic orthography, the same words being frequently written differently, at different times, and in the same letter. I thought it best to give a *facsimile* to all of these documents, without any change, with the exception only of the writing, which is inimitably obscure, and so difficult to read, that a good deal of practice is necessary to be able to do even that, as will appear by inspecting the letter, which is a lithographic facsimile of that of Drake, printed in page 145, and which is a correct specimen of his usual handwriting, and among the best, that is, the most legible, I could find.

Chapter One - Expedition of Hawkins to the West Indies - 1567-1568

It is the peculiar advantage of a British-born subject, that lowness of birth alone is no absolute bar nor disqualification for the attainment of wealth and honours; and the impediments, that are thrown in the way of advancement, are not of such a nature but may be overcome by steady good conduct, honest zeal, activity, perseverance, and, above all, by a determined resolution to surmount difficulties, and stand up manfully against misfortune; resolution being, as Dr. Johnson says, success. Of the happy effects of such conduct the life of Sir Francis Drake affords a striking and memorable example.

"This Drake," says Camden, "(to relate no more than what I have heard from himself) was born of mean parentage in Devonshire, and had Francis Russell (afterwards Earl of Bedford) for his godfather, who, according to the custom, gave him his Christian name. Whilst he was yet a child, his father, embracing the Protestant doctrine, was called in question by the law of the Six Articles made by Henry VIII. against the Protestants, fled his country, and withdrew himself into Kent" [1] "for," says Prince, "the sting of Popery still remained in England, though the teeth thereof were knocked out, and the Pope's supremacy abolished." [2]

In the dedication, "To the courteous Reader," of the relation of the 'Voyage Revived,' by Sir Francis Drake (the nephew), he gives some information of the family. "Honest reader, without apologie, I desire thee in this insuing discourse to observe with me the power and justice of the Lord of Hostes, who could enable so meane a person to right himself upon so mighty a prince, together with the goodness and providence of God, very observable, in that it pleased him to raise this man, not only from a low condition, but even from the state of persecution; his father suffered in it, being forced to fly from his house (neere South Tavistocke in Devon) into Kent, and there to inhabit in the hull of a shippe, wherein many of his younger sonnes were born; hee had twelve in all, and as it pleased God to give most of them a being upon the water, so the greatest part of them dyed at sea; the youngest, though he were as far as any, yet dyed at home, whose posterity inherits that which by himself, and this noble gentleman the eldest brother, was hardly, yet worthily gotten."

"After the death of King Henry," continues Camden, "he (the father) got a place among the seamen in the King's Navy, to read prayers to them; and soon after he was ordained Deacon, and made Vicar of the Church of Upnore upon the river Medway, (the road where the fleet usually anchoreth). But by reason of his poverty he put his son to the master of a bark, with which he used to coast along the shore, and sometimes to carry merchandise into Zeland and France.

"The youth, being painful and diligent, so pleased the old man by his industry, that, being a bachelor, at his death he bequeathed his bark unto him by will and testament." [3]

This honourable reward of his service is, as Dr. Johnson observes, "a circumstance that deserves to be remembered, not only as it may illustrate the private character of this brave man, but as it may hint to all those who may hereafter propose his conduct for their imitation, that virtue is the surest foundation both of reputation and fortune, and that the first step to greatness is *to be honest.*" [4]

The simple account given by Drake to Camden might be supposed to settle the question as to his parentage, coming as it does directly from himself, and recorded by one of the ablest and most faithful of our old historians: it sets aside the story of his father Edmund being merely a sailor; and the account that, when he retired into Kent, he inhabited the hull of a ship, in which several of the younger of his twelve sons were born, has been confirmed by his grandson Sir Francis Drake.

What indeed could a sailor have to do with the Six Articles, to make it necessary for him to fly from his country? He was more probably one who, in those days, bore the title of Preacher or Minister, who had received holy orders, but was without church preferment, and engaged in giving instruction to the neighbouring people, and reading prayers to them. Be that as it may, he must have been a well-educated man, if it be true that he was ordained Deacon, and then, as is said, was inducted to the vicarage of Upnore, on the river Medway. At any rate, it can scarcely be supposed that such a man, giving instruction to others, would neglect the education of his own twelve sons. We shall see, in the course of this memoir, abundant proof if good sense, correct expression, and sound argument will be admitted as proof that Sir Francis Drake was a man of superior education, and that two or three of his brothers, who partook of his adventures, were by no means deficient.

There is, however, some inconsistency in the foregoing account, as indeed has been noticed by the able editors of the *Biographia Britannica,* who observe, "if Drake was in his tender years, or childhood, when his father was persecuted on the score of the Six Articles, he must have been born a good while before the year 1539; and if so, how could Sir Francis Russell be his godfather, who was himself born in 1527?" Perhaps at that time they might not be very strict as to the age of sponsors; however, he certainly was not born a "good while" before 1539, but in, or after, 1539: there is an original portrait of him in Buckland Abbey, painted *Anno Domini* 1594; *aetatis suae* 53. According to this he must have been born in 1541, and Lord Francis Russell was then 14. But there is also a beautiful miniature portrait by Hilliard, sold lately at Strawberry Hill, and now in possession of the Earl of Derby, under which is written *Aetatis suae* 42; *Anno Dom.* 1581: which gives 1539 for the date of his birth. There is a doubt also of the name of the father, as it appears by the pedigree to be Robert (instead of Edmund), the third son of

John Drake of Otterton; but of the father we hear nothing whatever in the course of the numerous narratives published of the son's adventures, nothing where this old patriarch of twelve sons died, or when, or how he died; no memorial of him seems to have been left to posterity. But there is another mistake respecting the father: there is not now, nor ever was, either church or chapel at Upnor, but a small castle was built there by Elizabeth to protect the anchorage. At the present day there is a village of little cottages, inhabited chiefly by brickmakers. These points are of no further importance than as matters of fact.

For some time, it appears, young Drake continued to carry on his late master's line of traffic. But the narrow seas were too confined a prison for so large and aspiring a mind. He therefore sold his bark, and by the advice of Captain John Hawkins, a bold and adventurous seaman (who is called his kinsman, wherefore does not appear), was induced to try his fortune with him on a venture to the West Indies, in which he embarked the whole of his little property; a voyage that turned out disastrous enough for both, and one from which they both appear to have narrowly escaped with life.

Captain John Hawkins had previously made two voyages to Guinea and the West Indies, purchasing Negro slaves at the first place, and selling them to the Spaniards at the latter; - a trade that was carried on by virtue of a treaty, still subsisting, between Henry VIII. and Charles V. So far was this traffic then considered from being infamous, that every encouragement was given to it by Queen Elizabeth, who took Hawkins into her service, made him Paymaster of the Navy, and, to mark her sense of obligation and favour, gave him a coat of arms, "whose crest was a demi-moor properly coloured, bound by a cord," - the very symbol which, more than two hundred years afterwards, was made use of as a vehicle to stamp infamy and disgrace on those concerned in it, as well as abhorrence and detestation of the traffic itself, - that same traffic which, when carried on successfully, conferred, as we see in the case of Hawkins, badges of honour in the days of Elizabeth. That the adventurous spirit of Drake should have induced him cheerfully to join a man who had always been kind to him, and who was engaged in large mercantile concerns, on a voyage to the West Indies, cannot be wondered at. "Nothing," says Dr. Johnson, "was talked of among the mercantile or adventurous part of mankind but the beauty and riches of this new world. Fresh discoveries were frequently made, new countries and nations, never heard of before, were daily described; and it may easily be concluded that the relators did not diminish the merit of their attempts, by suppressing or diminishing any circumstance that might produce wonder or excite curiosity." [5]

These relations and descriptions were entirely congenial with Drake's feelings, as offering a field for adventure; and the idea of sharing the dangers and the fortunes of one, who had always befriended him in his earlier days, removed all doubt and hesitation from his mind, and induced him cordially to contribute his little all towards the equipment of the expedition.

But Drake was in fact already acquainted (to what extent we know not) with the West Indies and the coast of the Caribbean Sea. In the Preface to the Voyage (called his THIRD), revised, as we shall see, by Drake himself, and published by his nephew, he speaks of the wrong he suffered with Captain John Lovell, in the years 1565 and 1566, at Rio da Hacha; of his voyage to the West Indies with the Dragon and Swanne, in the year 1570, and in the Swanne alone, in 1571, for the purpose, it is said, of gaining intelligence of these countries; both being made subsequent to that with Hawkins which we are about to describe; but of which no particulars appear to have been at any time published; they were no doubt based on mercantile speculation, and perhaps, among other things, in the traffic for slaves, as an outward-bound cargo. Nor can there be any doubt that, by the knowledge acquired in the first of these voyages, he was enabled to be of service in the present adventure of Mr. John Hawkins.

The expedition consisted of one of the Queen's ships, which, as the strongest proof of her approbation of the voyage, she lent to Hawkins. It was called the Jesus of Lubeck, a ship of 700 tons, and commanded by the Admiral, - or, as the commander of an expedition was always in those days called, the *General,* - and who, in this instance, was Hawkins himself. To the Jesus was added the Minion, Captain John Hampton; the William and John, Captain Thomas Bolton; and the Judith, Captain Francis Drake, he being then, as stated, in the twenty-third year of his age, or, if the picture chronology of 1541 be correct, in the twenty-sixth. There were besides two very small vessels, the Angel and the Swallow. [6]

On the 2nd of October, 1567, they set sail from Plymouth, but met with a violent storm off Cape Finisterre, which lasted four days; the ships separated, the boats were all lost, arid the Jesus suffered so much as to be nearly disabled for the voyage. The storm ceasing, however, they were enabled to assemble the ships and to pursue their course; and having reached the Cape de Verde, Hawkins landed about 150 of his men, in the hope of obtaining a supply of negroes, where, however, they got but few, and those with great hurt and damage to their men, which chiefly proceeded from the envenomed arrows of the negroes; and "although in the beginning they seemed to be but small hurts, yet there hardly escaped any, that had blood drawn of them, but died in strange sort, with their mouthes shutte some tenne dayes before they died, and after their wounds were whole; when I myself," says Hawkins, "had one of the greatest wounds, yet, thanks be to God, escaped." Mr. Miles Philips, one of Hawkins's men that were afterwards left on the Spanish Main, tells us a little more; the seven or eight men with closed mouths, it would appear, died of lock-jaw, for he says, "we were forced to put sticks and other things into their mouths to keep them open." It appears also they were attacked by the negroes before they could succeed in carrying off their 150 slaves, to do which there was hard fighting. [7]

They next proceeded down the coast of Guinea, and after many difficulties, and the loss of several of their men, they succeeded in taking on board about 200 negro slaves more, and departed with this cargo of human beings on their voyage for the Spanish Islands of the West Indies, to sell them to the Spaniards, as Hawkins had done before, by virtue of the treaty above-mentioned, and which was still enforced.

Before, however, we allow Mr. Hawkins to proceed with his cargo to the West Indies, we must accompany him farther down the coast to St. Jorge da Mina, where he was to obtain gold for his merchandise, fitted, no doubt, for the slave-market; and we are the more desirous of doing so, to show in what manner the slave-trade was then carried on, and that the unsophisticated mind of young Drake must have seen it with abhorrence, for through the whole course of his future life he had no concern in this kind of traffic. At this place a negro king came to ask the assistance of Hawkins against a neighbouring king, promising him all the negroes that should be taken. An offer so tempting was not to be rejected, and 150 men were selected and sent to assist this black tyrant. They assaulted a town containing 8000 inhabitants, strongly paled round, and fenced after their manner, and so well defended that Hawkins's people had six slain and forty wounded. More help was called for: "Whereupon," says Hawkins, "considering that the good success of this enterprise might highly further the commodity of our voyage, I went myself; and with the help of the king of our side, assaulted the town both by land and sea; and very hardly, with fire (their houses being covered with palm-leaves), obtained the town and put the inhabitants to flight; where we took 250 persons, men, women, and children; and by our friend, the king on our side, there were taken 600 prisoners, whereof we hoped to have our choice; but the negro (in which nation is never or seldom found truth) meant nothing less; for that night he removed his camp and prisoners, so that we were fain to content us with those few that we had gotten ourselves." [8]

On this part of Hawkins's narrative it would naturally occur that Dr. Johnson, who, in his Life of Drake, rarely failed to make some beautiful moral reflection applicable to the subject in hand, has omitted altogether this atrocious proceeding, and not once touched on the subject of negroslavery; nor do we find in the whole of Boswell's volumes a single passage on slavery, except one, where Boswell says, "He had always been very zealous against slavery in every form, in which I, with all deference, thought that he discovered 'a zeal without knowledge.'" But he adds, "Upon one occasion, when in company with some very grave men at Oxford, his toast was, 'Here's to the next insurrection of the negroes in the West Indies;' Boswell qualifying it, as it were, by his violent prejudice against our West Indian and American settlers." [9]

On the 27th of March they came in sight of Dominica, coasted Margarita, Cape de la Vela, and other places, "carrying on, and without obstruction, a tolerable good trade," that is, of course, in selling their negroes for silver. But at Rio da Hacha all commerce with the inhabitants was strictly prohibited. Hawkins, deeming this to be an infraction of the treaty, and an unauthorized .and illegal proceeding, determined to attack the place, and having landed 200 men, the town was taken by storm with the loss of two men only, and no hurt is said to have been done to the Spaniards, because, after their volley was discharged, they all fled; they soon, however, returned, and then, Hawkins says, they were permitted to trade in secret and by night; and the Spaniards bought of them 200 negroes; "and at all other places where we traded," says Hawkins, "the inhabitants were glad of us, and traded willingly." [10]

From hence, in proceeding toward Cartagena, they were caught in a terrible storm, which continued four days, and so shattered the Jesus, that they cut down her upper works, her rudder was shaken, and she sprung a leak. Proceeding toward Florida, they encountered another storm, and were driven into the bay of Mexico, and entered into the port of San Juan d'Ulloa; in searching for which, he says, "we took on our way three ships, which carried passengers to the number of one hundred. I found in this port," continues Hawkins, "twelve ships, which had in them, by report, £200,000 in gold and silver; all which being in my possession, with the King's Island, and also the passengers, before in my way thitherward stayed, I set at liberty without taking from them the weight of a groat." [11] The Spaniards mistook the English ships for a fleet from Spain, which was daily expected, and the chief officers came on board, but being soon deceived, began to be greatly dismayed; "but when they saw our demand was nothing but victuals, they were re-comforted." [12]

To prevent any misunderstanding, Hawkins sent to Mexico, representing to the viceroy that he had put in here by stress of weather, in want of victuals, and his ships in great need of repair; and these wants, the English, as friends to King Philip, requested they might be supplied with for their money.

"On the morrow," says Hawkins, "we saw open of the haven thirteen great ships, and understanding them to be the fleet of Spain, I sent immediately to advertise the General of the fleet of my being there, giving him to understand, that before I would suffer them to enter the port, there should be some order of conditions pass between us, for our safe-being there, and maintenance of peace." [12] It is not easy to comprehend, in our times, that a commander of three ships, one, it is true, of 700 tons, one of 100, and a little bark of 50, would presume to dictate to thirteen great ships not yet in port, and twelve others in port, and that port belonging to the Spaniards, and guarded by a battery of brass guns; that a commander of such a miserable squadron should be bold enough to presume to talk of making conditions, before he would suffer them to enter their own port. It marks, however, most strongly, the wide difference in point of feeling between an English sea commander and a Spanish one.

Hawkins, however, began to consider that he had gone too far, and that his presumption was likely to have got him into a scrape; "and here," he says, "I began to bewail that which after followed, for now, said I, I am in two dangers, and forced to receive the one of them. That was, either I must have kept out the fleet from entering the port, the which with God's help I was able to do, or else suffer them to enter in with their accustomed treason, which they never fail to execute, where they may have opportunitie to compass it by any means; if I had kept them out, then had there been present shipwreck of all the fleet, which amounted in value to six millions, which was, in value of our money, £1,800,000, which I considered I was not able to answer, fearing the Queen's Majesty's indignation in so weighty a matter. Thus with myself revolving the doubts, I thought rather better to abide the jutt of the uncertainty than the certainty; the uncertain doubt, I account, was their treason, which, by good policy, I hoped might be prevented; and therefore, as choosing the least mischief, I proceeded to conditions." [13] The fact was, as he more clearly admits in another place, that besides the risk he ran of an unequal combat, he was fearful of taking on himself the responsibility of plundering from the king of Spain so immense a sum of money, which could not fail to bring her Majesty into collision with that sovereign.

The General therefore, on his part, fully resolved not to commit any act of hostility, or do anything that could be construed into a breach of the peace. All that he required of the Spaniards was the assurance of security for himself and all that belonged to him and his people, provisions to be supplied for money, and liberty to trade; moreover that, during his abode there, he should keep possession of the island with the eleven pieces of brass cannon that were planted upon it.   In the fleet was a new viceroy from Mexico, Don Martin Henriquez, who, after some demur, and somewhat misliking these conditions, at last agreed to them, the viceroy giving a writing signed with his hand, and sealed with his seal; each party giving and exchanging ten hostages for the due performance of the stipulations.

At the end of three days "the Spanish fleete entered the port, the ships saluting one another, as the manner the sea doth require; the morrow after, being Friday, we laboured," says Hawkins, "on all sides, in placing the English ships by themselves, and the Spanish ships by themselves, the captains and inferior persons of either part offering and shewing great courtesie one to another, and promising great amitie on all sides." (p. 171.) This pretended amity on the part of the Spaniards was soon discovered to be fallacious; they were observed to be placing additional guns on the fortifications of the island, and encreasing the crews of their ships. The viceroy having sanctioned this treason by leaving these matters to work without interfering, assured Hawkins that he would be their defence against all villainies. Fair words, however, were not sufficient to allay the apprehensions of the English. Men were secretly conveyed to the ships; and a: the master of the Jesus spoke Spanish, Hawkins sent him to the viceroy to inquire if his suspicions were correct; immediately the master was seized, the trumpet sounded, the English were taken by surprise, and the Spaniards most perfidiously falling upon

14

them, killed a great number of their men, seized, plundered, and burnt three of their ships, made several of their crews prisoners, and obliged the remainder, in the smaller ships, to retreat without necessaries, and in so miserable a plight, that scarcely a sixth part survived to reach England.

The English, however, did not come away wholly unrevenged; for the result of this singular adventure was, according to Hakluyt's account, which he says he had from Hawkins himself under his own hand, that "no sooner were the Jesus and the Minion got about two ships' length from the Spanish fleet, than the fight began to be so warm on all sides, that, in less than an hour, the Spanish Admiral was supposed to be sunk, the Vice-Admiral burnt, and another of their chief ships believed to be sunk, so that their ships were little able to annoy us." [14]

The cannon on the island being now in possession of the Spaniards, the masts, yards, and rigging of the Jesus were so shattered, that no hopes were left of carrying her off. With these cannon also the small ships of the English were destroyed. It was then proposed to place the Jesus between the fort and the Minion, and at night to tranship all the provisions and necessaries of the former into the latter, and to leave the Jesus behind.

But the Spaniards set fire to two of their large ships, and let them drive down upon those of the English. "Upon this," says Hawkins, "the men on board the Minion, without either the captain's or master's consent, set sail in such hurry and confusion, that it was not without great difficulty I was received on board." [15]

Mr. Miles Philips, one of the unfortunate men put on shore, as will be seen presently, gives a more detailed account. He says, "The Minion, which had somewhat before prepared herself to avoid the danger, hauled away, and abode the first brunt of the 300 men that were in the great hulke; then they sought to fall on board the Jesus, where was a cruel fight, and many of our men slain; but yet our men defended themselves and kept them out; for the Jesus also got loose, and joyning with the Minion, the fight waxed hote upon all sides; but they having won and got our ordinance did greatly annoy us. In this fighte there were two great shippes of the Spaniards sunke, and one burnte, so that with their shippes they were not able to harme us, but from the shore they beat us cruelly with our own ordinance in such sort that the Jesus was very sore spoyled, and suddenly the Spaniards, having fired two great shippes of their owne, they came directly against us, which bred among our men a marvellous feare. Howbeit the Minion, which had made her sayles ready, shifted for herself, without consent of the Generall, captaine, or master, so that very hardly our Generall could be received into the Minion, and those which the small boat was not able to receive were most cruelly slain by the Spaniardes.

"Of our shippes none escaped saving the Minion and the Judith; and all such of our men as were not in them were inforced to abide the tyrannous cruelty of the Spaniards. For it is a certain trueth, that whereas they had taken certaine of our men ashore, they took and hung them up by the armes, upon high postes, until the blood burst out of their fingers' ends: of which men so used, there is one Copston and certaine others yet alive, who by the merciful providence of the Almighty were long since arrived here in England, carrying still about with them (and shall go to their graves) the marks and tokens of those their inhuman and more than barbarous cruell dealings." [16] Hawkins says that most of the men that were left alive in the Jesus made shift t to follow the Minion in a small boat, but the rest who could not get into the boat were left to the mercy of the Spaniards.

Thus the Minion, with only one small bark of fifty tons, the Judith (Drake's ship), escaped the treachery of the Spaniards; but, he says, "the same night the Judith likewise forsook us. We were now left alone with only two anchors and two cables, our ship so damaged that it was as much as we could do to keep her above water, and a great number of us with very little provisions. We were besides divided in opinion what to do. Some were for yielding to the Spaniards, others chose rather to submit to the mercy of the savages; and again, others thought it more eligible to keep the sea, though with so scanty an allowance of victualls as would hardly suffice to keep us alive.

"In this miserable plight we ranged an unknown sea for fourteen days, till extreme famine obliged us to seek for land. So great was our misery that hides were reckoned good food; rats, cats, mice, and dogs, none escaped us that we could lay our hands on; parrots and monkeys were our dainties. In this condition we came to land, on the 8th of October, at the bottom of the bay of Mexico, where we hoped to have found inhabitants of the Spaniards, reliefe of victuals, and a proper place to repair our ship. But we found every thing just contrary to our expectation; neither inhabitants, nor provisions, nor a haven for the repair of our ship. Many of our men, nevertheless, being worn out with hunger, desired to be set on shore, to which I consented, and such as were willing to land I put them apart, and such as were desirous to go homewards I put apart; so that they were indifferently posted, a hundred on one side, and a hundred on the other side. These hundred men we set a-land with all diligence in this little place, before said, which being landed, we determined there to take in fresh water, and so with our little remains of victuals to take the sea.

"Of about two hundred souls which we then were, one hundred chose to seek their fortune on land, on which they were set with great difficulty; and with the remainder, after having watered, I again submitted to the mercy of the seas, and set sail on the 16th of October." [17]

Hawkins himself, with the rest of his company, were first endangered by a vehement storm, after that with famine, his men dying continually; so that the rest not being able to manage the ship, seeking to relieve themselves at Ponte Vedra, near Vigo, with fresh meat, they grew diseased, and many of them died. For fear of being a second time betrayed by the Spaniards they again put to sea, and arrived in England on the 25th of January. 1568/9.

16

Hawkins concludes his relation of this unfortunate expedition by saying, that "if all the miseries and troubles of this melancholy voyage were to be completely and thoroughly written, it would require a laborious man with his pen, and as much time as the author had, who wrote the lives and deaths of the Martyrs."

The following is a copy of a letter in the State Paper Office, from Hawkins, announcing his arrival in England from this disastrous voyage:

25th January 1568.

Right Honorable, my dewty most humbly consydered: yt may please your honor to be advertysed that the 25th day of Januarii (thanks be to God) we aryved in a place in Cornewall called Mounts bay, onelie with the Minyon which is left us of all our flet, & because I wold not in my letters be prolyxe, after what maner we came to our dysgrace, I have sent your honor here in-closed some part of the circumstance, and althoughe not all our meseryes that hath past yet the greatest matters worthye of notynge, but yf I shold wryt of all our calamytyes I am seure a volome as great as the byble wyll scarcelie suffyce: all which thyngs I most humblie beseeche your honour to advcrtyse the Queen's Majestic & the rest of the counsell (soch as you shall thinke mette).

Our voiage was, although very hardly, well acheived & brought to resona-ble passe, but now a great part of our treasure, merchandyze, shippinge and men devoured by the treason of the Spanyards. I have not moche or any thynge more to advertyse your honour, nore the rest, because all our busi-ness hath had infelycytye, mysfortune, and an unhappy end, & therefore wyll treble the Queen's Majestic, nor the rest of my good lords with soch yll new-es. But herewith pray your honour eftsoons to impart to soch as you shall thynke mete the sequell of our busyness.

I mynd with God's grace to make all expedicyon to London myselfe, at what tyme I shall declare more of our esstate that ys here omytted. Thus prayinge to God for your Honours prosperous estate take my leave: from the Mynion the 25th day of Januarii 1568.

Your's most humbly to command,

(Signed). JOHN HAWKINS.

To the Ryght Honorable Sir Wm Cycylle Knighte, & Principall Secretarie to the Queen's Majestic, gyve this. [18]

No mention whatever is made of the Judith, nor what became of her: her captain, however, arrived safe in England; but it is somewhat remarkable that the name of Drake never once occurs in any of the accounts of this very uninteresting and unfortunate voyage. Hawkins probably considered him in somewhat the same light that the commander of a man-of-war would a young midshipman he takes under his protection; there are, however, de-tached accounts of this voyage in which Drake is represented to have done wonders with the little Judith.

Hortop, one of the unfortunate men left on shore, says, that "the General willed Mr. Francis Drake to come in with the Judith and lay the Minion aboord, to take in men and other things needful, and then to goe out, and so he did." The truth seems to be that Hawkins considered the Judith to be of little use, and Drake, as we have hinted, merely a pupil of his, as in his earlier days he used to be. His letter shows how wholly his mind was occupied with the misery he suffered after the affair of St. Juan d'Ulloa.

Of the hundred men that were put on shore, and of the sufferings they underwent from the Indians and Spaniards, the industry of Hakluyt and Purchas has supplied very curious narratives, taken from the persons themselves, on their return to England. From that of Mr. Miles Philips an extract has been given, which bears evident marks of truth. From that of Mr. Job Hortop we shall also give a brief extract, as regards only the affair of St. Juan d'Ulloa. The miseries they were destined to undergo, the recital of the torture, the mutilations of those who survived, the inhuman cruelties which others endured when brought to the stake and murdered by the accursed Inquisition, are calculated to rouse a spirit of indignation against the whole Spanish nation, which was afterwards signally punished under a courageous and truly British Sovereign. But, as we have said, our extract must be confined to one particular object. "From Cartagena, by foule weather, wee were forced to seeke the port of Saint John de Ulloa. In our way thwart of Campeche we met with a Spaniard, a small ship who was bound for Santo Domingo; he had in him a Spaniard called Augustine de Villa Neuva: them we took and brought with us into the port of Saint John de Ulloa. Our Generall made great account of him, and used him like a nobleman; howbeit in the ende he was one of them that betrayed. When wee had mored our ships and landed, wee mounted the ordinance that wee found there in the Ilande, and for our safeties kept watch and warde. The next day after wee discovered the Spanish fleete, whereof Luçon, a Spanyard, was Generall: with him came a Spaniard called Don Martin Henriquez, whom the King of Spain sent to be his viceroy of the Indies. He sent a pinnesse with a flag of truce unto our Generall, to knowe of what countrie those shippes were that rode there in the King of Spaine's port; who sayd they were the Queene of England's ships, which came in there for victuals for their money; wherefore if your Generall will come in here, he shall give me victuals and all other necessaries, and I will goe out on the one side the port, and he shall come in on the other side. The Spanyard returned for answere, that he was a viceroy and had a thousand men, and therefore he would come in. Our Generall sayd, If he be a viceroy I represent my Queene's person, and I am a viceroy as well as he: and if he have a thousand men, my powder and shot will take the better place.

"Then the viceroy, after counsell among themselves, yeelded to our General's demand, swearing by his king and his crowne, by his commission and authority that he had from his king, that hee would performe it, and thereupon pledges were given on both parts.

"Our Generall bearing a godly and Christian minde, voyde of fraude and deceit, judged the Spanyards to have done the like, delivered to them five gentlemen, not doubting to have received the like from them; but the faithlesse Spanyardes, in costly apparell gave of the basest of their company, as afterwardes it was well knowen. These things finished, proclamation was made on both sides that on payne of death no occasion should be given whereby any quarrel should grow to the breach of the league, and then they peaceably entered the port with great triumph on both sides.

"The Spaniards presently brought a great hulke, a ship of five hundred, and mored her by the side of the Minion, and they cut out ports in their other ships, planting their ordinance towardes us; in the night they filled the hulke with men, to lay the Minion aboord, as the sequel did shew, which made our Generall doubtful of their dealings; wherefore, for that he could speake the Spanish tongue, he sent Robert Barret aboord the viceroy to know his meaning in those dealings, who willed him with his company to come in to him, whom he commanded presently to be set in the bilbowes, and forthwith a cornet (for a watch-word among the false Spaniards) was sounded for the enterprising of their pretended treason against our Generall, whom Augustine de Villa Neuva, sitting at dinner with him, should then presently have killed with a poynarde, which hee had privily in his sleeve, which was espyed and prevented by one John Chamberlayne, who tooke the poynarde out of his sleeve.

"Our Generall hastily rose up, and commanded him to be put prisoner in the steward's roome (and to be kept with two men).

"The faithlesse Spanyards, thinking all things to their desire had been finished, suddenly sounded a trumpet, and therewith three hundred Spanyards entred the Minion; whereat our Generall with a loude and fierce voyce called unto us, saying, 'God and Saint George! upon those traiterous villaines, and rescue the Minion; I trust in God the day shall be ours:' and with that the mariners and souldiers leapt out of the Jesus of Lubeck into the Minion, and beat out the Spaniards; and with a shot out of her fiered the Spaniards' Vice Admirall, [19] where the most part of 300 Spanyards were spoyled and blowen over-boord with powder. Their Admirall [19] also was on fire halfe an houre.

"We cut our cables, wound off our ships, and presently fought with them: they came upon us on every side, and continued the fight from ten of the clocke until it was night: they killed all our men that were on shore in the iland saving three, which, by swimming, got aboord the Jesus of Lubeck. They sunke the Generall's ship called the Angel, and tooke the Swallow. The Spaniards' Admirall (the flag-ship so called in those days) had above threescore shot through her: many of his men were spoyled; foure other of their ships were sunke. There were in that fleete and that came from the shore to rescue them, fifteene hundred: we slew of them five hundred and fourtie, as we were credibly informed by a note that came to Mexico.

"In this fight the Jesus of Lubeck had five shotte through her maynemast; her foremast was strooke in sunder, under the hounds, with a chayne shotte, and her hull was wonderfully pearced with shotte: therefore it was impossible to bring her away. They set two of their owne shippes on fire, intending therewith to have burnt the Jesus of Lubeck, which we prevented by cutting our cables in the halse; and winding off by our sternefast. The Minion was forced to set saile and stand off from us, and come to an anker without shot of the iland.

"Our General! couragiously cheered up his souldiers and gunners, and called to Samuel his page for a cup of beere, who brought it him in a silver cup; and hee, drinking to all men, willed the gunners to stand by their ordinance lustily like men. He had no sooner set the cup out of his hand but a demy culveriii shot stroke away the cup, and a cooper's plane that stoode by the mainemast, and ranne out on the other side of the ship; which nothing dismayed our Generall, for he ceased not to incourage us, saying, 'Feare nothing; for God, who hath preserved me from this shot, will also deliver us from these traitours and villaines.' Then Captaine Bland, meaning to have turned out of the port, had his mainemast stroke over boord with a chaine shot that came from the shore; wherefore he ankered, fired his ship, tooke his pinnesse with all his men, and came aboord the Jesus of Lubeck to our Generall, who said unto him that he thought he would not have runne away from him: he answered that he was not minded to have runne away from him, but his intent was to have turned up, and to have laid the weathermost ship of the Spanish fleete aboord, and fired his ship, in hope therewith to have set on fire the Spanish fleete. He said if he had done so he had done well. With this, night came on. Our Generall commanded the Minion, for safegard of her masts, to be brought under the Jesus of Lubeck's lee: he willed M. Francis Drake to come in with the Judith, and to lay the Minion aboord, to take in men and other things needefull, and to goe out; and so he did.

"At night, when the wind came off the shore, wee set sayle, and went out in despite of the Spanyards and their shot, where we ankered with two ankers under the iland, the wind being northerly, which was wonderfull dangerous, and wee feared every houre to be driven with the lee shore. In the end, when the wind came larger, we waied anker and set saile, seeking the river of Panuco for water, whereof we had very little; and victuals were so scarce that we were driven to eate hides, cats, rats, parrats, munkies, and dogges. Wherefore our Generall was forced to divide his company into two parts, for there was a mutinie among them for want of victuals; and some said that they had rather be on the shore to shift for themselves amongst the enemies, than to starve on ship-boord.

"He asked them who would go on shore, and who would tarry on ship-boord? Those that would goe on shore, he willed to goe on fore mast, and those that would tarrie, on baft mast: fourescore and sixteene of us were willing to depart.

20

"Our Generall gave unto every one of us five yards of Roane cloth, and money to them that demanded it. When we were landed, he came unto us, where, friendly embracing every one of us, he was greatly grieved that he was forced to leave us behind him; he counselled us to serve God, and to love one another; and thus courteously he gave us a sorrowfull farewell, and promised if God sent him safe home he would do what he could, that so many of us as lived should by some means be brought into England (and so he did)."

Miles Philips says, "Through the providence of Almighty God, after sixteen years' absence, having sustained many and great troubles and miseries, as by this discourse appeareth, I came home to this my native countrey of England in the year 1582, in the month of February, in the ship called the Landrer, and arrived at Poole."

Job Hortop was landed at Portsmouth, from the Dudley, on the 2nd day of December, 1590; was sent by the Lieutenant of Portsmouth to the Right Hon. the Earle of Sussex, and examined, &c.; and he concludes, "Thus having truly set down unto you my travels, misery, and dangers, endured the space of twenty-three years, I ende." [20]

[1] Camden.
[2] Prince's Worthies of Devon.
[3] Camden.
[4] Johnson's Works.
[5] Johnson's Works.
[6] Hakluyt.
[7] Hakluyt.
[8] Hawkins, in Hakluyt.
[9] Boswell's Johnson.
[10] Hakluyt.
[11] Ibid.
[12] Hawkins, in Hakluyt.
[13] Hawkins, in Hakluyt.
[14] Hakluyt.
[15] Hawkins, in Hakluyt.
[16] Narrative of Miles Philips, in Hakluyt.
[17] Hakluyt.
[18] MS. State Paper Office.
[19] Admiral and Vice-Admiral are the two chief ships, so named.
[20] Hakluyt.

Chapter Two - Third Voyage to the West Indies and the Spanish Main - 1572-1573

[1]

The treacherous and unjust conduct of the Spaniards towards the unfortunate adventurers in the late voyages, and to other traders to the West Indies and the coasts of the Spanish Main, roused such a flame of indignation, more especially in the mercantile and seafaring community, that the cry of vengeance and retribution was loudly expressed against these tyrants of the New World. Elizabeth was well disposed to encourage adventurers desirous of sharing in the riches extorted by Spain from the unfortunate princes of Mexico and Peru and their native subjects, from whom, by most unjust and tyrannical means, she obtained that wealth, which enabled her to domineer over a large portion of Europe. She was equally well disposed to break a lance with Philip, who was employing every discreditable means to seduce her subjects from their religion and allegiance; but the times made it inexpedient to commit the nation to anything that could be construed into a direct act of aggression. The two sovereigns were to each other in a state of peaceable antipathy, each "willing to wound," but each "afraid to strike." Elizabeth was a staunch Protestant; Philip the slave of the Pope and the tool of priests, Jesuits and inquisitors. But it was not just then the policy of England to risk hostilities at home or abroad. The power of Spain was besides too colossal, though weak, to provoke a war by attacking her vast kingdom or her colonies. At home, it embraced a sea-coast extending from the Mediterranean to the Netherlands, except that portion which belonged to France. Abroad, the West India Islands, and two-thirds of the vast continent of America, were under her control; and her galleons traded even to the East Indies.

What was at that time the state of England? Her naval and military forces were small, in comparison with those of Spain, both of them inferior in point of numbers; and her ships greatly inferior in point of magnitude; her mercantile marine too limited and insignificant to be of much use as an arm of power. The want of colonies, the great and constant source of commerce and of shipping, necessarily crippled the supply of seamen; but notwithstanding all these drawbacks, the inferiority in numbers and strength, when once "the youth of England are on fire," then may we exclaim:

"O England! model to thy inward greatness,
Like little body with a mighty heart!
What might'st thou do, that honour bids thee do."

When the spirit of adventure is afloat, the seamen of England, in particular, are never found wanting where honour or glory calls, or the nation requires their services - witness our brave fellows in the early periods of foreign navigation, proceeding in their miserable little barks of 40, 30, or even 20 tons, to encounter the frozen seas of the polar regions; the more recent discoveries made in the same quarter, and even that foolish, fatal, and expensive expedition up the swampy, sultry Niger! They require but a leader such as Ross now is, or Drake was, in whom they can confide.

The general narrative of this voyage of Drake to the West Indies, and to the very spot, *Nombre de Dios,* from whence the immense quantities of gold and silver, the produce of Peru and Mexico, were formerly accumulated and shipped for Spain, has been related by most of the old historians, [2] but whether the manuscript voyage taken from the reports of Mr. Christopher Ceely, Hickson and others, and drawn up by Mr. Philip Nicholls, preacher, all being on the voyage, may or may not be more full or more correct than the rest, the very fact of its having been revised by Drake himself, at a subsequent period of his life, must be considered as stamping a superior and authentic value upon it. [3] That Drake should have taken the trouble to revise this voyage in particular, when there is reason to believe he generally left his adventures to be related by others, may perhaps be owing to the circumstance, that this voyage first opened the way to, and laid the foundation of, his future fame and fortunes. That happy and unlocked for incident, that gave him a view of the wide Pacific Ocean, inflamed his imagination, inspired his mind, and elevated his hope that, at some future and not very distant day, he would be able to open to the commerce and navigation of his countrymen, that noble expanse of ocean for their enterprise and advantage.

It may appear strange, after the experience of what had happened to the Jesus of Lubeck, the Minion, and the Judith, in the attack made upon them by the Spaniards at St. Juan de Ulloa, that Drake should run the hazard a second time of having to contend, in still more diminutive vessels than these - vessels of 70 and 25 tons burthen - with immense galleons of 800 to 1000 tons or more; but with a foresight highly characteristic of the man, Drake had determined to place no dependence on his little vessels, and therefore provided for what he meant to do, by taking with him a number of pinnaces in frame, in which his anticipated operations were to be conducted.

The late Admiral Burney, however, thinks that "The smallness of this force for an enterprise of such magnitude is not so extraordinary as that a navigation which, on account of its difficulties and dangers, had been so many years discontinued, should be undertaken in vessels so diminutive;" [4] and yet the Admiral's experience must have taught him that *sea dangers,* at least, are quite as likely to befal the largest ships as the very smallest, in any sea, and that the latter, how small soever her size, with a flush deck and hatches well battened down, will cross the Atlantic or any other sea with safety.

The documents prefixed to this voyage are contained in the Sloane MS. in the British Museum, and are printed or "set forth" in the Introduction of the first edition, published in 1626, by Sir Francis Drake, Baronet, (the nephew of the first Sir Francis,) in a small *quarto,* now become a very rare book. It were to be wished that Sir Francis had taken the trouble to revise his other voyages, in the accounts of which he says, "Many untruthes have been published, and the certain trueth concealed." The title to this voyage is itself curious. "Sir Francis Drake Revived, Calling upon this dull or effeminate age to folowe his noble steps for Golde & Silver. By this memorable relation of the rare occurrances (never yet declared to the world) in a third voyage made by him into the West Indies, in the years 72 and 73:

"Faithfully taken out of the Reporte of Mr. Christopher Ceely, Ellis, Hixon, and others, who were in the same voyage with him, by Philip Nichols, preacher. Reviewed also by Sir Francis Drake himselfe before his death, and much holpen and enlarged, by divers notes, with his owne hand, here and there inserted."

DEDICATION

"To THE HIGH AND MIGHTY CHARLES THE FIRST OF GREAT BRITAIN, FRANCE, AND IRELAND, KING, ALL THE BLESSINGS OF THIS AND A BETTER LIFE.

"MOST GRACIOUS SOVERAIGNE,

"That this briefe treatise is yours, both by right and by succession, will appeare by the Author's and Actor's ensewing dedication. To praise either the Mistress or the Servant, might justly incurre the censure of *Quis cos unquam sanus vituperavit;* cither's worth having sufficiently blazed their fame. This present loseth nothing by glancing on former actions and the observation of passed adventures may probably advantage future imployments; Caesar writte his owne Commentaries, and this Doer was partly ye. Inditor: neither is there wanting living testimony to confirme its trueth; for his sake then cherish what's good and I shall willingly entertaine check for what 's amisse: Your favourable acceptance may incourage my collecting of more neglected notes, however, though vertue (as Lands) be not inheritable, yet has he left of his name one that resolves, and therein joyes to approve himself

"Your most humble
"And loyall
"Subject,

"FRA: DRAKE (nephew)."

"To THE QUEENE'S MOST EXCELLENT MAtie

"MY MOST DREAD SOVERAIGNE,

"MADAM, Seeing diverse have diverslie reported and written of these voyages and actions, which I have atempted and made, every one endeavouringe to bring to light whatsoever Incklings or Conjectures they have had, whereby many untruthes have been published, and the certaine trueth concealed, as I have thought it necessary myselfe, as in a Card to prick the principall points of the Counsails taken, attempts made, and successe had, during the whole course of my employment in these services against the Spaniard, not as setting saile for maintayning my reputation in men's judgment, but onlie as sitting at Helme, if occasion shall be, for conducting the like actions hereafter: So I have accounted it my dutie to present this discourse to your Matie as of right, either for itselfe being the first fruits of your Servants Penne, or for the matter, being service done to your Matie by your poor Vassail, against your great Enemy, at such tymes, in such places, and after such sorte, as may seeme strange to those that are not acquainted with the whole cariage thereof, but will be a pleasing remembrance to your highnes, who take th' apparent height of th' Almighties favour toward you by these events, as truest Instruments, humbly submitting myself to your gracious censure, both in writing and presenting, that Posteritie be not deprived of such helpe as may hapilie be gained thereby, and our present Age at least may be satisfied in the rightfulnes of these Actions, which hitherto have bin silenced, and your servants labour not seeme altogether lost, but only in travell by sea and land, but also in writing the Report thereof, a worke to him no lesse troublesome, yet made pleasant and sweete, in that it hath bin, is, and shall be, for your M<small>ats</small> content, to whom I have devoted myslefe, live or die.

"FRA: DRAKE.

"Jan: I.
"1592."

"A RELATION OF THE RARE OCCURRENCES, &c."

This reviewed Relation states briefly what Drake had hitherto done, and commences thus:

"As there is a general vengeance which secretlie pursueth the doers of wrong, and stiffereth them not to prosper, albeit no man of purpose impeach them: Soe there is a particular indignation ingrafted in the bosome of all that are wronged, which ceaseth not seeking by all meanes possible to redresse or remedie the wrong received, in so much that those great and mighty men, in whom their prosperous estate hath bredde such an overweening of themselves that they do not onlie wronge their Inferiours, but despise them, being injured, seeme to take a verie urifitt course for their own safety and farre unfitter for their rest. For as Aesop teacheth, Even y<small>e</small> FLY hath her spleene, and the EMMET is not without her choller: and both together many tymes finde meanes, whereby though the EAGLE lay her Eggs in JUPITER'S lappe, yet by one way or other she escapeth not requital of her wrong done to the EMMET.

"AMONG the manifold examples hereof which former ages have committed to memorie, or our tyme yealded to sight, I suppose there hath not bin any more notable then this in hand, either in respect of the greatness of the Person by whom the first Injurie was offered; or the meanenes of him who righteth himself: the one being (in his owne conceit) the mightiest MONARCH of all the world; the other an English CAPTAINE, a meane subject of her Majesties, who, (besides the wronges received at Rio DA HACHA with Captaine JOHN LOVELL in the years 65: and 66:) having bin grievously indamaged at ST. JOHN DE ULLOA in the Bay of MEXICO with CAPTAINE JOHN HAWKINS in the years 67: and 68: not only in the losse of his goods of some value, but also of his kinsmen and friends, and that by the falsehood of DON MARTIN HENRIQUEZ then the Vice Roy of MEXICO, and finding that no recom pence could be recovred out of Spaine by any of his owne meanes or by her Maiesties letters: he used such help as he might by two severall voyages into the WEST INDIES; the first with two ships the one called the DRAGON, the other the SWANNE, in the year 70: The other in the SWANNE alone, in the yeare 71: to gaine such intelligence as might further him to get some amende for his losse: And having in those two voyages gotten such certaine notice of the persons and places aymed at, as he thought requisite, and thereupon with good deliberation resolved on a third voyage (the description whereof wee have now in hand), he accordinglie prepared his ships and companie, and then taking the first oportunity of a goode winde had such successe in his proceedings, as now follows further to be declared.

25

"On WHITSON Eve, being the 24th of May in the yeare 1572, CAPTAINE DRAKE in the PASCHA of PLYMOUTH of 70 Tonnes, his Admirall, with the SWANNE of the same Porte of 25 Tonnes, his ViceAdmirall, in which his brother JOHN DRAKE was CAPTAINE, having in both of them, in men, and boyes, 73: all voluntarilie assembled, of which the eldest man was 50: all the rest under 30: so divided that there were 47 in one ship and 26 in the other, both richlie furnished with victuals and apparel for a whole yeare: and no lesse heedefully provided of all manner of Munition, Artillery, stuffe and tooles that were requisite for such a man of WARRE, in such an attempte, but especiallie having three daintie Pinnaces made in Plimouth, taken asonder all in pieces, and stowed aboard, to be set up (as occasion served) set saile from out of the SOUND of PLYMOUTH with intent to land at NOMBRE DE DIOS." [5]

"This City," says Prince, in his Worthies of Devon, "was then the Granary of the West Indies, wherein the golden harvest brought from Peru and Mexico to Panama was hoarded up till it could be conveyed into Spain."

On the 2nd of July, they came in sight of the high land of Santa Martha, and directed their course to Port Pheasant, "which," says the narrative, "our Captaine had so named it in his former voyage, by reason of the great store of those goodlie foules, which hee and his companie did then dailie kill and feede on in that place. When we landed here, we found by evident marks that there had been latelie there an Englishman of Plimouth called John Garrett, who had been conducted thither by certaine English Mariners which had been there with our Captain in some of his former voyages, who, on a plate of lead, fastened to a very great tree, greater than any foure men joyning hands could fathom about, left these words engraven:

"Captain Drake, If you fortune to come into this port make haste away; for the Spaniards which you had with you here last year have betrayed this place, and taken away all that you left here. I departed hence this present 7th July 1572.

"Your very loving friend, JOHN GARRET." [6]

Notwithstanding which warning, Captain Drake resolved to build his pinnaces in this convenient port; which were finished in seven days. Here he fortified himself on a plot of three-quarters of an acre of ground to make some safety for the present, "by felling of great trees and bowsing and trailing them together with great pullies and halsers, until they were enclosed to the water, and then letting other fall upon them, until they had raised with trees and boughs thirty foot in height round about, leaving only one gate to issue at, neare the water side, which every night was shut up, with a great tree drawne athwart it."

"The next day after we had arrived, there came also into that Bay an English Barque of the Isle of Wight, of Sir Edward Horsey's, wherein James Rause was Captaine and John Overy Maister, with 30 men, of which some had bin with our Captaine in this same place the year before. They brought in with them a Spanish Carvell of Sevill which he had taken the daie before, also one shallop with oares which he had taken at Cape Blanche. This Captaine Rause, understanding our Captaine's purpose, was desirous to joyne in consort with him, and was received on conditions agreed upon between them." [7]

"22nd July. Drake disposing there of all his companies according as they enclined most, he left the three ships and the Carvell with Cap: Rause, and chose into his four pinnaces (Cap: Rause's shallop made the fourth) besides 53 of his own men, 20 to atchieve what he intended, especially having proportioned, according to his owne purpose, and the men's disposition, their severall armes: namely, 6 Targetts; 6 Fire Pikes; 12 Pikes; 24 Muskets and Callivers; 16 Bowes and 6 Partizans; 2 Drums and 2 Trumpets." With this force Drake proceeded for Nombre de Dios and reached the Isles of Pinos on the 22nd of July. Here Drake met with certain black men who had fled from the Spaniards their masters, and were known by the name of Simerons, who had enrolled themselves under two kings or chiefs. Drake, thinking to make good use of these people, set them on shore, that they might make their way to the Isthmus of Darien.

These Simerons are not negroes, but the native Indians of this part of the continent, who had fled from their tyrannical persecutors, not very dissimilar either in manners or character from the maroons of Jamaica, whom it was found necessary to put down by bloodhounds imported into that Island from Cuba, but in the latter case there was a mixture of the negro race among them. Drake silently by night came before Nombre de Dios; and finding his people were talking of the greatness of the town, and what their strength was, particularly from the report of the negroes whom they took at the Ile of Pinos, thought it best to put these conceits out of their heads, and therefore took the opportunity of the rising moon, to persuade his people that it was the dawn of day. "By this occasion we were at the towne, a longe hower sooner than was first purposed. For we arrived there by three of the clock after midnight; at what time it fortuned that a ship of Spaine of sixtie tunnes, laden with Canary wines "and other commodities, which had but lately come into the Bay, and had not yet furled her sprit-say le, espying our foure Pinnaces, sent away her Gundeloe towards the towne to give warning." [8]

Drake, however, perceiving this, "cut betwixt her and the Towne, forcing her to goe to the other side of the Bay," whereby they landed without impeachment, although they found one gunner upon the platform in the very place where they landed.

"On landing on the platform, we found six great pieces of brass ordinance mounted upon their carriages, some demy, some whole Culverins; we presentlie dismounted them, the Gunner fledd, the Towne tooke Alarum, (being verie ready thereto by reason of their often disquieting by their neare neighbours the Symerons,) as we perceived not onelie by the noise and cryes of the people, but by the Bell ringing out, and drums runninge up and downe the towne. Our Captaine sent some of our men to stay the ringing of the Alarum bell, which had continued all this while, but the Church being verie strongly built, and faste shutte, they could not without firing (which our Captaine forbad) get into the steeple where the Bell hung." [9]

In the market-place the Spaniards saluted the party with a volley of shot: Captain Drake returned their greetings with a flight of arrows, (the best ancient English compliments, says Prince,) which drove their enemies away. Here he received a dangerous wound; though he valiantly concealed it a long time, knowing, if the General's heart stoops, the men's will fail; and that if so bright an opportunity once setteth, it seldom riseth again. Drake left twelve of his men to keep their pinnaces and secure their retreat, and having strengthened the port, sent the rest to view the town. He then commanded his brother and John Oxenham with sixteen men to go above the King's Treasure-house, and enter near the East End of the market-place, himself with the rest designing to march up the broad street, with trumpets sounding and drums beating, to the market-place, the fire-pikes being divided between both companies, which no less affrighted the enemy than they gave light to the English. After a skirmish with the Spaniards, they seized upon two or three who were ordered to conduct them to the Governor's house, where usually all the mules, which brought the king's treasure from Panama, were unladen, though the silver only was kept there, the gold, pearls, and jewels being carried to the Treasury hard by.

From hence Drake and his party went to the Governor's house, and found the door open, a candle lighted on the stairs, and a fine Spanish horse ready saddled; by means of this light they saw a vast heap of silver in the lower room, consisting of bars of silver, piled up against the wall, (as nearly as they could guess) seventy feet in length, ten in breadth, and twelve in height, each bar between thirty-five and forty pounds' weight. If the eye-measurement of silver be nearly the truth the heap must have been about the value of a million sterling. He next proceeded to the King's Treasure-house, telling his people, "That he had now brought them to the mouth of the Treasury of the World; which if they did not gain, none but themselves were to be blamed." [10]

After this, he commanded his brother with John Oxenham, and their company, to break open the Treasure-house: the rest to follow him, to keep the strength of the market-place, but as he stept forward, his strength, and sight, and speech failed him, and he began to faint from loss of blood, which was then perceived had issued in great quantity from a wound in his leg; which he had hitherto concealed lest he should discourage his company. He lost so much blood "that it soon filled the verie prints which our footsteps made, to the great dismay of all our company, who thought it not credible that one man should be able to lose so much blood and live." [11] At sight of this his men were much troubled, and giving him somewhat to drink to recover his spirits, they bound up his wound with his scarf, and persuaded him aboard for his recovery; the which he refusing, they added force to their entreaties, and so carried him to his pinnace.

Divers of his men, besides himself, were wounded, though but one, and he a trumpeter, slain. Many of them got good booty before they left the place. But the wines in a Spanish ship, which they found in the harbour, they took along with them for the relief of their Captain and themselves. They carried off their prize to an island, which they called the Island of Victuals, where they staid two days to cure their wounded men, and refresh themselves in the gardens they found there, abounding with all sorts of roots, fruits, poultry, and other fowls no less strange than delicate. [12] During their short stay there, a gentleman belonging to the garrison, called an Hidalgo, came to visit them, protesting that his coming was only to see and admire the courage of those who, with so small a force, had made so incredible an attempt. This gentleman pretended that his visit was only to honour their bravery; yet they were afterwards satisfied that he came directly from the governor to discover, whether the Captain was the same Drake who had been the two last years on their coast. And because many of the Spaniards were wounded with arrows, he desired to know "Whether the English poisoned them, and how they might be cured?" To whom the Captain returned answers, "That he was the same Drake they meant; that it was never his custom to poison arrows; that their wounds might be cured with ordinary remedies; and that he wanted only some of that excellent commodity, gold and silver, which that country yielded for himself, and his company, and that he was resolved, by the help of God, to reap some of the golden harvest, which they had got out of the earth, and then sent into Spain to trouble the earth."

To this answer, unlocked for, this gentleman replied, "If he might without offence move such a question, what should then be the cause of our departure from that town at this time, where there was above 360 tonnes of silver ready for the Fleet, and much more gold in value resting in iron chests in the King's Treasure House?"

"But when our Captain had showed him the true cause of his unwilling retreat on board, he acknowledged that we had no less reason in departing than courage in attempting.

"Thus with great favour and courteous entertainment, besides such gifts from the Captain as most contented him, after dinner he was in such sort dismissed to make report of that he had seen, that he protested he was never honoured so much of any in his life." [13]

Being thus refreshed, Captain Drake and his people proceeded to the Isle of Pinos, where their ships were left under the charge of Captain Rawse. After consulting then, with this captain, as to further proceedings, he stated many difficulties, and thought it no longer safe to continue on the coast now that they were discovered. Drake was quite willing to discharge him, being resolved to attempt some other exploit; and Captain Rawse, having received full satisfaction for the use of his men, and the trouble he had taken in guarding the ships, took his leave on the 7th of August.

Drake now dispatched his brother and Ellis Hixon to examine the River

Chagre, where he had been the year before, but wished to have further notice of it. On their return, he departed with his two ships and three pinnaces for Cartagena, where he arrived on the 13th, and the same day took two Spanish ships, one of which was 240 tons.

Here he came to anchor with his two ships, in the evening, in seven fathoms water, between the Island of Caresha and St. Barnard's. Drake led the three pinnaces about the island into the harbour of Cartagena, where, at the very entrance, he found a frigate at anchor, on board of which was only one man, who, being demanded where the rest of his company was, answered, that they were gone ashore in their gondelo that evening to fight about a mistress; and he involuntarily related to the Captain that, two hours before night, there past by them a pinnace, with sail and oars, as fast as ever they could row, calling to them whether there had not been any English or Frenchmen there lately? and upon answer that there had been none, they bid them look to themselves; that within an hour that this pinnace was come to the other side of Cartagena, there were many great pieces shot off, whereupon, one going to the top, to descry what might be the cause, espied over the land divers frigates and small shipping, bringing themselves within the castle.

This report was credited by Drake, the rather for that himself had heard the report of the ordnance at sea, and perceived sufficiently that he was now descried; notwithstanding, in further examination of this old mariner, he understood that there was within the next point a great ship of Seville, which had here discharged her lading, and was riding now with her yards across, being bound the next morning for St. Domingo. The Captain took this old man into his pinnace to verify that which he had informed, and rowed towards this ship, which, on coming near it, hailed them, asking whence the shallops were? the answer was, from Nombre de Dios: "straightway they raised and reviled; no heed was given to their words; but every pinnace, according to the Captain's orders, one on the starboard-bow, the other on the starboard quarter, and the Captain in the mid-ships, on the larboard side, forthwith boarded her, though all had some difficulty to enter by reason of her height; but as soon as all entered upon the decks, they threw down the gratings and spardecks to prevent the Spaniards from annoying them with their close fights; who then perceiving the English were possessed of their ship, stowed themselves all in hold with their weapons (except two or three younkers which were found afore the bits), when having sight of the pinnaces, there was no danger of the enemy remaining. Having cut their cables at halse, with the three pinnaces they towed her without the island into the sound, right afore the town, without danger of their great shot.

"Meanwhile the town, having intelligence hereof by their watch, took the alarum; rung out their bells, shot off about thirty pieces of great ordnance; put all their men in a readiness, horse and foot, came down on the very point of the wood, and discharged their calivers in going forth."

August 14. - "Drake considering that he was now discovered upon two of the chiefest places of all the coast, and yet not meaning to leave it till he had found the Symerons, and made his voyage as he had conceived, which would require some length of time, and the sure manning of his pinnaces, he therefore determined with himself to burn one of his ships, and make of the other a storehouse, that his pinnaces (which could not otherwise) might be thoroughly manned, and so he might be able to abide for any length of time. But knowing the affection of his company, how loath they were to leave either of their ships (being both so good sailers and so well furnished), he purposed in himself, by some policy, to make them most willing to effect that which he intended. To accomplish this, therefore, he sent for one Thomas Moone (who was carpenter of the Swan), and taking him into his cabin, charged him to conceal for a time a piece of service, which he must in any case consent to do aboard his own ship that was, in the middle of the second watch, to go down secretly into the well of the ship, and with a great spike-gimlet to bore three holes, as near to the keel as he could, and lay something against it, that the force of the water entering might make no great noise, nor be discovered by boiling up.

"Thomas Moone at the hearing hereof, being utterly dismayed, desired to know what cause there might be to move him to sink so goodly a bark of his own, new and strong, and that by his means, who had been in two so rich and gainful voyages in her with himself heretofore; if his brother, the master, and the rest of the company, should know of such his fact, he thought verily they would kill him. But when the Captain had imparted to him his cause, and persuaded him with promises that it should not be known, till all of them should be glad of it, he undertook it, and did it accordingly." [14]

"Next morning, August 15," says the 'English Hero, or Drake Revived,' "Drake going early a fishing in his pinnace, and falling aboard the Swan, calls for his brother to go with him, who, rising hastily, replied, he would instantly follow, or attend him if he pleased to stay. The Captain, perceiving the business done, would not hasten him, but rowing away carelessly, demanded of them 'Why their ship was so deep in the water?' Upon which his brother sent to the steward to know whether there was any water in her, or what might be the cause; the steward, stepping hastily down his usual scuttle, was wet up to the waist, and getting up again with much affright, cried out, 'the ship was full of water!'"

There was no need of hastening them - some went to pump, and others to search for the leak, which the master observing, instantly followed his brother, certifying him of the strange accident befallen them that night; that whereas they had not pumped in six weeks before, they had now six feet water in hold, and therefore desired to be excused from fishing, to search and remedy the leak; and the Captain offering his assistance, his brother answered, they had men enough aboard, desiring him to continue his fishing that they might have part thereof for dinner.

His brother returning found the company had taken much pains, but had freed the water very little, yet having much love to the ship (as Drake foresaw), they used their utmost diligence till three in the afternoon, when, perceiving that though they had assistance from the Captain's ship, yet they were not able to free above one foot and a half of water, and were very unlikely to find the leak, they were much discouraged, and desired Drake's advice how to remedy it; who therefore persuaded them to take their goods out of her, and then set her on fire, to prevent her falling into the enemy's hands; that himself would sail in the pinnace, till he could provide some handsome frigate, and his brother should be captain of the Admiral (or chief ship of the squadron), together with the master. This advice seemed strange at first, yet was instantly put in execution that night, Drake having his desire, and men enough now to strengthen his pinnaces.

The next day, August 16, they resolved to seek out a place, in the Sound of Darien, to leave their ship at anchor, safe and undiscovered, that the enemy might judge them quite gone from the coast, and the meanwhile to prosecute their design with the pinnaces: Drake going with two to the Rio Grande, and his brother taking the third to find out the Symerons. In pursuance hereof they, in five days, privately recovered the Sound, when the Captain employed them to clear a spacious plot of ground from trees and bushes, to build houses large enough for their lodgings, and one particularly for their public assembling, wherein the natives, well acquainted with the country and buildings, did them much service, the rest of the company recreating themselves with shooting at butts, bowls, quoits, nine-pins, or what they pleased, half of them working one day, and the rest the next; and likewise in providing fresh victuals of fish, fowls, hogs, deer, rabbits, and the like, whereof there was great plenty.

"Having continued here fifteen days to silence the noise of their discovery, Drake, leaving his ship with his brother, went with two pinnaces for the River Grande, as was formerly concluded on; and passing by Cartagena, out of sight, and coming within two leagues of the river, they landed on the mainland westward, and saw much cattle which they obtained from the Indians, being in want of fresh victuals." [15]

Cruising about in his pinnaces, between Cartagena and Tolon, "they took six frigates laden with hogs, hams, and maiz; of whom they got what intelligence they could of the preparations against them, and then discharged four of them and all the men, retaining only two well stored with good provisions.

"Three days after, they arrived at Port Plenty, in the Island of Pinos, (where their Captain chose at first to leave his ship,) so called, because they usually brought thither all the stores which they took, going that way for victualling Cartagena and Nombre de Dios." [16] Drake now resolved to go with three pinnaces to Cartagena, leaving his brother John Drake to govern those who remained with the Symerons to finish the fort, and to fetch boards and planks from the prize he left at Cativas.

On that night Drake came to an island he called the Spurkite Island, because they found store of birds like kites, but very delicate meat. Next day, *October* 8, they recovered a large island where they got great quantity of fish, especially of a great shell-fish, two feet long, which they called whelks. On the 14th they chased two frigates ashore near the Island of St. Bernard's, from whence they proceeded to Tolon, and landed near the town, in a garden where certain Indians gave them bows and arrows, and presented them with the dainty fruit and roots therein. From hence they quickly went to Caresha, an island near Cartagena, and with a full gale sailed towards the city, casting anchor between the island and the continent, right against the goodly garden island, in which the Captain would not suffer them to land; because he knew the Spaniards sent soldiers thither, when they heard any men-of-war on their coast, which happened accordingly; for three hours after, passing by the points of the island, they had a volley of a hundred shot from them, yet not one of their men hurt.

On the 20th October, the Spaniards sent out two frigates from Cartagena without any cargo in them, evidently for the purpose of being taken by Drake, in the hope probably that he would divide his small force in order to man them; however, he was not to be thus inveigled, but burnt one of them and sunk the other, in sight of two full manned frigates, which came out but soon retired. He now sprung on shore from one of his pinnaces, in spite of the troops, which were on the hills and hovering in the woods, but were afraid to come within shot of his pinnaces. "To leap upon an enemy's coast," says Johnson, "in sight of a superior force, only to show how little they were feared, was an act that would in these times meet with little applause; nor can the general be seriously commended, or rationally vindicated, who exposes his person to destruction, and, by consequence, his expedition to miscarriage, only for the pleasure of an idle insult, an insignificant bravado. All that can be urged in his defence is, that perhaps it might contribute to heighten the esteem of his followers; as few men, especially of that class, are philosophical enough to state the exact limits of prudery and bravery; or not to be dazzled with an intrepidity, how improperly soever exerted. It may be added, that perhaps the Spaniards, whose notions of courage are sufficiently romantic, might look upon him as a more formidable enemy, and yield more easily to a hero, of whose fortitude they had so high an idea." [17]

That evening they went to sea, and next morning took a bark, and found that the captain, his wife, and principal passengers, had forsaken her, and were gone ashore in their gondelo, so that they boarded her without resistance, though very well provided with swords, targets, small shot, and iron guns: she was about 50 tons, with ten mariners, five or six negroes, great store of soap and sweet-meats, bound from St. Domingo to Cartagena, the captain having left behind him a silk ancient, with his arms, at his hasty departing.

Nov. 3rd. - "Drake returned towards Rio Grande. On their way they fell in with a Spanish ship of about 90 tons, which they joyfully expected to be their own, but, on being hailed, she despised their summons and gave them a gun. The sea went very high, so that they could not attempt her, but after a great shower a calm ensuing, they pursued and quickly took her, which, being laden with victuals well powdered and dried, they received them as sent by the mercy of Heaven." [18]

The account of this capture is given as follows: "We espied a sail plying to the westward with her two courses, to our great joy, who vowed together that we would have her, or else it should cost us dear; bearing with her, we found her to be a Spanish ship of above 90 tons, which being *wheaved amayne* by us, despised our summons, and shot off her ordnance at us. The sea went very high, so that it was not for us to attempt to board her, and therefore we made fit small sail to attend upon her and keep her company, to her small content, till fairer weather might lay the sea. We spent not past two hours in our attendance till it pleased God, after a great shower, to send us a reasonable calm, so that we might use our pieces and approach her at pleasure, in such sort that in short time we had taken her, finding her laden with victuall well powdred and well dryed, which at that present we received as sent us of God's great mercy." [19]

"The sickness which now began to make its appearance, and which was supposed to have been occasioned by the cold the men had got lately in the pinnaces, was attended with the death of one man, but the rest of the company, though ill, recovered their health." [19]

"The sickness," says the Relation, "which had begun to kindle amongst us two or three days before, did this day shew itself in Charles Chibb, one of our quarter-masters, a very tall man, and a right good mariner, taken away to the great grief both of captain and company. What the cause of this malady was we know not of certainty; we imputed it to the cold which our men had taken, lying without succour in the pinnaces. But, however, it was thus it pleased God to visit us, and yet in favour to restore unto health all the rest of our company that were touched with this disease, which were not a few."

On the 27th of November they returned in their pinnaces to the ships. "Within four or five days," says the Relation, "we came to our ship, where we found all other things in good order, but received very heavy news of the death of John Drake, our captaine's brother, and another young man called Richard Allen, which were both slain at one time as they attempted the boarding of a frigate, within two days after our departing from them.

"The manner of it, as we learned by examination of the company, was this: when they saw the frigate at sea, the company were very importunate on him to give chace and set upon this frigate, which they deemed had been a fit booty for them, but he told them that they wanted weapons to assail: they knew not how the frigate was provided; they had their boat laden with planks to finish what his brother had commanded. But this would not satisfy them: they still urged him with words and supposals; 'if ye will needs (said he) adventure, it shall never be said that I will be hindmost, neither shall you report to my brother that you lost your voyage by any cowardice you found in me.' [20]

"Thereupon every man shifted as he might for the time, and heaving the planks overboard, they took such few weapons as they had: namely, a broken pointed rapier, one old fisgee, and a rusty calliver: John Drake took the rapier, and made a gauntlet of his pillow: Richard Allen took the fisgee, both standing at the head of their pinnace, called the Lion: Robert Cluich took the calliver, and so boarded. But they found the frigate armed round about with a close fight of hides, full of pikes and callivers, which were discharged in their faces, and deadly wounded those that were in the foreship: John Drake in his belly, and Richard Allen in his head. But notwithstanding their wounds, they, with care, shifted off the pinnace and got clear of the frigate, and with all haste recovered their ship; where, within an hour after this, the young man of great hope ended his days, greatly lamented of all the company." [21]

January 3rd. - "Six of the company fell sick and died within two or three days, yea, they had thirty at a time sick of a calenture, occasioned by a sudden change from cold to heat, or from salt or brackish water, taken in at the mouth of the river, by the sloth of those seamen who would not go further up. 'Among the rest,' says the 'Relation,' 'Joseph Drake, another of our Captain's brothers, died in our Captain's arms of the same disease, of which that the cause might be the better discerned, and consequently remedied to the relief of others, by our Captain's appointment, he was ript open by the surgeon, who found his liver swollen, his heart as it were sodden, and his gutts all fair. This was the first and last experiment that our Captain made of anatomy in this voyage.' [22]

"The surgeon that cut him up overlived him not past four days, although he were not toucht with that sickness of which he had been recovered a month before, but only of an overbold practice which he must needs make upon himself, by receiving an over-strong purgation of his own device, after which, once taken, he never spake, nor did his boy recover the health which he lost by tasting it, till he saw England." [23]

Drake now made his arrangements for proceeding by land to Panama. Preparation of all necessaries were made on the 3rd February, being Shrove Tuesday; "at what time there had died 28 of our men." They began their journey with most of their company, leaving only a few sound men to secure the ships and tend the prisoners. They were in all 48, whereof 18 were English, and the rest Symerons. In a few days they reached Venta Cruz.

The King, or Chief of these people (for one was yet left), dwelt in a city sixteen leagues south-east of Panama, and was able to raise seventeen hundred righting men. They had towns of about sixty families, in the which the people lived cleanly and civilly. [24]

Captain Drake being informed of a great number of *recoes,* or companies of mules and people travelling, consisting of sometimes thirty, sometimes fifty, sometimes seventy, in a recoe, on which they carry the King of Spain's treasure to the ports, coming either across the isthmus from Panama, or from Venta Cruz to Nombre de Dios; he, with his party, way-laid them in the road. But, owing to one of his own people having taken a little too much aqua-vitae, and starting up to look at a Spanish horseman passing by, they were discovered. Drake, however, resolved to fight his way through the enemy's forces; and, upon their flight, pursued them as far as the town of Venta Cruz, into which he entered with them: where, such was his humanity and prudence, he strictly charged the Symerons, and all his company, that they should on no account hurt any female, or unarmed man; an order which they all faithfully obeyed. [25]

In their way hither it happened that Captain Drake was informed of a certain tree, from whose top he might at once discern both the North Sea from whence they had come, and the South Sea whither they were desirous of going. Being arrived near the spot where this tree stood (which was on the summit of a very high hill), one of the chief Symerons, taking Captain Drake by the hand, desired him to walk up to this famous tree, - "that goodlie and great high tree," as the manuscript says, in the trunk of which there were cut divers steps, to facilitate the ascent, almost to the top; and in the midst of the branches they had constructed a convenient arbour, in which twelve men might sit; and from thence, without difficulty, might plainly discern both the North and South Atlantic Oceans. [26]

Captain Drake having thus ascended this famous tree, and (the weather being fair) taken a full view of that sea, of which he had heard such golden reports, with great solemnity besought God "To give him life, and leave, once to sail an English ship in those seas;" and, adds the historian, "he was heard in what he asked, as will hereafter appear." Camden gives the following account of this discovery:- "That Drake, roving for a time up and down in the parts adjoining, discerned from the mountains the South Sea. Hereupon, the man, being influenced with ambition of glory and hopes of wealth, was so vehemently transported with desire to navigate that sea, that falling down there upon his knees, he implored the Divine assistance that he might, at some time or other, sail thither and make a perfect discovery of the same; and hereunto he bound himself with a vow. From that time forward, his mind was pricked on continually night and day to perform his vow." [27]

This, however, was not the first discovery of the great South Sea. In the year 1513, six years previous to the voyage of Magelhaens, Vasco Nunnez de Balboa, a Spanish Commander of Darien, to verify the intelligence he had received, marched with a body of Spaniards, and with Indian guides, across the isthmus. He was opposed on the passage by the natives. They demanded who the bearded strangers were, what they sought after, and whither they were going? The Spaniards answered, "They were Christians, that their errand was to preach a new religion, and to seek gold; and that they were going to the Southern Sea." This answer not giving satisfaction, Balboa forcibly made his way. On arriving at the foot of a mountain, from the top of which he was informed that the sea he so anxiously wished to discover was visible, he ordered his men to halt, and ascended alone. As soon as he had attained the summit, he fell on his knees, and, with uplifted hands, returned thanks to heaven for having bestowed on him the honour of being the first European that beheld the sea beyond America. Afterwards, in the presence of his followers and of many Indians, he walked up to his middle in the water, with his sword and target; and called upon them to bear testimony that *he took possession of the South Sea, and all which appertained to it,* for the King of Castile and Leon. [28]

A similar account of Balboa's discovery is mentioned by Southey, but in a more solemn and impressive manner; "falling prostrate on the ground, and raising himself again upon his knees, as the manner of the Christians is to pray, lifting up his eyes and hands towards heaven, and directing his face towards the new-found South Sea, he poured forth his humble and devout prayers before Almighty God, as a spiritual sacrifice with thanksgiving, that it pleased his Divine Majesty to reserve unto that day the victory and praise of so great a thing unto him, being but a man of small wit and knowledge, of little experience, and base parentage." And having beckoned his companions to come to him, he again "fell to his prayers as before, desiring Almighty God and the blessed Virgin to favour his beginning, and to give him good success to subdue those lands to the glory of his Holy name, and increase of his true religion; all his companions did likewise, and praised God with loud voices for joy." Then Vasco, with no less manly courage than Hannibal of Carthage showed his soldiers Italy from the promontories of the Alps, exhorted his men to lift up their hearts, and to behold the land even now under their feet, and the sea before their eyes, which should be unto them a full and just reward of their great labours and travails now overpast. When he had said these words, he commanded them to raise certain heaps of stones in the stead of altars, for a token of possession. [29]

The same relation nearly is given by Ramusio, who says that Vasco Nunnez, after returning thanks to God and all the saints of heaven, addressed himself to the Southern sea, "*O mare del sur,* Rege gli altri mari, fá che placido et quieto riceva la mià venuta!" &c. [30]

But to return to the party of Drake. Being by the folly and carelessness of this one drunken man disappointed of a very rich booty, it fell out that Drake became more fortunate afterwards: for, going back from the neighbourhood of Panama, and having ended their business at Venta Cruz (which they took and rifled), between Rio Francesco and Nombre de Dios, they intercepted a recoe of fifty mules, each carrying three hundred pounds' weight of silver, and some bars and wedges of gold; of which, carrying off what they could, they left several tons of silver behind them, buried in the sand; which, one of his soldiers being taken by the enemy, was, by torture, compelled to discover to the Spaniards. So that, at their return, they found it was almost all gone, the place having been digged up for a mile round about. Captain Drake, having thus performed his journey, hoped to meet with his pinnaces at the appointed place; coming thither, however, instead thereof, looking towards the sea, they saw seven Spanish pinnaces, that appeared to have been searching all the coasts thereabouts, which made him greatly doubt whether his own might not have been discovered and burnt, or taken possession of.

Being now also under great apprehension lest his frigate and ships might also be lost, it was very doubtful in such a case, if he and his company should ever return to their own country; in this extremity he resolved upon what appears to have been a desperate adventure. He caused a raft to be made with the fallen trees, which the river had brought down to the spot in its current: these were fitted and fast bound together, and a sail, made of a biscuit sack, was adapted to a pole as a mast, and an oar, shaped out of a young tree, served for a rudder to direct their course: this being completed, Drake, with three others, put out in their raft to sea; and having sailed and rowed about six hours, sitting always up to the middle in water, and at every wave up to their arm-pits, by God's wonderful providence they had sight of their pinnaces coming towards them. But the pinnaces, not perceiving the raft, nor suspecting any such thing, were forced by the wind and the approach of night to run for shelter behind a point of land. Drake seeing this, and judging they would anchor there, ran his raft ashore, and he and his party walked over land to the other side of the point, where he to his great joy found them. Proceeding from hence to Rio Francesco, he took in the rest of his company, with their treasure; and made such expedition, that in a short time they recovered their frigate and their ships; which done, Drake resolved to dismiss the Symerons, and return to England.

Upon their parting, Pedro, who proved himself to be an eminent person among the Symerons, and one who had been greatly serviceable to Captain Drake, could not be sent away without some remuneration for himself and his party. It was apparent that he took a great fancy to a rich cimeter which the Captain possessed, but was too modest to ask it, and the more so, lest Drake himself should so value it as to be unwilling to part with it. As soon as this impression was conveyed to the Captain, he freely and at once presented it to him. Pedro was overwhelmed with joy, and, anxious to make a grateful return, entreated Drake to accept from him four wedges of gold, as a pledge of his friendship and thanks; Drake refused to take them, but the importunity of the grateful Indian was so great that he was unable to resist, and received them with all courtesy; but threw them into the common stock, observing, "That it was only just, that those, who bore part of the charge with him, in setting him to sea, and in sharing in all the dangers, should likewise enjoy their full proportion of the advantage, at his return." An argument, says the narrator, of a generous and an honest mind.

The Episode of the French Captain Teton, who joined Drake at Cattivas and was relieved by him with water and provisions of which he stood in need, and had entreated permission to be Drake's confederate in the last expedition, is here omitted. This brave fellow, for so he appeared to be, was wounded in the scuffle, was unable to proceed on their return, was caught in the woods by the Spaniards, and is supposed to have suffered; the eighteen men he supplied, on the return of the expedition, shared in the prize to their full content.

The cimeter that was given to Pedro was a present to Drake from Mons. Teton, in acknowledgment of the kind treatment he had met with from him, and some other trifles he had received at Drake's hands. The Frenchmen and the Symerons took leave of Drake with deep regret. [31]

Being now resolved for England, and fully prepared for sea, they sailed, steered a direct course for home, and proceeded with so prosperous a gale, that in twenty-three days they passed from Cape Florida to the Isles of Scilly, and arrived at Plymouth on Sunday the 9th of August, 1573, during sermon time. The news of Drake's return being carried into the church, there remained few or no people with the preacher; all running out to witness the blessing of God upon the dangerous adventures and enterprises of the Captain, who had spent one year, two months, and some odd days, in this voyage; [31] "all (says the narrator) hastening to see the evidence of God's love and blessing towards our gracious Queene and countrey, by the fruite of our Captaine's labour and successe.

SOLI DEO GLORIA" [32]

We may append to this narrative, as a curiosity, an abstract from a whimsical drama of Sir William Davenant, Poet-Laureate to Charles II., founded on this expedition of Drake, which he calls "The History of Sir Francis Drake, expressed by instrumental and vocal music, and by art of Perspective in Scenes, &c."

The incidents of this voyage are pretty correctly told in rhyme, accompanied with appropriate scenery, songs, dances, and choruses, by the Mariners, and the Symerons, Pedro performing a principal part. The first scene is Port Pheasant, the men busied setting up the pinnaces, &c., and the arrival of Captain Rause is announced by the Boatswain.

Boatswain. The Lion Rause is landed here,
　　　　　　I'll run to meet him at the pier.
　　　　　　　　A ton of yellow gold,
　　　　　　　　Conceal'd within our hold,
　　　　　　For half my share I scorn to take,
　　　　　　When he is joined with Dragon Drake.

In the fourth "Entry" (or scene) we have "hills, a wood, and a tree of extraordinary compass and height."

Drake.	Is this that most renown'd of Western trees
	On whose main-top
	Thou gav'st me hope
	To view the North and South *Atlantick* Seas?
Pedro.	It is; therefore, with speed,
	Thither, my chief, proceed,
	And when you, climbing, have attained the height,
	Report will grow authentick, by your sight.
Drake.	When from those lofty branches, I
	The South *Atlantick* spy,
	My vows shall higher fly,
	'Till they with highest heav'n prevail,
	That, as I see it, I may on it sail.
Drake Jun.	No English keel hath yet that Ocean plowed.
Pedro.	If prophecie from me may be allow'd,
	Renown'd Drake, Heaven does decree
	That happy enterprize to thee,
	For thou of all the Britons art the first
	That boldy durst
	This Western World invade;
	And as thou now art made
	The first to whom that Ocean will be shown,
	So to thy Isle thou first shall make it known. [33]

This dramatic sketch is so far curious, as showing that the history of Drake, or a small portion of it, was considered interesting enough to amuse a public audience, a century after the event, as his adventures will no doubt ever be, so long as the lives of our brave and fearless seamen continue to be cherished, and had in that degree of respect and consideration by their countrymen, to which they are so eminently entitled.

[1] So called by Sir F. Drake (nephew), but is in fact the Fifth of Drake to the West Indies.

[2] Camden, Hakluyt, Purchas, Strype, &c.

[3] Report of this Voyage in the Sloane MS. British Museum.

[4] Burney's Discoveries in the South Sea.

[5] Sloane MSS. British Museum.

[6] Drake Revived.

[7] Drake Revived.

[8] Drake Revived.

[9] Drake Revived.

[10] Drake Revived.

[11] Drake Revived.

[12] Drake Revived.

[13] Drake Revived.

[14] Sloane MS.; and Drake Revived.

[15] Drake Revived.

[16] Drake Revived.

[17] Johnson's Works.

[18] Drake Revived.

[19] Sloane MS.; and Drake Revived.

[20] Sloane MS; and Drake Revived.

[21] Sloane MS.

[22] Ibid.

[23] Sloane MS.

[24] Prince's Worthies of Devon.

[25] Drake Revived.

[26] Camden; Prince; Drake Revived, &c.

[27] Camden.

[28] Burney, from *Gomara Istoria de las Indias.*

[29] Southey, from *Eden's translation of Peter Martyr.*

[30] Ramusio.

[31] Drake Revived.

Chapter Three - The Voyage Round the World - 1577-1580

"Five years," says Camden, "after his return from a former voyage, to wit, in the year 1572, when Drake had gotten a pretty store of money, by playing the seaman and the pirate, he, to lick himself whole of the damage he had received from the Spaniards (which a divine belonging to the fleet had easily persuaded him to be lawful), set sail again for America." [1]

There can be little doubt that Captain Drake did return from his late voyage with "a pretty store of money," after discharging all demands upon it; and admitting it to be so, it was not likely that a person of his active and vigorous mind would sit down quietly, and lapse into a state of listless indolence, but rather be on the look out for some fresh employment congenial with his enterprising disposition. He betrayed no haste, however, to embark on a new voyage. Previous to the last, he had made the acquaintance of the Earl of Essex, who was now appointed Governor of the province of Ulster, with the view of quelling the rebels, more particularly in the district of Clandeboy, by means of volunteer adventurers, which he was himself to raise, and for which they were to be rewarded by grants of land.

Drake, thinking he might be of material assistance to his friend, and perhaps with a view to his own interest, "furnished," says Stow, "at his own proper expense, three frigates with men and munition, and served voluntary in Ireland under Walter Earl of Essex; where he did excellent service both by sea and land, at the winning of divers strong forts." [2] We are not, however, to suppose that a frigate in those days had any resemblance or analogy to the frigate of ours. A *fregata* was a small pinnace moved by sails and oars, of five, ten, or fifteen tons measurement, in use mostly in the Mediterranean. There was no such *name* as *frigate* in our navy at that time.

The project, however, failed. We learn from Rapin that, "in 1573 Walter Devereux, Earl of Essex, had leave to go Ireland, to conquer the country of Clandeboy, at his own expense. But his enterprise was not crowned with success, because he was privately hindered by the Earl of Leicester, his enemy." [3] An Irish historian, McSkimmin, tells us a little more. "In the same year (1573) came the Right Hon. the Earl of Essex into this land, as Captain General and Governor of Ulster, and was, at this time, the chief of a band of military adventurers. He drove the Scots out of Clandeboy, and took the Castle of Lifford from Con. O'Donnell; but making little progress, and receiving many angry messages from court, at the instigations of Lord Leicester, who was his greatest enemy, he resigned his command, and retired to Dublin, where he died of a broken heart, in September, 1576, at the early age of 36."

This visit, however, of Drake's undoubtedly led to the establishment of his future reputation, by the introduction it procured for him to Sir Christopher Hatton, then Vice-Chamberlain, and by him to the Queen, who, being apprized of his adventurous expedition and success against her bitterest enemy, gave him a most flattering reception, and encouraged him to follow up his brave and successful attacks upon the Indian colonies of Spain; and some of his historians add, that she gave him a commission to make reprisals. This would have been equivalent to a declaration of war, and therefore is not credible; still less so that she should say to him at the first interview, as the old chroniclers mostly have it, and repeated in the "World Encompassed," "I account that he who striketh thee, Drake, striketh me." Such an expression might have escaped the royal lips, not always discreetly closed, at a future period, after his return from this circumnavigation voyage, when she condescended to visit the "Golden Hind" at Deptford, and when Drake *had been stricken* by certain of his own countrymen, - she might have then assuaged the pain that envy had inflicted, by the balm of an expression of such soothing kindness, - but she did enough at once to raise his fortune and reputation; and it had that effect.

When we regard the early period of our foreign voyages, in which the present one was about to be made, the means by which it was made, and the success with which it was crowned, it must ever be, as it has long been, a splendid memorial of one of the most daring and adventurous enterprises, and the most glorious in its result, that the naval exploits of England, many and brilliant as they are, can supply. We mean not to compare it to one of those gallant conflicts with an enemy, where the forces are nearly equal, and victory or disgrace must be the result; this is an exploit of a different character, and admits not of such comparison; but, to undertake a voyage on a sea hitherto unknown and unnavigated; to attack advisedly an enemy's distant territory, with scanty and inadequate means; to perform what had but once been attempted, and had failed; and to return triumphantly home, are exploits worthy of that high distinction and renown which it procured for him. And with what means were they achieved? with five small ships, the largest of one hundred, the smallest of fifteen tons, and the average of the whole only fifty-five tons. With these he started on a voyage round the world, which had never been done but once, passed through the Straits of Magelhaens, which had never been passed but once, and "accounted so terrible in those days that the very thought of attempting it was dreadful;" the other half of the world was passed over with his own single ship; and all this, be it recollected, undertaken by a private individual, known but by a single successful adventure, made with two miserable vessels, unassisted by any public patronage, and fitted out, from any thing that appears to the contrary, entirely at his own expense, or upon his own credit with a few friends. Yet on this voyage, conducted by himself and his two brothers, both of whom perished on the occasion, he laid the solid foundation of his future fame and fortune.

From the luxurious manner in which it is stated that Drake fitted out his own ship, for the present voyage, it may be concluded that there was no want of funds. His ships were supplied with all manner of necessaries and provisions for the long and hazardous voyage in contemplation; nor were they confined to such as were absolutely necessary. Articles were provided to administer, not merely to his comforts, but also to his pleasures and amusement. The furniture of his own little ship, the Pelican, is described as being sumptuous; all the vessels for his table, and some of them even in the cook-room, are said to have been of silver, probably part of his prizes. He took with him, besides, musicians who could play on different instruments. With all this, however, Drake is described as a man of plain and simple habits, and had therefore, no doubt, some special object in view when he, in this instance, departed from them. He might have considered it politic to display the wealth and taste of his country, in the distant parts of the world to which he was about to proceed; and perhaps also, at the same time, to indulge a little feeling of vanity on his own account.

The present voyage was published by Sir Francis Drake (nephew of the Admiral), under the title of "The World Encompassed," carefully collected, as the preface tells us, "out of the notes of Master Francis Fletcher, Preacher in this employment, and divers others his followers in the same: Offered now, at last, to publique view, both for the honour of the actor, but especially for the stirring up of heroick spirits, to benefit their countrie, and eternize their names by like noble attempts." [4]   He begins by informing the reader, that "the main ocean by right is the Lord's alone, and by nature left free for all men to deal withall, as very sufficient for all men's use, and large enough for all men's industry. And therefore that valiant enterprize, accompanied with happy success, which that right rare and thrice worthy Captaine, Francis Drake, achieved, in first turning up a furrow about the whole world, doth not only overmatch the ancient Argonauts, but also outreach eth, in many respects, that noble mariner Magelhaens, and by farre surpasseth his crowned victory. But hereof let posterity judge." [5]

It is said, that such secrecy was observed by Drake in making preparations for this voyage, that its destination was concealed from his intimate friends, and that his little squadron put to sea avowedly for a very different part of the world to that which was advisedly intended. The result of this concealment was, that the voyage to Nombre de Dios, and the other places about the isthmus of Darien, was anticipated by another adventurer. It has been seen that, in the late voyage, was one John Oxenham, who served under Drake, as a soldier, sailor, and cook, and was actively and usefully employed by him on various occasions. This man was so attached to Drake, that he declared his readiness to go with him on any future voyage and to any part of the world; but having waited above two years, and not knowing of Drake's intentions, he, with some others, scraped together money enough to fit out a ship of a hundred and forty tons' burden, bearing twenty seamen, with which they sailed in the year 1575, for the isthmus of Darien; and, on arriving at Porto Bello, Oxenham learned from the Indians that a convoy of muleteers was expected to come to that place from Panama. He accordingly marched with his company to meet them, having only two small guns and some muskets, with six Indians for their guides, and proceeded about twelve leagues over the mountains, to a small river that falls into the South Sea. [6] Here he built a pinnace, and dropped down in her into the Bay of Panama, and thence to the Pearl Islands, as the place near which the plate ships from Peru usually pass for Panama. Before long a small bark from Quito arrived at the island, of which Oxenham took possession, and found in her sixty pounds' weight of gold, [7] and a large supply of provisions. At the end of six days he took another bark from Lima, in which he found a hundred pounds' weight of silver in bars. [8] He then went in search of pearls on the island; found a few, and returning to his pinnace, re-entered the river, first, however, dismissing his two prizes.

The delay of fifteen days, on Pearl Island, was the cause of all his misfortunes. The Indians of the island went, the same night he left them, to Panama, to give intelligence of what had happened. Captain Ortega was dispatched with four barks, in search of him; and, in their way to Pearl Island, fell in with the two liberated prizes, from whom Ortega learned that Oxenham had gone up the river. It seems this river had three branches, and Ortega was doubtful which of them to take; but having observed a quantity of fowl feathers swimming down one of the streams, he took that branch, and, after four days' rowing, discovered Oxenham's pinnace upon the sands, with only six men in her, of whom his party killed one, but the other five escaped. In the pinnace, however, they found nothing but provisions. He therefore left twenty of his men to guard her, and his two barks; and, with the other eighty, set out to explore the country. They had not proceeded more than half a league, before they discovered a hut, made of boughs, in which they found all the Englishmen's goods, together with their booty of gold, pearls, and silver. Satisfied with having recovered the treasure, Ortega was about to depart, when Oxenham came down upon them with his men, and about two hundred Symerons, and attacked the Spaniards with great fury; but the latter got the better of the English party, killed eleven of them, together with five Indians, and took seven prisoners, having only two of their men killed and five wounded. [9] Oxenham escaped, and made the best of his way to his ship.

Information had been sent from Panama, over the isthmus to Nombre de Dios, of all that had passed; four barks were fitted out, found Oxenham's ship, and carried her back to their port. In the meantime the Viceroy of Peru had ordered 150 men to scour the mountains, in search of the English. When found, as they speedily were, some of them were sick and made prisoners; the rest fled. But, being betrayed by the Indians, they were soon taken and conveyed to Panama. Here Oxenham was examined as to what authority he had from the Queen; and being unable to produce any power or commission, he and his comrades were sentenced to suffer death, as pirates and common enemies of mankind; and were accordingly executed, with the exception of Oxenham, who, with his master, pilot, and five boys, were carried to Lima, where the three men likewise suffered, but the boys were pardoned. And thus terminated this ill-conducted and unfortunate adventure. [10]

This young man deserved a better fate. Drake had the highest opinion of him, and he was beloved by the whole crew. Prince says there is a family of considerable standing of this name at South Tawton, near Oakhampton, of which is this strange and wonderful thing recorded: "That at the death of any of them, a bird with a white breast is seen for a while fluttering about their beds, and then suddenly to vanish away." [11] The same is told in the "Beauties of England," article Devon; and Southey quotes, from Howell, several inscriptions on a tombstone, giving the names of the family to whom the bird had appeared, - to the mother, a son, two sisters, and some others. "To all these there be divers witnesses, both squires and ladies, whose names are engraven upon the stone." [12]

Drake of course knew nothing of all this regarding Oxenham, which occurred while he was busily fitting out his little squadron for the same scene of action. It consisted of the Pelican, 100 tons, Captain Drake; the Elizabeth, 80 tons, Captain John Winter; the Mary gold, 30 ditto, Captain John Thomas; the Swan, Flyboat, 50 ditto, Captain John Chester; the Christopher, pinnace, 15 ditto, Captain Thomas Moone; manned with 163 stout and able seamen. They left Plymouth on the 15th November, 1577; but a violent storm overtook them, which obliged them to put into Falmouth, and thence return to Plymouth to have their damages made good. As soon as they were refitted, Drake set sail from Plymouth, a second time, on the 13th December. On the 27th they called at Mogador, on the coast of Barbary, for refreshments; and here Drake set up one of his pinnaces which he had carried with him in frame. The inhabitants showed signs of friendship, and promised to bring them, the following day, sheep, fowls, and other provisions; and accordingly they came down with camels laden with various articles, not only of provisions, but merchandise: but on their approaching the coast an unlucky accident occurred. One of the crew, in the boat, John Fry, leaping hastily on shore, and wishing to give some of them a hearty shake of the hand, so surprised and alarmed the Moors that they seized him, and, to prevent his making any resistance, held a dagger to his throat, laid him across a horse, and carried him off.

This act of violence, as it afterwards appeared, was only to ascertain to whom the ships belonged; whether they were Portuguese, who were at war with them; and when the chief before whom the man was brought was informed they were English, he was immediately sent back with presents to the Captain; but the ships having unfortunately departed before his return, he was sent back to England by the first opportunity. In the meantime the little squadron, proceeding along the coast, fell in with three Spanish fishing craft called *caunters,* which they took, and after that with three caravels at Cape Blanco. Drake gave up two of the fishermen's boats, and the third, of about 40 tons, he kept, but gave the owner the Christopher in exchange. Here Drake remained four days, taking in water and provisions, and mustering and exercising his men.

The squadron next proceeded to the Cape de Verd Islands, and calling at Mayo, they landed, and "found a town not far from the water's side, of a great number of desolate and ruinous houses, with a poor naked chapel or oratory, being to small purpose, and as it seemeth only to make a shew, and that a false shew, contrary to the nature of a scarecrow which feareth birds from coming nigh; but this enticeth such as pass by to come in and look for commodity, which is not at all to be found there." [13] Having here taken in fruits and refreshments, they next stood in for Porto Pray a, in the island of St. Jago, but, from distrust of the inhabitants, did not anchor. Here they fell in with, and chased, two Portuguese vessels, one of which they captured, laden with wine and other valuable articles. She had also several passengers on board, who requested to remain in her, on learning that the squadron was bound for the Brazils; but the crew he dismissed, and put twenty-eight of his own men into her, retaining the master, Nuno de Silva, in order to make use of him as a pilot on the Brazil coast: and he appointed Mr. Doughty, a friend and volunteer on the expedition, to the command of this Portuguese prize. To his great mortification, however, a complaint was shortly afterwards preferred against Doughty, of which the General lost no time in making an investigation. But of this transaction the Rev. Mr. Fletcher thus reports the issue.

"Into this Shipp the Generall sent one Tho: Doubty, Gentleman, to be Captain; there, not long after his entering into his charge, he was charged and accused by John Brewer, Edward Bright, and some others of their friends, to have purloined, to his proper use, to deceave the voyage from things of great value, and therefore was not to be put in trust any longer, least he might rob the voyage and deprive the company of their hope, and her Majesty and other adventurers, of their benefit, to inrich himself and make himself greater to the overthrow of all others. In regard whereof, the General speedily went on board the Prize to examine the matter, who finding certain pairs of Portugal Gloves, some few pieces of money of a strange coin, and a small Ring, all which one of the Portugals gave him out of his chest in hope of favour, all of them being not worth the speaking of. These things being found with him, not purloined but only given him, received in the sight of all men, the General, in his discression, deposed him from his place, and yet sent him in his own stead to the Admiral (meaning the ship) as commander of that company for the tyme, in his absence; and placed Thomas Drake, his brother, in the Prize, Captain in the room of Thomas Doubty, yet remained there himself till he had discharged the Portugals.

"In the mean time the said Thomas Doubty, being aboard the Admirall, was thought to be too peremptory and exceeded his authority, taking upon him too great a command, by reason whereof such as had him in dislike tok advantage agaynst him to complain a second tyme, which were heard with expedition to their own contentation; for the Portugals, being set in one pinnace with necessary provisions of victual, whereof they rejoiced that they scaped with their lives, thinking Ships and Goods, as they said, well bestowed, to arrive where they would. The General came aboard the Admiral, and upon the second complaint, remooved the said Doubty a prisoner into the fly boat with utter disgrace." [14]

The next island they passed by was the island of Fuego, which was then throwing out volcanic flames; and Brava next, near which mariners speak of the sea being very deep, 120 fathoms close to the shore. The island, however, is described as a sweet and pleasant abode; the trees always green, and the soil almost full of trees; figs always ripe, cocos, plantains, oranges, lemons in abundance; silver streams of sweet and wholesome water, which with boats may easily be taken in. [15] And now, drawing near the equator, Drake, being always very careful of his men's health, let every one of them blood with his own hand. [16]

Here the ships were as usual becalmed; they had much thunder and lightning; and made little or no progress for the space of three weeks; an occurrence not unfrequent not only at the time in question, but for two centuries afterwards; owing to the invariable practice of trying to make a direct and straight course across the line, instead of, as is now done, crossing it from 20° to 24° of west longitude, where ships are very rarely becalmed. The consequence was, that Drake saw no land for fifty-five days, when the coast of Brazil presented itself to his view.

Drake here did little more than look into the great river La Plata, as the object of his voyage did not lie in that river. He observed it encumbered with multitudes of seals, which Camden calls sea-calves, and of which they killed many, and found them good and acceptable meat, both as food for the present, and as a supply of provisions for the future. [17] Standing to the southward, they anchored in a bay in 47° S. lat., all but the Swan and the Portuguese prize, (now named the Mary,) which had separated. Some natives were seen, to whom they made a signal by hoisting a white cloth, which they answered by gestures and speech, but kept at a distance.

Near the rocks were found, in places made for the purpose, dried fowls and above fifty ostriches (cassiowaries); the thighs of the latter equal in size "to reasonable legs of mutton." They do not fly; but with the help of their wings run swiftly, taking such large strides that no man can overtake them. Leaving this port they found a better, somewhat less than a degree to the southward. The General sent the Elizabeth, Capt. Winter, with the steward, to look for the missing ships, the Swan and Mary; the former he met with and brought her in. Here they trafficked with the natives. These people had no other covering than a skin, which, when sitting or lying in the cold, was thrown over their shoulders, but which, when in motion, was bound round their loins.

They painted themselves all over; some had one shoulder painted white, and the other black; and similar contrasts were exhibited with their sides and legs; in the black parts were white moons, and in the white parts black suns. This fanciful style of painting may have been intended for decoration; [18] but Dr. Johnson, in this part of his life of Drake, seems to ascribe the custom to its being a protection against cold. He says, -

"It is observable that most nations, amongst whom the use of clothes is unknown, paint their bodies. Such was the practice of the first inhabitants of our own country. From this custom did our earliest enemies, the Picts, owe their denomination. As it is not probable that caprice or fancy should be uniform, there must be doubtless some reason for a practice so general, and prevailing in distant parts of the world, which have no communication with each other. The original end of painting their bodies was, probably, to exclude the cold; an end which, if we believe some relations, is so effectually produced by it, that the men thus painted never shiver at the most piercing blasts. But doubtless any people so hardened by continual severities would even, without paint, be less sensible of the cold than the civilized inhabitants of the same climate. However, this practice may contribute in some degree to defend them from the injuries of winter, and in those climates where little evaporates from the pores may be used with no great inconvenience; but in hot countries, where perspiration in greater degree is necessary, the natives only use unction to preserve them from the other extreme of weather: so well do either reason or experience supply the place of science in savage countries." [19]

Practically, it may be doubted whether reason or experience bears out the theory of this great moral philosopher. The uncivilized beings of moderate climates, like the Hottentots of the Cape of Good Hope, rub their bodies with the powder of Buccho (Diosma), mixed with a little grease. The savages of the tropical regions bathe in the water, and amuse themselves with tattooing each other's skins; and those of the Polar regions wrap their bodies up in the furry skins of the native animals. It is not probable that painting the body with suns, and moons, and other devices, could in the least degree contribute to expel the cold in any of these climates.

"Magelhaens, it is observed, was not altogether deceived in naming them giants, for they generally differ from the common sort of men, both in stature, bigness, and strength of body, as also in the hideousness of their voice; but yet they are nothing so monstrous or giant-like as they were reported, there being some Englishmen as tall as the highest of any that we could see; but, peradventure, the Spaniards did not think that ever any Englishmen could come thither to reprove them; and thereupon might presume the more boldly to lie: "the name *Pentagones,* five cubits, namely, 7½ feet, describing the full height, (if not somewhat more,) of the highest of them." [20]

Modern voyagers have described these people as a strong and powerful race, but by no means exceeding the ordinary size of Europeans.

It is curious to find how very differently different people are apt to view the same objects, seen even at the same time and on the same spot. Cliffe (the writer of Winter's Voyage) says, "the people were of mean stature, well limbed, but very sly. One of them," he says, "as the General stooped, snatched off his hat, which was of scarlet, with a gold band, and ran away with it, and that the General would not suffer his people to hurt any of them by way of resenting the injury." Mr. Fletcher, on the contrary, writes that these people were of large stature; that the hat was a gift from the General; and that the Indian, proud of the gift, wore it every day. These people are well made, handsome, and strong; their dispositions cheerful, and much addicted to merriment. Commodore Byron calls one of these Patagonians a "frightful colossus," not less than seven feet. Mr. Cummings, who was 6 feet 2 inches high, he calls a pigmy among giants, for "indeed," says he, "they may more properly be called giants than tall men." But Cook and Sir Joseph Banks decided the question; and ascertained the average height to be from 5 feet 4 to 5 feet 8 inches, and which recent voyagers have confirmed.

Leaving Seal Bay, as it was called, on the 3rd of June, they anchored in another on the 12th, where they unloaded the little fishing skiff, and turned her adrift. On the 20th their whole force having joined, they anchored in Port St. Julian. Here, in a foolish trial of skill with bows and arrows, Drake lost two of his most valuable men. Robert Winter, partly in sport, and partly to show English dexterity, on pulling the string of his bow with violence, broke it; and while busying himself with fixing it again, some natives shot their arrows at him, and wounded him in the shoulder; and another arrow pierced his lungs; he survived these wounds but two days. The gunner, Oliver, took aim at them with his musket, but it missed fire, and he was slain outright by an arrow.

It seems the natives became short of arrows, "which the General perceiving, he then took the fowling-piece in hand, and priming it anew, made a shot at him which first began the quarrel, and striking him in the pancy with hail shot, sent his guts abroad with great torment, as it seemed by his cry, which was so hideous and terrible a roar, as if ten bulls had joined together in roaring." [21]   This seems to have dispersed the giants, as well it might. On recovering one of the dead bodies, Fletcher says, - "When our men came to him, the enemies had thrust into one of his eyes one of our arrows as deep as they could." [22] A sermon was preached, and the bodies "buried with such honours as in such case martial men used to have when they are dead, being both laid in one grave, as they both were partakers of one manner of death, and ended their lives together by one and the self-same kind of accident."

One of the first objects that caught attention was a gibbet, which had been set up, as was supposed, seventy years before, by Magelhaens, for the execution of certain mutineers; no one supposing that a similar occurrence was at hand in the fleet of Drake, within the same port. It has been mentioned that Mr. Doughty was removed from the Portuguese prize for malversation. The melancholy history of this unfortunate man has been told, with more or less appearances of guilt, by all the narrators of Drake's adventurous voyages; but a considerable doubt is still left on the mind of the reader, which is now perhaps too late to be cleared up. But as the story would seem to leave a blot on Drake's general kind disposition and humanity, it may be right to repeat what the several writers have told of the circumstances of this transaction. And first let us give what the oldest and most respectable of Drake's historians says on the subject:-

"In this very place," says Camden, "John Doughty, an industrious and stout man, and the next unto Drake, was called to his trial for raising a mutiny in the fleet, found guilty by twelve men, after the English manner, and condemned to death, which he suffered undauntedly, being beheaded, having first received the holy communion with Drake. And, indeed, the most impartial persons in the fleet were of opinion that he had acted seditiously; and that Drake cut him off as an emulator of his glory, and one that regarded not so much who he himself excelled in commendations for sea matters, as who he thought might equal him. Yet wanted there not some, who, pretending to understand things better than others, gave out that Drake had in charge from Leicester to take off Doughty, upon any pretence whatsoever, because he had reported abroad that the Earl of Essex was made away by the cunning practices of Leicester." [23]

The next most ancient and independent authority is that of Hakluyt.

"In this port (St. Julian) our General began to inquire diligently of the actions of Mr. Thomas Doughty, and found them not to be such as he looked for, but tending rather to contention of mutiny, or some other disorder, whereby (without redress) the success of the voyage might greatly have been hazarded; whereupon the company was called together and made acquainted with the particulars of the cause, which were found partly by Mr. Doughty's own confession, and partly by the evidence of the fact, to be true: which, when our General saw, although his private affection to Mr. Doughty (as he then in presence of all sacredly protested) was great, yet the care he had of the state of the voyage, of the expectation of her Majestic, and of the honour of his countrie, did more touch him (as indeed it ought) than the private respect of one man; so that the cause being thoroughly heard, and all things done in good order, as neere as might be to the course of our laws in England, it was concluded that Mr. Doughty should receive punishment according to the qualitie of the offence. And he, seeing no remedie but patience for himself, desired before his death to receive the communion, which he did at the hands of Mr. Fletcher, the minister, and our General himself accompanied him in that holy action; which being done, and the place of execution made ready, he, having embraced our General, and taken his leave of all the companie, with prayer for the Queen's Majestic and our realm, in quiet sort laid his head to the block, where he ended his life." [24]

In speaking of the evil disposition of the people of St. Julian, which is ascribed to the cruelties of the Spaniards, who had visited this place, the narrator, in the "World Encompassed," says, "To this evil, thus received at the hands of the infidels, there was adjoined and grew another mischief, wrought and contrived closely among ourselves, as great, yea, far greater, and of far more grievous consequence than the former; but that it was, by God's providence, detected and prevented in time, which else had extended itself, not only to the violent shedding of innocent blood, by murdering our General, and such others as were most firm and faithful to him, but also to the final overthrow of the whole action intended, and to divers other most dangerous effects."

The person here alluded to, for his name is never once mentioned throughout the whole transaction in the "World Encompassed," is the same spoken of by Camden and Hakluyt and others, - Mr. Thomas Doughtie, - who is accused of having conceived the murder of the General, and some of his immediate friends - a plot which, it states, "was laid before the departure of the expedition from England, and which was made known to the General at Plymouth, who would not believe that a person whom he so dearly loved would conceive such evil purposes against him; till, at length, perceiving that the manifold practices grew daily more and more, even to extremities, and that lenity and favour did little good, he thought it high time to call these practices into question, and before it were too late to call any question of them into hearing; and therefore, setting good watch over him, and assembling all his captains, and gentlemen of his company together, he propounded to them the good parts which were in the gentleman, the great good will and inward affection, more than brotherly, which he had ever, since his first acquaintance, borne him, not omitting the respect which was had of him among no mean personages in England; and afterwards delivered the letters which were written to him, with the particulars from time to time which had been observed, not so much by himself, as by his good friends; not only at sea, but even at Plymouth; not bare words, but writings; not writings alone, but actions, tending to the overthrow of the service in hand, and making away of his person.

"Proofs were required and alleged, so many, and so evident, that the gentleman himself, stricken with remorse of his inconsiderate and unkind dealing, acknowledged himself to have deserved death, yea, many deaths; for that he conspired, not only the overthrow of the action, but of the principal actor also, who was not a stranger or illwiller, but a dear and true friend unto him; and therefore, in a great assembly openly besought them, in whose hands justice rested, to take some order for him, that he might not be compelled to enforce his own hands, against his own bowels, or otherwise to become his own executioner.

"The admiration and astonishment hereat, in all the hearers, even those which were his nearest friends, and most affected him, was great, yea, in those which, for many benefits received from him, had good cause to love him: but yet the General was most of all distracted; and therefore withdrew himself, as not able to conceal his tender affection, requiring them that had heard the whole matter to give their judgments, as they would another day answer it unto their prince, and unto Almighty God, judge of all the earth." [25]

We are then told that "they all, after duly weighing the evidence, above forty in number, the chiefest in place and judgment in the whole fleet, with their own hand, under seal, adjudged that he had deserved death; and that it stood by no means with their safety to let him live; and therefore they remitted the manner thereof, with the rest of the circumstances, to the General. Therefore they then proposed to him (the still unnamed person) this choice: Whether he would take to be executed in this island? or to be set upon land on the main? or return into England, there to answer his deed before the Lords of her Majesty's Council? He most humbly thanked the General for his clemency extended towards him in such ample sort; and craving some respite, to consult thereon and so make his choice advisedly; the next day he returned answer that, 'Albeit he had yielded in his heart to entertain so great a sin, as whereof he was now justly condemned; yet he had a care, and that excelling all other cares, to die a Christian man, and therefore besought the General most earnestly he would not counsel him to endanger his soul by consenting to be left among savage infidels; and as for returning to England, he must first have a ship, and men to conduct it, with sufficient victuals, if any men could be found to accompany him on so disgraceful an errand; yet the shame of return would be more grievous than death; and therefore he preferred that, with all his heart, he did embrace the first branch of the General's offer, desiring only this favour, that they might once again receive the holy Communion together before his death, and that he might not die other than a gentleman's death.'" [26]

"No reasons," we are told, "could persuade him to alter his choice: seeing he remained resolute in his determination, his last requests were granted; and the next convenient day a Communion was celebrated by Mr. Francis Fletcher, preacher and pastor of the fleet at that time. The General himself communicated in this sacred ordinance with this condemned penitent gentleman, who shewed great tokens of a contrite and repentant heart. After this holy repast they dined also at the same table together, as cheerfully in sobriety, as ever in their lives they had done aforetime, each cheering up the other, and taking their leave, by drinking each to other, as if some journey only had been in hand." [27]

After dinner, all things being ready prepared, by a provost-marshal appointed for the occasion, Mr. Doughtie, without any dallying or delaying the time, "came forth, and kneeled down, preparing at once his neck for the axe, and his spirit for heaven, which having done, without long ceremony, as one who had before digested this whole tragedy, he desired all the rest to pray for him, and willed the executioner to do his office, not to fear nor spare." [28]

Such is the account given of this transaction by Mr. Thomas Drake, who is believed to be, and no doubt was, the chief compiler or reviser of the "Voyage round the World," (though published by his son, Sir Francis,) especially of the part in question, as it appears in the narrative of the "World Encompassed:" but which is somewhat too theatrical to obtain general belief; and this conclusion will be come to, from the extraordinary and mysterious manner in which it is evidently got up. But there is a strong and irresistible testimony against a very essential part of the story. The manuscript relation of Mr. Francis Fletcher differs materially from the foregoing representations, and is wholly omitted in the printed voyage. Nothing appears in it, of any choice being given to Mr. Doughtie, between death and life, upon any terms. But it is best to give Mr. Fletcher's own account of this melancholy story, in his own words, from his own manuscript, or rather the certified manuscript copy of it contained in the Sloane MSS. in the British Museum. He thus goes on with his narrative, after his story of the giants.

"This bloudy Tragedie being ended, another more grievous ensueth. I call it more grievous because it was among ourselves begun, contrived, and ended; for now, Thomas Doubty, our countryman; is called in question, not by giants but by Christians, even ourselves. The original of dislike against him you may read in the storye off the Iland of Cape Verde, upon the coast of Affrick, at the taking of the Portugal prize, by whom he was accused - and for what? But now more dangerous matter, and of greater weight, is layed to his charge, and that by the same persons, namely, for words spoken by him to them, being in England, in the General's garden in Plymouth, long before our departure thence, which had been their parts and dutyes to have discovered them at that tyme, and not to have consealed them for a tyme and place not so fitting; but how true it was wherewith they charged him upon their oathe, I know not; but he utterly denied it, upon his salvation, at the hour of communicating the Sacrament of the body and blood of Christ, at the hour and moment of his death, affirming that he was innocent of such things whereof he was accused, judged, and suffered death for. Of whom I must needs testifye the truth for the good things of God I found in him, in the tyme we were conversant, arid especially in the time of his afflictions and trouble, till he yielded up the spirit to God - I doubt not, to immortality: he feared God, he loved his word, and was always desirous to edify others, and conforme himselfe in the faith of Christ. For his qualityes, in a man of his tyme, they were rare, and his gifts very excellent for his age: a sweet orator, a pregnant philosopher, a good gift for the Greek tongue, and a reasonable taste of Hebrew; a sufficient secretary to a noble personage of great place, and in Zealand an aproved soldier, and not behind many in the study of the law for his tyme; and that with it a sufficient argument to prove a good Christian, and of all other things, a most manifest witness of a child of God to men, that he was delighted in the study, hearing, and practice of the word of God; daily exercising himselfe therein by reading, meditating to himselfe, conferring with others, instructing of the ignorant, as if he had been a minister of Christ, wherein he profitted so much, that long before his death he seemed to be mortifyed, and to be ravished with the desire of God's kingdom, yea to be dissolved and to be with Christ, in whose death so many vertues were cutt off as dropps of blood new shedd, - who being dead was buried neer the sepulchre of those which went before him, upon whose graves I set up a stone, whereon I engraved their names, the day of their buriall, and the month and the yeare, for a monument to them which shall fall with that place in tyme to come." [29] "These thinges, with dropps of blood from the hartes of some, thus ended, wee went about our other business and necessarie affaires." [30]

It is evident that Mr. Fletcher speaks of Mr. Doughtie in terms of more than common regard; and, in giving his character, has described him as a man of extraordinary endowments. What possible object Doughty could have in murdering his friend, and others, is difficult to conceive. Suppose him to have succeeded; what next would he have done? He had neither friends nor confederates in the ship nor in the squadron (besides Fletcher); and Drake was beloved by the whole crew; all that he could possibly expect, after such a deed, would be to be instantly torn in pieces by the crew. On this transaction Dr. Johnson has made the following reflexions:

"How far it is probable that Drake, after having been acquainted with this man's designs, should admit him into his fleet, and afterwards caress, respect, and trust him; or that Doughtie, who is represented as a man of eminent abilities, should engage in so long and hazardous a voyage, with no other view than that of defeating it, is left to the determination of the reader. What designs he could have formed with any hope of success, or to what actions worthy of death he could have proceeded without accomplices, for none are mentioned, is equally difficult to imagine. Nor, on the other hand, though the obscurity of the account, and the remote place chosen for the discovery of this wicked project, seem to give some reason for suspicion, does there appear any temptation from either hope, fear, or interest, that might induce Drake, or any commander in his state, to put to death an innocent man upon false pretences." [31]

That Drake should take shelter during the winter season in the same port where Magelhaens had wintered so many years before, and, like him, should there execute one of his officers upon a charge of mutiny, are circumstances of coincidence which have not escaped notice in the early accounts.

If any blame be attached to the mode of proceeding, it should be recollected that no court of Martial Law existed in Queen Elizabeth's time, nor was there any court established for the trial of high criminal offences committed at sea; that we now have dates not further back than the 13th of the reign of Charles II., when an Act was passed "for establishing Articles and Orders for the Regulating and better Government of His Majesty's Navies, Ships of War, and Forces by Sea," on which the "Articles of War" are grounded. A ship therefore, in ancient times, floating on the ocean, or in the port of a foreign or savage land, must have carried with her some who understood law or custom of the sea. The crew had to look only for their protection to the captain or commander; but to protect them he must have the power to keep them in order; and to effect this, he must also have the power of punishment. Every seaman enters a ship under this implied condition, fully convinced it is for his own and his messmates' advantage and protection. "The seaman is willing," says Sir William Monson, "to give or receive punishment deservedly, according to the laws of the sea, and not otherwise, according to the fury or passion of a boisterous, blasphemous, swearing commander;" and he adds, what has only been recently ordained in our Navy, "punishment is fittest to be executed in cold blood, the *next day* after the offence is committed and discovered."

Sir William moreover specifies what the ordinary punishments were in his time. "A captain," he says, "is allowed to punish according to the offence committed; to put men in the bilbows during pleasure; keep them fasting; duck them at the yardarm; or haul them from yard-arm to yard-arm, under the ship's keel; or make them fast to the capstan, and whip them there; or at the capstan or main-mast, hang weights about their necks till their hearts and backs be ready to break; or to gagg or scrape their tongues for blaspheming or swearing. This will tame the most rude and savage people in the world." [32]

These are indeed most brutal punishments, and such as would not be tolerated at the present day: and though they were in use in Drake's time, we may be assured that they never were practised by that Commander, nor in any ship that he commanded. He was a mild, indulgent and humane man, universally beloved by the seamen; in all his expeditions seamen crowded to join under his command; and it may fairly be argued from this, that punishments in his ship were rare and mild; some imperious necessity must therefore have governed his conduct in the case of Doughty. This is the plea set up by Captain Slidell McKenzie of the American ship Somers, when he hanged three of his crew without trial. "In the necessity of my position," he says, "I found my law." But as the proverb goes, necessity *has* no law; *ergo*, these men were hanged not by *any* law. He might have had recourse to a court-martial. In Drake's time no such court existed.

But it has been said that his putting Doughty to death was a great stretch of his authority. In mutiny it has at all times been lawful. Sir William Monson, the highest naval authority for the time we can appeal to, tells us, that "a Captain under a General (which Drake was not, but he was commanding an expedition of several ships, and was himself therefore, General, and so called) has lawful authority to punish offences committed within his ship; or if his company grow mutinous or stubborn, he may have recourse to the General, who will inflict more severe punishment, as *death,* if they deserve it, which no private captain can do."

Kindness and benevolence, as has been said, were the characteristics of Drake's disposition; and it cannot be supposed that he would sacrifice a friend, whom he esteemed, and towards whom he took the very earliest opportunity on the voyage to show his esteem, by distinguishing and benefiting him in an appointment to the command of the very first prize they took, but which he abused by misconduct. Is it not then a probable presumption that Mr. Doughty, from a feeling of pique and resentment at his removal, and at the disgrace of being sent back to his former ship, may have been guilty of what he was accused, a criminal design against his Captain, and the officers and crew? though there does not appear to have been any mutiny. He had not, indeed, either associates or confederates, nor was there any public feeling against Drake or in favour of the deceased, either here or on the return of the ship to England. Still a mystery hangs over the whole proceeding, - an irregular court held, - a civilian criminally accused, but no crime specified, - no charge produced, - no defence set up - no evidence on either side - no proceedings put on record, - the prisoner condemned and executed by an unusual process, - and not a word said about it. "In the island," says the narrative, "as we digged to bury this gentleman (still without a name), we found a great grinding stone, broken in two parts, which we took and set fast in the ground, the one part at the head, the other at the feet, building up the middle space with other stones, and turfs of earth, and engraved on the stones the names of the parties buried there, with a memorial of our General's name in Latin, that it might the better be understood of all that should come after us." [33] "In this place our stay being longer than we purposed, which chanced by the accidents before remembered, our diet began to wax short, and small mussells were good meat, yea, the sea-weeds were dainty dishes; by reason whereof we were driven to seek corners very narrowly for some refreshing, but the best we could find was shells instead of meat; we found the nests, but the birds were gone: that is, the shells of the cockells upon the sea shore where the giants had banqueted, but could never chance with the cockells themselves in the sea. The shells were so extraordinary that it would be incredible to the most part: for a pair of shells did weigh four pounds, and what the meat of two such shells might be, may easily be conjectured. I make account it weighed a pound, at least, so that it was a reasonable bit for a giant. The figure of the cockell you shall find in the end of this story of Port St. Julian." [34]

"Other things in this place we found not worthy remembrance, save only that whereas Magelhaens, performing the first voyage about the world, falling in with this port, as we did, did first name it Port St. Julian; and making some abode there, had a mutiny against him by some of his company, for the which he executed divers of them upon a gibbett, close by the sea, upon the main land over against the Hand: part of which gibbett being of fir wood, we found there sound and whole; of the wood of which gibbett, being fifty years, at the least, before the tyme of our coming thither, our cooper made tankards or canns for such of the company as would drink in them. Whereof for my owne part, I had no great likeing, seeing there was no such necessity." [35]

The Portuguese prize, the Mary, being leaky, was unloaded and broken up, and the fleet reduced to three, the Pelican, the Elizabeth, and the Marigold; and, on the 20th August, Drake came to the mouth of the Strait of Magelhaens, being an inland sea thick set with islands, and enclosed with high cliffs and mountains, which in that latitude render the air extremely cold, the summits being covered with snow. At the Cape forming the entrance, "Our General caused his fleet, in homage to our sovereign Lady the Queen's Majestic, to strike their topsails upon the bunt, as a token of his willing and glad mind, to shew his dutiful obedience to her highness, whom he acknowledged to have full interest and right in that new discovery; and withal in remembrance of his honourable friend and favourer, Sir Christopher Hatton, he changed the name of the ship, which himself went in, from the Pelican to be called the 'Golden Hind.' Which ceremonies being ended,, with a sermon and prayers of thanksgiving, they entered the narrow strait with much wind, frequent turnings, and many dangers. They observed on one side an island like Fogo, burning aloft in the air in a wonderful sort without intermission." [36]

On the 6th September (that is, in sixteen days), having passed the strait, they entered into the open South Sea (which they call the Pacific, or calm sea); but found it rough and turbulent above measure; and a terrible tempest carried the fleet about a hundred leagues westward, and separated them. Here it is noticed, that an eclipse of the moon happened on the 15th September, at six o'clock in the afternoon, (which, says Camden, I note for the mathematicians' sakes.) "It was observed also, contrary to what some had written, that that part of the heaven next to the southern pole was bedecked with but few stars, and those of a smaller magnitude; and that there were but only three of any remarkable bigness to be seen in that hemisphere, which England hath not beheld. But two small clouds were noticed, of the same colour with the *Via lactea,* and far distant from the pole, which the men called Magelhaens's clouds." [37] (Nebula Magellanicae.)

But we cannot allow Drake to pass this remarkable strait, being but the second time it was ever gone through, without a word or two of this bold and well-executed undertaking. Crooked and narrow in many places, with creeks and rivers branching off in all directions, the tides irregular and rapid, the shores steep and rocky, a burning island, like Fuego, on their left, flaming without intermission, peaks of snow on all sides, no chart to guide them in the right direction, the tide rising and falling thirty feet, and running like a rapid torrent, - such were the formidable obstacles, compensated only by the consolation of calm weather. Observing, near the western outlet, a cluster of three islands that appeared large and fruitful, the General, with some of his people, went on shore, and called the island they landed on, Elizabetha, and took possession of it in the Queen's name.

The crew amused themselves with taking penguins, of which they killed three thousand in one day. They observed many fruitful valleys, full of grass, and herds of very strange creatures feeding there. The trees were green, and the air temperate, the water pleasant, and the soil agreeable for any of our country grain; "and nothing wanting," says Drake, "to make an happy region, but the people's knowing and worshipping the true God." [38] Among the anomalies of creation, in this wild and desolate region, surmounted with ice and snow, were found valleys full of evergreens; of these we may mention the evergreen beech tree, and the winter bark; and above all other curiosities, in such a situation, thousands of little humming-birds.

It is a remarkable fact that, in sixteen days, they passed through this most intricate and troublesome navigation, which, on an average, requires a fortnight for one of our square-rigged vessels to accomplish, with all the advantages of modern knowledge, improvements in ships, nautical instruments, and the theory of navigation. The General now finding the health of some of the men impaired, had resolved at once to hasten towards the line and the warm sun; but it pleased God to disappoint him. A terrific tempest arose, and the ships were driven to the south, even as far as 57°, to the southward of Cape Horn, by which Drake had the opportunity of seeing the union of the Atlantic and Pacific oceans. On trying to regain their lost ground, the wind still blowing strong, the Marigold, Captain John Thomas, parted and was no more heard of; in fact, she was lost, and all on board must have perished.

On the 7th of October, the Admiral and the Elizabeth under slow sail stood into a bay near the western entrance of the strait, where they hoped to have found shelter from the bad weather; but in a few hours, after coming to an anchor, the cable of the Admiral parted, and she drove out to sea, and was thus separated from the Elizabeth, which remained in the port without any attempt to follow the Admiral. On the contrary, the next day, taking advantage of his absence, Captain Winter re-entered the strait, and having refreshed the crew, Mr. Cliffe, who was one of them, says, that on the 1st of November "they gave up their voyage, by Captain Winter's compulsion, full sore against the mariners' minds."

The Admiral being now left entirely alone, except with the little pinnace, was driven back once more into the latitude of 55° south, in which he got among some islands, perhaps some of those to the north of Terra del Fuego, where the ship was anchored, and the crew were refreshed with wholesome herbs and good water. After two days, however, they were driven from their anchorage, and the little shallop or pinnace lost sight of the ship. There were eight men in her, who had provisions only for one day; but by good fortune they reached the shore, procured water and roots, and in the course of a fortnight, entered the Strait of Magelhaens, and Drake heard nothing more of them.

These poor creatures, however, found the means of subsisting themselves on dried and salted penguins, then of proceeding to Port Julian, and thence to Rio de la Plata. Six of the party here went into the woods, and two remained to take care of the boat. A party of Indians met with them in the woods, shot their arrows at them, wounded all and took four prisoners; the other two escaped to the boat. They moved to an island two or three leagues from the shore, where the two wounded men died; the shallop was dashed in pieces against the rocks.

The remaining two, Peter Curder and William Pitcher, staid on this island two months, subsisting on small crabs, eels, and a fruit like an orange, but they had no water. The misery they endured from want of this indispensable necessary of life induced them, by means of a plank and a couple of paddles, to endeavour to reach the main land, which they accomplished in three days and two nights; when Curder says they found a rivulet of sweet water, "where Pitcher, my only comfort and companion, (although I endeavoured to dissuade him,) being pinched with extreme thirst, over-drank himself; and, to my unspeakable grief, died within half an hour, whom I buried as well as I could in the sand." Purchas, who dearly loves a pun, even on the most solemn occasions, adds in the margin of the page, "Pitcher breaks." [39]

The General, with his solitary Golden Hind, was now completely alone with a reduced crew. To ordinary minds, a more forlorn situation than that in which Drake now found himself can hardly be conceived. Deprived of all his ships, his companions and a great part of his crew, driven by a succession of tempests to the very southern extremity of the great continent of America, which had never been visited by any civilized human being - for he was the first to discover Cape Horn - tossed about on a sea utterly unknown, suffering from severe wounds, and, as he might reasonably suppose, every hope, that had carried him thither, as to his ulterior views, utterly destroyed; under all these deplorable circumstances, more than sufficient to crush the spirits and suppress the hopes of ordinary mortals, Drake's condition might indeed be considered as most calamitous. "Being driven from the first place of anchoring, so unmeasurable was the depth of the sea that 500 fathoms would fetch no ground. So that the violence of the storm without intermission; the impossibility to come to anchor; the want of opportunity to spread any sail; the most maddened seas; the lee shore; the dangerous rocks; the contrary and most intolerable wind; the impossible passage out; the desperate tarrying there, and the inevitable perils on every side, did present so small a likelihood to escape present destruction, that if the special providence of God himself had not supported him, he never could have endured that woeful state, as being environed with most terrible and most fearful judgments round about." [40]

The moment that a genial breeze sprung up from the south, he weighed his anchor on the 30th October, "departing thence," says Mr. Fletcher, "from the southernmost part of the world known or like to be known," and sailed to the north-west, towards that part of the world, where he had laid his plan of operations, and made a vow, that with the blessing of God, he would perform them. Drake, or his historian, observes, that "if the ship had retained her old name of Pelican, which she bore at our departure from home," she might now indeed have been said to be as "a Pelican alone in the wilderness." [41]

Although the storm abated and enabled Drake, on the 30th October, to proceed to the northward in his solitary ship, towards the place he had appointed for the rendezvous of his squadron, namely in 30° south, every search for them was of course unavailing, but of this he could not be aware, and consequently was kept in a state of constant anxiety. The next day he fell in with two islands, well stocked with fowls, of which he laid in a quantity for the crew, and thence coasted along till he came to 38°; and finding no intelligence of his companions, nor any convenient place to anchor in, he stood to the island Macho, a little to the northward, which in the narrative is called *Mucho*, "by reason of the greatnesse and large circuit thereof." This island was inhabited by native Indians of the same sort as the Patagonians of St. Julian's, (on the opposite side of the continent,) whom the cruelties of the Spaniards had driven from the mainland. Here he intended to water his ship, and entered into friendly communication with the natives, treating them with small presents such as he thought might best please them. In return they presented him with fruits, and two sheep, and pointed out a place where he would obtain fresh water.

The next morning, according to agreement, the men landed with their water-casks, and sent a couple of the crew forward towards the place, who were suddenly attacked by the Indians, and immediately slain; nor were the boat's crew free from danger, as four or five hundred men sprung up from behind the rocks, discharged a volley of arrows into the boat, and wounded every man of the crew before they could free themselves, or come to the use of their weapons; Drake himself was shot in the face by an arrow, under his right eye, which pierced him almost to the brain, and he also received another wound in the head. The rest, being nine persons in the boat, were deadly wounded in divers parts of their bodies, "if God, almost miraculously, had not given cure to the same; for our chief surgeon being dead, and the only remaining one absent in the Vice-Admiral's ship, so that being left to the care of a boy who had little experience and no skill, we were little better than altogether destitute of such cunning and helps as so grievous a state of so many wounded bodies did require;" but, by the favour of Providence, they all recovered, and yielded God the glory thereof. The only reason assigned for this treachery, and not an unreasonable one, was, that one of the crew having made use of the word *aqua*, they mistook them for Spaniards, against whom, for the robberies and cruelties practised against them, they entertained an inveterate hatred, and delighted with every opportunity of taking revenge. [42] Mr. Fletcher, however, gives a very different account of these barbarians. "Having landed upon the Maine, the inhabitants shewed themselves in divers companyes, upon severall hills not farr from us, with leaping, danceing, and great noies, and cries, with voices like the bulls of Basan; expecting that we should answer them with the like, and do as they did, to satisfy them as well as we could, by imitating their gestures, that we were friends and not enemies; such notwithstanding we did accordingly, yet would they have none of our company, til such time they were warranted by oracle from their god Settabos [did Shakespeare get Caliban's god from Macho?] - that is the divell, whom they name their great God.

"In the mean time, with what expedition we could, the boate was manned again, and sent to see if happily any help might be had for our men whom the enemy had taken, but all in vain and impossible, for when our men came in view of them, the multitude was great, by estimation 2000 persons, well-appointed with bows, darts, spears, shields, pikes, and other weapons, most of them headed with pure silver, which, in the light of the sun, made a wonderful show and glittering; among these, and many others of the common people, were our two men in their execution and torments, the manner whereof, as they perceived, or conceived at the least, was in this sort; - the men being fast bound were laid upon the ground among them, and the people cast themselves into a ring round about them, hand in hand, with a dance, still turning or going about with a song. In the mean time, tormentors, working with knives upon their bodies, cut the flesh away by *gubblets,* and cast it up into the air, the which falling down, the people catched in their dancing, and like dogs devoured it, in most monstrous and unnatural manner, even most horrible to nature, and thus continued till they had picked their bones, life yet remaining in them." [43]

It is difficult to reconcile such extraordinary discrepancies. The sacred character of Fletcher forbids us to disbelieve what he has recorded, though his eyes may, to a certain extent, have deceived him, as they certainly did with regard to the giants, which he also describes these people to be. The nonsense of John Conyers, the copyist and annotator of Fletcher, who calls himself "pharmacopolist, citizen, and apothecary of London," respecting these giants, is at least amusing; it is appended to, and at the conclusion of the MS. of Fletcher.

"Now as the transcriber may here make inquiry why som (in these days, 1677) may accompte the storye of these giants fabulous, so it may be answered that som may pretend only to have been so farr as these parts, and have not, either having asserted the contrary in globes and mapps, therefore are loth to have it contradicted. Now, it may be considered these giants are here said to feed upon a gigantick foule, viz., ostridges, and it seemes they have large cockles and mussells, and larger than ordinary hearbes of the same kind with us, such as marjorom, thyme, scurvye grass, - then why not large-grown men and women? That these giants have bowes and arrows to kill ostridges, and it's likely for defence of themselves from the rest of the Indians that, so long as they remained in that country undisturbed, their bodyes becam gigantick from their ease and the nature of the place, and from the virtue communicated by the use of the oyle of ostridges upon their children as aforesaid." [44]

On the 30th, Drake dropped anchor in a bay called St. Philip, when a boat's crew having landed, brought away an Indian they had fallen in with, clothed in a long white gown, of manners exceedingly mild and gentle. Drake treated him with the utmost kindness, and dismissed him with presents, ordering his boat to set him safe on shore. "In him we might see a most lively pattern of the harmless disposition of that people; and how grievous a thing it is that they should, by any means, be so abused as all those are, whom the Spaniards have any command or power over." [45] This man so courteously entertained, gave to his countrymen so flattering a description of his kind reception, that within a few hours they came down to the boat with fowls, eggs, and a hog, and with them one of their captains, who desired to be conveyed on board the English ship. He lamented they were unable to furnish the English with such supplies as they stood in need of, but volunteered to pilot the ship to a port a little to the southward, where they could procure all that they wanted. Drake assented to receive him, and he took the ship to a place named by the Spaniards Volpariza, where he met with everything he wanted of stores, provisions, and wine; and, after spending three days in taking on board the necessary supplies, he landed the Indian pilot where he first received him, having rewarded him amply for his trouble and kindness.

On the 19th December, Drake entered a bay near to a town named Cyppo, when as soon as he was discovered, there came down about three hundred men, Spaniards and Indians, of whom one hundred at least were Spaniards, every one well mounted upon his horse; the rest being Indians, "running as dogs at their heels, all naked, and in most miserable bondage." Drake's crew hastened to their boat, with the exception of one foolish man, who, refusing to retire with the rest, was shot by the Spaniards, and, by way of brutal triumph, was drawn to the shore, his carcass placed in full sight of his companions, his head and hands cut off, the heart torn out, and then the Indians were ordered to shoot their arrows into every part of the body. Proceeding from hence a little further to the north, Drake found a convenient and quiet harbour, where he caused a pinnace to be set up, in order that he might look with it into the creeks for intelligence of his missing ships. [46]

The next place they fell in with, and landed at, was Tarapaca, in about 20° S. lat., where, in searching for water, they found a Spaniard asleep, with a bundle consisting of thirteen silver bars lying by his side, to the value of about four thousand ducats. Drake would not suffer any violence to be done to his person, but allowed his people to carry away the treasure without doing him any harm. Some of them jokingly said, he ought to be thankful to them for freeing him of his heavy charge, and easing him of his burden. [47] In another place a Spaniard was found driving eight Peruvian sheep, or lamas, each laden with an hundred pounds' weight of silver, which they also seized, and drove down to their boats. Further on was a small Spanish town, where the Spaniards agreed to traffic with Drake, and supplied him with provisions of different kinds, and some lamas, whose necks are like camels, and their heads resemble those of sheep. [48]

Coasting along, still in the hope of meeting with his friends, Drake arrived, on the 7th of February, before Arica, where he took barkes, laden with about eight hundred weight of silver. On the 15th he arrived at Calloa, the port of Lima, and entered the harbour without resistance, though about thirty ships were lying there, seventeen of which were prepared for their voyage. Whether these ships were manned and armed, or what their size might be, is not stated; but there is something very remarkable that Drake, with his single ship, should have been able to disarm all resistance, and strike such dismay into the Spaniards, that they suffered the plunder of their seventeen loaded ships to be carried on without the least attempt at opposition. One cannot decide which to admire most, the temerity of Drake, or the panic or cowardice of the Spaniards, who calmly looked on from the shore; but there was not even a boy on board the ships, such was the fancied security of these people, so remote from Europe, or the visits of any foreign people. [49]

In one of these ships they found fifteen hundred bars of silver; in another, a large chest of coined money; and valuable lading of different articles in the rest, of which the Spaniards suffered Drake's people to take away whatever they pleased, and, if they had been so disposed, they might have set fire to the whole of the ships; but Drake was satisfied in obtaining booty for himself and his crew, in compensation for former wrongs on the part of the Spanish people.

Drake, however, in order to secure himself against an immediate pursuit, ordered the cables of the ships to be cut that they might float about the harbour. He had here received intelligence of a very rich ship, that was laden with gold and silver, and had sailed from hence just before his arrival, and bound for Panama. Her name was the Cacafuego, "the great glory of the South Sea;" and as he was in full chase in the direct course for Panama, he fell in with and boarded a brigantine, out of which he took eighty pounds' weight of gold, a crucifix of the same metal, some emeralds, and some cordage. In a few days after, near Cape St. Francis, in 1° lat., he got sight of the Cacafuego, about one hundred and fifty leagues from Panama. On coming up with her, a shot or two carried away one of her masts, when she was boarded and easily carried. Besides a large quantity of pearls and precious stones, they took out of her eighty pounds' weight of gold, thirteen chests of silver, coined and rough silver enough to ballast a ship. Having transferred all this to the Golden Hind, the total amount of which was calculated at three hundred and sixty thousand pieces of eight, or nearly ninety thousand pounds, they let the Cacafuego go but not without a joke from the master, or, as is said more probably, from the boy, "You may let your ship for the future be called Cacafuego, and ours the Cacaplata." [50]

Standing out to the westward to avoid Panama, where the name of Drake must have been well known, they fell in with another ship, from which they obtained some linen, cloth, porcelain dishes, and silk. The owner of this ship, a Spanish gentleman, was on board, from whom Drake is said to have received a falcon, wrought in pure gold, with a large emerald set in its breast; but whether by seizure, by purchase, or as a present, is not mentioned: the name of Drake would sanction any one of them. After taking out the pilot for his own service, he suffered the ship to proceed on her voyage.

He now continued his course; and keeping close to the coast of North America, on the 15th of April came to the port of Aguapulca, in latitude about 15½° N. Having here taken in some bread and other provisions, he prepared to depart northwards; but, as the narrative says, "Not forgetting, before we got a shipboard, to take with us also a certain pot (of about a bushell in bignesse) full of ryalls of plate, which we found in the towne, together with a chaine of gold, and some other jewels, which we entreated a gentleman Spaniard to leave behind him, as he was flying out of the towne." [51]

At this place the Admiral set on shore Nuna de Silva, the Portuguese pilot, whom he had taken from the Cape de Verde Islands, and who, on his arrival at Mexico, gave to the governor a narrative of all the circumstances that had happened on the voyage, though not perhaps quite circumstantial, yet with great correctness; and it was published by Hakluyt. There was also here a ship proceeding to the southward, which Drake, ever anxious and mindful about his missing ships, thought too good an opportunity to interest the captain of her in his search for them, and therefore entreated him to take charge of a letter he had written, of which the following is a copy:-

"MASTER WINTER, if it pleaseth God that you should chance to meete with the ship of Sant John de Auton, I pray you use him well, according to my word and promise given unto them; and if you want any thing that is in this ship of Sant John de Auton, I pray you pay them double the value for it, which I will satisfie againe, and command your men not to doe her any hurt; and what composition or agreement we have made, at my return into England, I will by God's helpe performe; although I am in doubt that this letter will never come to your hands: notwithstanding, I am the man I have promised to be, beseeching God, the Saviour of all the world, to have us in his keeping, to whome onely I give all honour, praise, and glory.

"What I have written is not only to you, Master Winter, but also to M. Thomas, M. Charles, M. Caube, and M. Anthonie, with all our other good friends, whom I commit to the tuition of him that, with his blood, redeemed us, and am in good hope that we shall be in no more trouble, but that he will helpe us in adversitie, desiring you, for the passion of Christ, if you fall into any danger, that you will not despaire of God's mercy, for he will defend you and preserve you from all danger, and bring us to our desired haven, to whom be all honour, glory, and praise, for ever and ever. Amen.

"Your sorrowfull captain, whose heart is heavy for you,

"FRANCIS DRAKE." [52]

[1] Camden.
[2] Stow's Annals.
[3] Rapin's History of England.
[4] The World Encompassed.
[5] The World Encompassed.
[6] Hakluyt.
[7] Camden.
[8] Ibid.
[9] Hakluyt. - Purchas - from Lopez Vaz.
[10] Hakluyt. Purchas.
[11] Prince's Worthies of Devon.
[12] Southey, from Howell.
[13] World Encompassed.
[14] Sloane MSS. in British Museum.
[15] Hakluyt.
[16] World Encompassed.
[17] Camden.
[18] World Encompassed.
[19] Dr. Johnson's Works.
[20] World Encompassed.
[21] World Encompassed.
[22] Fletcher's MS.
[23] Camden.
[24] Hakluyt.
[25] World Encompassed.
[26] World Encompassed.
[27] World Encompassed.
[28] World Encompassed.
[29] Fletcher's MS.
[30] Fletcher, in Sloane MS.
[31] Johnson's Works.
[32] Monson's Naval Tracts.
[33] World Encompassed.
[34] *Note.* - Various drawings accompany Fletcher's MS.
[35] Sloane MS. Fletcher's Journal.
[36] World Encompassed.
[37] Camden.
[38] World Encompassed.
[39] Purchas, from Curder's narrative.
[40] World Encompassed.
[41] Fletcher's MS.
[42] World Encompassed.
[43] Fletcher's MS.
[44] Sloane MS., British Museum.
[45] World Encompassed.
[46] World Encompassed; Hakluyt.
[47] Camden; Hakluyt.
[48] Hakluyt; World Encompassed.
[49] Hakluyt.
[50] World Encompassed - Hakluyt.
[51] World Encompassed.
[52] Hakluyt.

Chapter Four - Continuation of Voyage Round the World - 1577-1580

While Drake's little bark of 100 tons, which had sustained so many perils and adventures, was undergoing a complete refit at Aguapulca, he was anxiously revolving in his mind the next step it would best behove him to pursue. His ship was already nearly laden with treasure alone; in addition to this, he was about to take in stores and provisions for a voyage of uncertain duration, but which, in its extent, whatever track he might pursue, was nearly equal to half the circumference of the globe. If he returned the way he had advanced hitherto, he would have to repass Magelhaen's Strait; for Cape Horn, which is now the usual route, had never yet been doubled; and the Spaniards had industriously given it out that a return by them, from the westward, was next to impossible; and little therefore could he suppose that one of his own inferior ships had actually so repassed them. Besides, he wisely considered that his voyage, and the fame of his exploits, must have reached Spain, or at all events be well known throughout her Indian colonies, and that the natural consequence would be, the sending a fleet to guard the entrance of the Strait, a preparation for which turned out to be actually the case.

What then was the next thing to be considered? The people began to manifest signs of uneasiness. "Being now sufficiently rich," says Dr. Johnson, "and having lost all hopes of finding their associates, and perhaps beginning to be infected with that desire of ease and pleasure, which is the natural consequence of wealth obtained by dangers and fatigues, they began to consult about their return home." But Drake required not much time to make up his mind. Columbus thought that by sailing westward he should arrive at the Indies; Cabot had found no difficulty in reaching Newfoundland; Sir Hugh Willoughby had attempted a North East passage to the Indies, and Drake had seen the two great oceans united at the southern extremity of America! Why then should not the Pacific and Atlantic be also united on the northern part of America?   This was the obvious and natural conclusion; but Drake had stronger grounds to go upon than mere theoretical conjectures. Various papers from learned cosmographers had endeavoured to prove that a communication existed between the Northern Atlantic and the Pacific, and Martin Frobisher, the friend, and subsequently the colleague, of Drake, had actually made the attempt, and returned at the end of 1576, a whole year before Drake left England, "highly commended of all men for his greate and notable attempt, but specially famous for the greate hope he brought of the passage to Cathaia." [1]   Drake therefore - perhaps encouraged by the "greate hope of the passage" - boldly resolved to try whether he could not reach home by proceeding in a contrary direction, that is to say, by that of North East. He failed in the attempt; but so did Cook, or rather the survivors of Cook, fail in the same pursuit in after times; but his friend Frobisher's anticipations may yet one day be realized.

It has now been proved, beyond a doubt, that there is a clear water communication between the Northern Atlantic and Pacific Oceans, with the partial intervention of patches of ice in some parts of the mid-sea, and perhaps not much there. The openings at the two extremities in Baffin's Bay and Behring's Strait have been passed, and the remaining parts, as seen from every portion of the high sea-shore of North America, consist of an unbounded ocean as far as the eye can reach, free from land.

It is probable therefore that the attention of Drake, even before he set sail from England, had been called to the question of an eastern passage from the northern part of the Pacific, by which his return voyage would be greatly shortened. But even if it were known that such a communication actually existed, the attempt, under his circumstances, was a bold and daring undertaking. A small and lonely vessel, with a diminished and feeble crew, destitute of every medical aid, should sickness or accident overtake him; cut off from all communication with not only civilized, but most probably with human beings in any shape; moreover, in this ship was contained the whole of his wealth; - under such circumstances therefore, it must be considered as one of the most daring and courageous attempts in the records of navigation; the more so, as not a ship of any nation had as yet the opportunity, and perhaps it never entered into any man's head, to search for such a passage *on that side* of America, though it is most likely that, by taking that course, it may be found. Such an opinion might now be correct, when we know that a sure and certain open passage exists through Lancaster Sound into Baffin's Bay; but without such knowledge, it would have been madness to dash through Behring's Strait, with an open sea and a fair westerly wind, not knowing what course to steer, and whether there was any opening at all, and in what quarter to the eastward. But it will be done from one side or the other. There is one man, the first and foremost among Purchas's "Marine Worthies," whose return from the Antarctic regions, with his two ships ready fitted, manned with officers and crew that will not desert him, in full health and vigour, none of whom, it is reported, have had so much as a *finger-ache* during two voyages among fields of ice - Captain James Ross is the man for whom this accomplishment of the North-West passage is reserved; an object which three centuries nearly of repeated trials have not yet completed. Seven long and severe winters in the northern ice; a march amid ice and snow of some hundred miles to approach the magnetic pole; a volunteer winter voyage to the Greenland Seas, to relieve the whaling ships frozen up; three attempts to approach the Southern Pole; this is the bold and talented officer to go from the Atlantic to the Pacific, round the northern coast of America.

Drake's endeavours however were strangely crossed by the unexpected severity of the weather, at a low comparative latitude, of which the Rev. Francis Fletcher has given a long detailed account, and which it may be as well to set down in his own words:

"From Guatulco we departed the day following, namely, April the 16th, setting our course directly into the sea; whereupon we sailed 500 leagues in longitude to get a wind, and between that and June 3d, 1400 leagues in all, till we came in 42 degrees of north latitude, wherein the night following we found such an alteration of heat into extreme and nipping cold, that our men, in general, did *grievously* complain thereof; some of them feeling their healths much impaired thereby; neither was it that this chanced in the night alone, but the day following carried with it not only the marks, but the stings and force of the night going before, to the great admiration of us all; for besides that the pinching and biting air was nothing altered, the very ropes of our ship were stiff, and the rain which fell was an unnatural and frozen substance: so that we seemed rather to be in the frozen zone than anyway so near unto the sun, or these hotter climates.

"Neither did this happen for the time only, or by some sudden accident, but rather seemed indeed to proceed from some ordinary cause, against the which the heat of the sun prevails not; for it came to that extremity, in sailing but two degrees further to the northward in our course, that though seamen lack not good stomachs, yet it seemed a question to many amongst us, whether their hands should feed their mouths, or rather keep themselves within coverts from the pinching cold that did benumb them." [2]

"Neither could we impute it to the tenderness of our bodies, though we came lately from the extremity of heat, by reason whereof we might be more sensible of the present cold, insomuch that the dead and senseless creatures were as well affected with it as ourselves. Our meat, as soon as it was removed from the fire, would presently in a manner be frozen up; and our ropes and tacklings in a few days were grown to that stiffness, that what three men before were able with them to perform, now six men, with their best strength, and utmost endeavours, were hardly able to accomplish; whereby a sudden and great discouragement seized upon the minds of our men, and they were possessed with a great mislike and doubting of any good to be done that way; yet would not our General be discouraged; but as well by comfortable speeches of the Divine Providence, and of God's loving care over his children, out of the scriptures, as also by other good and profitable persuasions, adding thereto his own cheerful example, he so stirred them up to put on a good courage, and to acquit themselves like men, to endure some short extremity to have the speedier comfort, and a little trouble to obtain the greater glory; that every man was thoroughly armed with willingness and resolved to see the uttermost, if it were possible, of what good was to be done that way." [3]

In admiring the good sense and kindly feeling of Drake, it is impossible at the same time not to be struck with the absurd and utterly incredible account of the Rev. Mr. Fletcher, of whose intellect some delusion must unquestionably have taken possession, or he would not have recorded such nonsense, in direct contradiction to the usual ordination of nature, in such a latitude and at such a period of the year; it may therefore be fearlessly pronounced impossible. But as the "World Encompassed" is avowedly taken from Fletcher's manuscript, it cannot be wondered that they should be identically the same.

"The land in that part of America," he continues, "bearing farther out into the west than we before imagined, we were nearer on it than we were aware, and yet the nearer still we came unto it, the more extremity of cold did seize upon us. The 5th day of June we were forced by contrary winds to run in with the shore, which we then first descried, and to cast anchor in a bad bay, the best road we could for the present meet with, where we were not without some danger by reason of the many extreme gusts and flaws that beat upon us; which if they ceased and were still at any time, immediately upon their intermission there followed most vile, thick, and stinking fogs, against which the sea prevailed nothing, till the gusts of wind again removed them, which brought with them such extremity and violence when they came, that there was no dealing or resisting against them.

"In this place was no abiding for us, and to go further north, the extremity of the cold (which had now utterly discouraged all our men) would not permit us, and the wind being directly against us, having once gotten us under sail again, commanded us to the southward whether we would or no." [4]

This no doubt was hailed with gladness, for the idea of a northern passage, it is quite clear, was not at all relished by either the chaplain or the crew. On this account the wind that drove them to the southward was not an ill wind, for it blew them good.

"From the height of 48°, in which now we were, to 38°, we found the land, by coasting it, to be but low and reasonably plain; every hill (whereof we saw many, but none very high), though it were in June, and the sun in the nearest approach unto them, being covered with snow." [5]

"And here, having so fit occasion (notwithstanding it may seem to be beside the purpose of writing the history of this our voyage), we will a little more diligently inquire into the causes of the continuance of the extreme cold in these parts, as also into the probabilities or unlikelihood of a passage to be found that way." [Still harping, Mr. Fletcher, on the passage, which has evidently caused you much uneasiness; but for your explanation.] "Neither was it (as hath formerly been touched) the tenderness of our bodies coming so lately out of the heat, whereby the pores were opened, that made us so sensible of the colds we here felt. In this respect, as in many others, we found our God a provident Father and careful Physician to us; we lacked no outward helps nor inward comforts to restore and fortify nature, had it been decayed and weakened in us: neither was there wanting unto us the great experience of our General, who had often himself proved the force of the burning zone, whose advice always prevailed much to the preserving of a moderate temper in our constitutions; so that even after our departure from the heat, we always found our bodies not as sponges, but strong and hard, more able to bear out cold though we came out of excess of heat, than a number of chamber-companions could have been, who lie on their feather beds till they go to sea, or rather, whose teeth, in a temperate air, do beat in their heads at a cup of cold sack and sugar by the fire." [6]

The account which is here given from the Fletcher MS., and printed in the "World Encompassed," by Sir Francis Drake (nephew), is the more extraordinary, as all our navigators, from Cook and Vancouver downwards, speak favourably of the Californian climate. The very last who has recently published says, "To the north, the climate is even and temperate; the winters are mild and of short duration, and snow appears on the loftier hills, and the summers have an agreeable warmth, with the atmosphere clear and transparent." [7]

"The inhabitants of this place," [not named, but a fit harbour in 38° 30' latitude,] "the inhabitants," says Fletcher, "who had never been acquainted with warmer climates, in whom custom of cold was as it were a second nature, used to come shivering in their warm furs, crowding close together, body to body, to receive heat one from another, and to shelter themselves under lee banks; and afterwards (when they became more familiar with the English) they endeavoured, as often as they could, to shroud themselves for warmth under the garments of the Englishmen."

This puts one in mind of Trinculo, who, in the thunder-storm, crept under the gaberdine of Caliban - "Misery acquaints a man with strange bedfellows!" Indeed, the whole scene among these innocent savages cannot fail to remind one of parts of the "Tempest."

The several accounts of the voyage state that the natives of the north-west shores of America regarded Drake and his people as gods. "They returned our presents," says the "World Encompassed," "because they thought themselves sufficiently enriched and happy that they had found so free access to see us. They stood as men ravished with admiration at the sight of such things as they had never before heard of, nor seen, seeming rather to reverence us as deities than mortal men." [8] They might have exclaimed with Caliban, -

"These be fine things, an if they be not sprites.
 That's a brave god, and bears celestial liquor;
 I will kneel to him."
"I'll kiss thy foot, I'll swear myself thy subject."

As Shakespeare is known to have borrowed much from Holinshed and the old chroniclers, it is not improbable that Drake's voyage on the northwest coast of America may have furnished hints for some of his scenes in the "Tempest."

Drake being thus driven to the southward, and finding a convenient harbour on the 17th June, in lat. 38½° north; the land inhabited, and the houses of the natives close to the water's side, he decided on remaining there to put his little ship to rights, and in the hope of refreshing his crew. From the moment of their arrival, numbers of the natives had been seen on shore, and a single man in a canoe came off to the ship. On approaching, he made a long oration, and having finished his harangue, with great show of reverence, he returned to the shore. The ship had sprung a leak on her passage, which made it necessary to lighten her, and bring her as close to the shore as could be done with safety. Tents were landed for the men, and something like a fort erected for the protection of the stores and the crew. [9]

The people of the country looked on for a time: when they saw that the strangers were establishing themselves, they came down in great numbers; but on approaching within a small distance, remained perfectly quiet, looking attentively at what was going on, and, though armed, manifested not the least symptom of hostile intentions. Signs were made to them to lay down their bows and arrows, which they at once did. The General, with the view of securing their good will, distributed little presents among them, and they, in return, presented the General with feathers, net-work, arid skins. In the evening they returned quietly to their village, near a mile distant, where they kept up a loud clamour for some time, the women shrieking in a most dolorous manner. [10]

"For two days after the night mostly spent in lamentations, none of them came near the tents; but on the third day, a much more numerous assemblage than before appeared on the summit of the hill, which was nearest to the English fort. Here one of them made a loud and long oration, at the end of which they all laid down their bows and arrows, which they left upon the hill, and came down to the tents. The women however remained on the hill, 'tormenting themselves lamentably, tearing the flesh from their cheeks, whereby we perceived they were about a sacrifice.' In the meantime our General with his companie went to prayer, and the reading of the Scriptures, at which exercise they were attentive, and seemed to be greatly affected with it: but when they were come unto us, they restored again unto us those things which before we bestowed upon them," [11]

"Presently came down from the country a great multitude, and among them a man of goodly stature, and comely personage, who was the King himself, accompanied by many tall and warlike men. Before his majesty advanced, two ambassadors presented themselves to the General to announce his approach, but continued speaking for about an hour; at the end of which the Hioh or King, making as princely a show as he possibly could, with all his train, came forward; in the course of which they cried continually, after a singing manner, with a lusty courage. As they drew nearer and nearer towards us, so did they more and more strive to behave themselves with a certain comeliness and gravity in all their actions."

Indeed, they appear to have been a harmless and inoffensive people, the Chief and all his men joining in a song, and moving in a kind of dance. The harmless manner of their approach took from the General all suspicion, and he gave directions for their being admitted within the enclosure of their tents without interruption; and they entered the fort singing and dancing. Amid this festivity, the King or Chief placed a feathered cap of network on the General's head, a chain around his neck, and saluted him by the name of *Hioh,* which was supposed to be his own, or to signify the chief. By this act it was not unreasonable in Drake to suppose that it was meant to convey the whole country and themselves to the new comers. The General of course gave them to understand, in the best way he was able, that he accepted them in the name, and for the use of, the Queen of England.

"After they had satisfied, or rather tired themselves in this manner (singing and dancing, and the women tearing themselves, till the face, breasts, and other parts were bespatted with blood), they made signs to our General to have him sit down." The following ceremony then took place:- First, "both the King and divers others made several orations, or rather, indeed, if we had understood them, supplications, that he would take the province and kingdom into his hand, and become their king and patron; making signs that they would resign unto him their right and title in the whole land, and become his vassals in themselves and their posterities; which, that they might make us indeed believe that it was their true meaning and intent, the King himself, with all the rest, with one consent, and with great reverence, joyfully singing a song, set the crown upon his head; enriched his neck with all their chains;

and offering unto him many other things, honoured him with the name of *Hioh;* adding thereto, as it might seem, a song and dance of triumph: because they were not only visited of the gods, (for so they still judged us to be,) but that the great and chief god was now become their god, their king and patron, and themselves were become the only happy and blessed people in the world." [13]

Admiral Burney seems to have some doubt, and well he may, whether this ceremony was so clearly understood as to warrant the interpretation put upon it by the writer of the narrative. "The invariable custom," he observes, "adopted by Europeans, of claiming and taking formal possession of every new land they meet with, whether it is inhabited or uninhabited, never entering into the consideration, no doubt disposed Drake to credit (if it is true that he did credit it) that these people simply and for no cause, value received, or other consideration, made a voluntary gift of themselves and their country to him, a perfect stranger. Such is stated to have been the fact; and against allegations of fact, incredulity is no proof." [14]

"The English," says Burney, "were certainly regarded by the natives here with an uncommon degree of favour, for which two very natural reasons may be assigned. This part of the American continent had been visited by Juan Rodriguez Cabrillo, and by no other European. His interview with the natives was of the most friendly kind. No intervening circumstance could have occurred to change the nature of the impressions left by Cabrillo; and this disposition, so favourable to Europeans, the conduct of Drake, friendly and humane towards them, confirmed." [15]

The men were naked, but their bodies painted with different colours. Their character is thus described in the 'World Encompassed:' - "They are a people of a tractable, free, and loving nature, without guile or treachery. Their bows and arrows would do no great harm, being weak, and fitter for children than for men; and yet the men were so strong of body, that what two or three of our people could scarcely bear, one of them would take upon his back, and, without grudging, carry it up hill and down hill, an English mile together." It was remarked that the women were "very obedient and serviceable to their husbands."

"Before we went from hence, our General caused a post to be set up on shore, a monument of our being there; as also of her Majesty's and successor's right and title to that kingdom, namely, a plate of brass, fast nailed to a great and firm post; whereon is engraven her Grace's name, and the day and year of our arrival there, and of the free giving up of the province and kingdom, both by the King and people, into her Majesty's hands; together with her Highness's picture and arms in a piece of sixpence, current English money, showing itself by a hole made of purpose through the plate: underneath was likewise engraven the name of our General, &c." [16]

To show respect to his own country, and because white cliffs were observed on the coast, Drake gave to all the land he had seen in this part of

America the name of *New Albion*. As the time approached for departure, the friendly natives appeared to be deeply affected, and to wish for their speedy return; and the separation was accompanied with every token of mutual good will towards each other.

Drake remained here thirty-six days in port, which seems to have been a place so perfectly secured against storms, that the winds in all that time are never once mentioned.

"There is reason," says Burney, "to conclude, that the *Port of Drake* was that which is now known by the name of *Port San Francisco*, the latitude of which is 37° 48'½ N." For, as he says, the latitude given in the Famous Voyage is 38° N., and in the "*World Encompassed*" 38° 30', and the latitude of *Port San Francisco* is 37° 48' N.; there can be little doubt they are one and the same. Burney adds in a note, - "Allowing them to be the same, it is remarkable that both the most northern and the most southern ports at which Drake anchored in the course of his voyage, should afterwards by the Spaniards, doubtless without any intended reference to the name of *Francis* Drake, be named *San Francisco*." [17]

Thus we may observe that this portion of the west coast of America was indeed discovered, and taken possession of in the usual manner, by an Englishman, in the name of his sovereign, full 200 years before the United States of America had any existence; and yet they have the modesty to lay claim to it, on the assumption that a Captain Grey, or White, or some other colour, discovered it some few years ago - but discovery, or prescription, as Queen Elizabeth justly said, "is little worth without actual possession;" if it were not so, what indeed would become of our title to Australia and Van Diemen's Land, with a host of Dutch names staring us in the face?

On the 23rd of July, Drake left the western coast of America, and, while in sight of it, the kind natives kept up fires on the hills. Whatever the original intention of Drake had been, in the attempt of an eastern passage round the northern part of America, if no other motive induced him to abandon it, the advanced season of the year, and the extreme degree of cold they had already experienced in so low a latitude as 48°, no doubt had determined him to cross the Pacific, which however was a long and most extensive tract of ocean, as unknown to him as the passage of the Strait of Magelhaens had been. Fortunately, however, he had obtained from the master of a trading ship from Panama to the Philippine Islands, 'a sea-card' (no doubt a chart of the route), and therefore the best they could do was to direct their course for the Philippines.

"Having nothing," says the narrative, "in our view but air and sea, without sight of any land for the space of full sixty-eight days together, we continued our course through the main ocean till September the 30th following, on which day we fell in kenne of certain islands, lying in about 8 degrees to the northward of the line." [18] The natives came off in their canoes, each hollowed out of a single trunk of wood, bringing cocoa-nuts, fruits, and fish. The first that came appeared to be peaceably disposed, but others acted dishonestly, carrying off articles that were once put into their hands. The English therefore would have nothing to do with them in the way of trade; and to manifest their resentment, they began to attack the ship with stones, with which they had provided themselves. A gun was fired over their heads, the noise of which frightened them, but none being hurt they returned, and were more insolent than before. It may be supposed that the patience of Drake was exhausted, and that he ordered some muskets to be fired at them; for, it is observed, that they could not be got rid of till they were made to feel some smart as well as terror." Drake gave to them the name of the *Islands of Thieves*. Admiral Burney seems to think, from the description of the natives, the time of the passage to them, and the latitude, that they are the Islands that in our time have been called the Pellew Islands.

Leaving these islands, they sailed westerly, from the 3rd to the 16th of October, without seeing any land, till they made the Philippine Islands, coasting them to the 21st, when they anchored and watered the ship at the largest of them called Mindanao; and sailing from thence about eight leagues, they passed between two islands south of Mindanao, and on the 3rd of November had sight of the Moluccas, and steered for Tidore; but having received information from a boat, by which they were informed that the Portuguese had been driven out of Ternate, and had taken up their quarters at Tidore, Drake determined to proceed to Ternate, at the entreaty of the people in the boat, finding that Drake was not a friend to the Portuguese.

On anchoring at Ternate, the capital of the Moluccas, Drake sent a messenger with a velvet cloak to the King, with a request to be supplied with provisions, and allowed to trade for various kinds of spices. The King himself came off, preceded by three large and magnificent canoes, each having eighty rowers, who paddled to the sound of brass cymbals. On each side of every vessel was a row of soldiers, every one having a sword, dagger, and target, and in each canoe was a small piece of ordnance, mounted on a stock. Drake received him in great state, with a splendid display of finery, guns firing, and trumpets sounding. The King was a tall, corpulent man, with a good countenance. His attendants showed him great respect, speaking to him only in a kneeling posture.

On taking leave, he promised to visit the General the following day, and that the ship should be supplied with provisions; and accordingly abundance of rice, fruits, and poultry were sent off, together with a small quantity of cloves. The King, however, did not keep his promise, but sent his brother with an excuse and an invitation to the General to land; this, however, he declined, but some of his officers waited on the King, the brother being detained on board as a pledge for their safety. The officers were received with much parade, the king being covered with ornaments of gold and jewels.

"The King being yet absent, there sate in their places 60 grave personages, all which were said to be of the king's counsel. There were besides 4 grave persons, apparalled all in red, downe to the ground, and attired on their heads like the Turkes, and these were said to be Romanes, and Ligiers there to keep continual traffike with the people of Ternate. There were also 2 Turks Ligiers in this place, and one Italian. The king at last came in guarded with 12 launces covered over with a rich canopy, with embossed gold. Our men, accompanied with one of their captaines called Moro, rising to meet him, he graciously did welcome and entertaine them. He was attired after the manner of the country, but more sumptuously then the rest. From his waste down to the ground, was all clothe of golde, and the same very rich: his legges were bare, but on his feet were a paire of shooes, made of Cordouan skinne. In the attire of his head were finely wreathed hooped rings of gold, and about his necke he had a chaine of perfect golde, the linkes whereof were great, and one folde double. On his fingers hee had six very faire jewels, and sitting in his chair of estate, at his hand stood a page with a fanne in his hand, breathing and gathering the ayre to the king. The fanne was in length two foote, and in breadth one foote, set with 8 saphyres, richly embroidered, and knit to a staffe 3 foote in length, by the which the page did hold, and moove it. Our gentlemen having delivered their message, and received order accordingly, were licensed to depart, being safely conducted backe againe by one of the king's counsell." [19]

Drake appears by his conduct to have gained golden opinions from all he had to deal with here. The son of the King of Ternate, after the death of his father, writes to King James, soliciting his friendship and aid, in lieu of the Dutch. "Hearing," he says, "of the good report of your Majesty by the coming of the great Captain, Francis Drake, in the time of my father, which was about some fifty years past; by the which Captain my predecessor did send a ring unto the Queen of England, as a token of remembrance between us; which, if the aforesaid Drake had been living, he could have informed your Majesty of the great love and friendship of either side; he in behalf of the Queen, my father for him and his successors; since which time of the departure of the foresaid Captain, we have daily expected his return, my father living many years after, and daily expecting his return; and I, after the death of my father, have lived in the same hope, 'til I was father of eleven children; in which time I have been informed that the English were men of so bad disposition, that they came not as peaceable merchants, but to dispossess us of our country; which, by the coming of the bearer hereof, (Captain Middleton,) we have found to the contrary, which greatly we rejoice at, &c." [20]

He then goes on to say that, as the English failed them, they were obliged to call in the Dutch to expel their enemies the Portuguese out of the forts they held at Amboyna and Tidore; a bad exchange for England, we may add, when the horrible massacres by the Dutch at Amboyna are called to recollection.

What the king states in his letter, concerning the promises of Drake, is probably true; for we find from Hakluyt that Drake received many offers of friendship from the king, and proposed, if he would enter into a treaty of amity and commerce, the trade of Ternate should be reserved exclusively for England. It was in fact this sovereign who dispossessed the Portuguese of the dominion they had so long enjoyed at Ternate. Drake, having furnished his ship with provisions, and procured as many cloves as he desired, on the 9th November sailed from the capital of the Moluccas.

On the 11th they anchored at a small island near the eastern part of Celebes, where they repaired their ship; and the island being uninhabited they remained here for weeks undisturbed, with tents erected and a forge set up on shore. The island was one continued wood; and most of the trees were large, lofty, and straight, without throwing out a branch till near the top. No fresh water was found on the island, but they received a supply of this necessary article from an adjoining one.

"Among the trees night by night, through the whole land, did shew themselves an infinite swarm of fiery wormes flying through the ayre, whose bodies being no bigger than our common English flies, make such a shew and light, as if every twigge or tree had been a burning candle. In this place breedeth also wonderful store of bats, as bigge as large hennes; of cray - fishes also heere wanted no plentie, and they of exceeding bignesse, one whereof was sufficient for four hungry stomachs at a dinner, being also very good and restoring meate, whereof we had experience; and they dig themselves holes in the earth like conies." [21]

It is impossible not to admire the boldness and the skill of this able navigator, steering his solitary vessel through unknown seas, without a pilot and without a chart, (for the only one he had was from the coast of America to the Philippines,) to conduct his little ship in safety thus far through an intricate navigation, among rocks and islands, far more intricate even than the passage through the Strait of Magelhaens; but on their course to the westward they got entangled with such a number of small islands and shoals among the Celebes, that in order to extricate themselves, they stood off to the southward, where there appeared to be a more clear sea, when on the night of the 9th January, 1580, running under all sail set, and the wind blowing moderately fresh, the ship all at once struck on a rocky shoal and stuck fast.

Here the Golden Hind remained firmly fixed all night; at daylight every exertion was made to get her off; the water was of such a great depth on every side of the shoal as to make it impossible to get out an anchor to heave her off. In this state of distress, the whole ship's company was summoned to prayers, "commending ourselves into the merciful hands of our most gracious God: for this purpose we presently fell prostrate, and with joined prayers sent up to the throne of grace, humbly besought Almighty God to extend his mercy unto us in his son Christ Jesus; and so preparing, as it were, our necks unto the block, we every minute expected the final stroke to be given unto us." [22]

That duty performed, it was determined to lighten the ship of part of her lading. Three tons of cloves, eight of the guns, and a quantity of meal and beans, were thrown overboard, but without producing any visible benefit. Burney slily observes, "It does not appear that, during their apprehension of danger, the idea was once entertained of lightening the ship at the expense of any part of the treasure on board, which was the heaviest part of their cargo." Fortunately it happened that, at low water, in falling over on one side, she slipped off from the ledge of the rock, and floated into deep water.

On the 14th of March they had arrived, one hardly knows how, at some port at the south side of Java, where they remained till the 26th, and procured every kind of supply they stood in need of. Their time was here passed in feasting and jollity with the native chiefs, who then were not fettered by any Dutch masters. "This island," says Hakluyt, "is governed by five kings whom they called Rajah, who live as having one spirit and one minde." [23]

From Java they put to sea for the Cape of Good Hope, which they passed without stopping, though it was the first land they fell in with, notwithstanding, Hakluyt says, "we ranne hard aboord the Cape, finding the report of the Portirigals most false, who affirm that it is the most dangerous cape in the world, never without intolerable stormes and present danger to travaillers which come neere the same." [24]

On the 22nd July, they put into Sierra Leone, on the coast of Africa, where they stopped two days to take in water, and obtained there oysters and fruit. On the 24th, they again put to sea, and on the 26th September, 1580, "which," says the narrative, "was Monday in the just and ordinary reckoning of those that had stayed at home, in one place or country, (but in our computation was the Lord's day or Sunday,) we safely, with joyful minds and thankful hearts to God, arrived at Plimouth, the place of our first setting forth, after we had spent two years, ten months, and some odd days beside, in seeing the wonders of the Lord in the deep, in discerning so many admirable things, in going through with so many strange adventures, in escaping out of so many dangers, and overcoming so many difficulties, in this our encompassing of this nether globe, and passing round about the world, which we have related.

Soli rerum maximarum Effectori,
Soli totius mundi Gubernatori,
Soli suorum Conservatori,
Soli Deo sit semper gloria." [25]

[1] Frobisher's Voyage.
[2] The World Encompassed; Fletcher's MS.
[3] World Encompassed; Fletcher's MS.
[4] World Encompassed; Fletcher's MS.
[5] Ibid.
[6] Fletcher's MS.; World Encompassed.
[7] Belcher's Voyage round the World.
[8] World Encompassed.
[9] World Encompassed; Hakluyt.
[10] World Encompassed.
[11] World Encompassed.
[12] Hakluyt.
[13] World Encompassed.
[14] Burney's South Sea Discoveries.
[15] Ibid.
[16] World Encompassed.
[17] Burney's South Sea Discoveries.
[18] World Encompassed.
[19] Hakluyt.

[20] Purchas East India Voyage.
[21] Hakluyt.
[22] World Encompassed.

[23] Hakluyt.
[24] Ibid.
[25] The World Encompassed.

Chapter Five - Drake on Shore, Visit to London - 1580-1585

As soon as Drake's arrival with his single ship at Plymouth was known, the inhabitants hastened in crowds to the shore to welcome their old friend. On landing he was received by the Mayor and civic authorities, the bells of St. Andrew's church ringing a merry peal, which was prolonged during the whole day. The general joy was extreme, for a very common impression had gone forth, after the arrival of Captain John Winter, who had deserted him, that some fatal disaster had befallen Drake. The day was spent in feasting and rejoicing. But his first visit, on the following day, was to his native village near Tavistock; an act which proved, that no degree of celebrity nor change of fortune could divert this brave and right-minded man from performing an act of pious devotion to the once residence of his old parents, in which most probably he first drew his breath, and from which those parents had been driven by religious persecution - so strong is the affection generally felt for the abode of one's early youth.

Having been fêted for some days by the authorities of Plymouth and the neighbouring gentry, and rejoined his little bark, the Golden Hind, that had borne him through so many perils and adventures, and with which, as one of the old writers observes, "he ploughed up a furrow round the world," - he set sail for Deptford. The report of his arrival had of course preceded his appearance in London; where, it may be supposed, his adventures on the first voyage round the globe, by an Englishman, were not alone the topic of conversation, but that it was also combined with the most exaggerated account of the immense wealth he had brought back, and that various opinions were held as to the manner in which it had been acquired. But that which must have affected him most deeply, was the total silence of the court, where, before his departure, he had been so cordially received, and his projected enterprise had met with such flattering encouragement. No intimation was now given that his appearance there would be acceptable. The first Englishman, and the second of any country, that had circumnavigated the globe, might have been considered an object of curiosity, if of no higher consideration, and as one not unworthy of his sovereign's special notice. It is said, indeed, that in less dignified circles, the cool reception that Drake met with was too marked to be misunderstood; and that some were squeamish enough to refuse the acceptance of any little trifling gift or curiosity at his hands, lest it might not have been honestly come by; or that the wealth he had brought home had not been honestly or legitimately obtained. Stow appears to be the only writer of the time who enters into the case, and being a contemporary

78

with, and having survived, Drake, and a collector by profession, as it were, of all that was going forward, the following account may not be considered uninteresting. After stating Drake's arrival at Plymouth, "being very richly fraught with golde, silver, silke, pearls, and precious stones," he goes on to say,

"The newes of this his great wealth so far fetcht, was miraculous strange, and of all men held impossible and incredible, but both proving true, it fortuned that many misliked it and reproached him: besides all this there were others that devised and divulged all possible disgraces against Drake and his followers, deaming him the master thiefe of the unknowne world; yet neverthelesse, the people generally, with exceeding admiration, applauded his wonderful long adventures and rich prize, chiefly for some such reasons following.

"The Queene, not yet persuaded to accept and approve his unknowne purchase, paused a while and heard every opinion, which at that time were many; the principal points whereof were, that if this action of Drake should be justified, it would call in question the late piracy of Captayne Christmasse: the staying of the Spanish king's treasure by Martine Frobisher: hinder commerce: break the league: raise reproach: breede warre with the house of Burgundy: and cause imbargo of the English shippes and goodes in Spayne. Whereunto answer was made, that it was neither prize, nor piracy, nor civill policy, to cast so much treasure out of their possession: neither could any prince or private subject rightly challenge it: nor by it any offence committed, or intended to any Christian prince or state.

"And that it was very necessary to retaigne it, as well for further triall of the Spanish malice, shewed to the English merchants in Spayne; as for the descrying of secret enemies at home, against both which, it would prove a present remedy: as also that if warres ensued, which the Spanyards long threatened, then the same treasure of itself would fully defray the charge of seaven yeares warres, prevent and save the common subject from taxes, loanes, privy seals, subsidies and fifteenes, and give them good advantage against a daring adversary: the which said opinion strongly prevayled.

"Yet Captaine Drake, all this while, being therewithal, and by his friends much encouraged, rested doubtful of the event, untill the day that the Queen's Majesty came aborde his weather-beaten barke; where being as highly graced as his heart coulde wish, with knightly honors, princely commendations and encouragements, he forthwith visited his friendes in courte, towne and countrey, his name and fame became admirable in all places, the people swarming dayly in the streets to beholde him, vowing hatred to all that durst mislike him. Books, pictures and ballades were published in his prayse, his opinion and judgment concerning marine affayres stoode currant." [1]

It must be noticed, however, that Drake had for five months been held in suspense, as to the side of the scale into which the Queen would throw her weight, and upon which his future fame would mainly depend. He was now, however, to be highly honoured and amply gratified.

Stow continues the history, more fully, of the favourable reception Drake met with from the Queen. "They came home into England," he says, "in the year 1580; and in the year next following, to wit, 1581, on the 4th of April, her Majesty dining at Deptford, after dinner entered the ship which Captain Drake had so happily guided round about the world, and being there, a bridge which her Majesty had passed over, brake, being upon the same more than two hundred persons, and no man hurt by the fall; and there she did make Captain Drake Knight, in the same ship, for reward of his service; his armes were given him, a ship on the world, which ship, by her Majestie's commandment, is lodged in a dock at Deptford, for a monument to all posterity, of that famous and worthie exploite, whereof a worshipfull gentleman, Maister William Borough, in his preface to a book entitled 'A discourse of the variation of the compasse or magnetical needle,' hath these words: 'So now at length (saith he) our countrieman Sir Francis Drake, for valorous attempt, prudent proceeding, and fortunate performing his voyage about the world, is not only become equal to any of them that live, but in fame farre surpassing." [2]

It is quite true that the Queen did bestow on Drake the honour of knighthood on board his own ship, "an honour," says Dr. Johnson, "in that illustrious reign not made cheap by prostitution, nor ever bestowed without uncommon merit."

The Queen, it appears, expressed herself strongly that the Golden Hind should be preserved, as a striking monument of his own and his country's glory; and for a long series of years it remained in Deptford dock yard as an object of curiosity and admiration. One of our old chroniclers, Holinshed, says, "it were to be wished, that in memorie of this gentleman's incomparable achievement, some monument might remain to succeeding ages, and none more fitted than the brittle bark wherein he arrived safe and sound, which, as a Knight of good account and rarelie qualified, thought meete to be fixed upon the stumpe of Paul's steeple, in lieu of the spire, that, being discerned farre and neere, it might be noted and pointed at of people with these true termes: Yonder is the barke that hath sailed round about the world." [3]

"The gentleman," he says, "whom this remembrance concerneth, preferring the honour of his country before his own life, with magnanimitie undertooke unwonted adventures, and went through the same with wonderful happiness; were it not then injurie to burie his name in oblivion, matters of no moment compare to this noted in our annales? Wherefore 'til time produce a more sufficient commemoration of him, let this serve the turne; whereto we will add a few verses written in his fame, and so leave him unto the blessed successe whereunto he is by God's most gracious appointment (no doubt) reserved."

Holinshed follows up his encomium on Drake, and invokes the muse in the following "few verses" - "aut per se aut per alium;" - by the Knight, perhaps, 'rarelie qualified:'

"Ante *Dracum* multi heroes freta multa Britanni
 Non sine laude citis sulcârunt salsa carinis;
 Nee potuere tamen votis potirier: alti
 Nee reserare vias pelagi (sors omnia versat,)
 Quamvis mente pia imbuti atque ingentibus ausis:
 Dracus at ex multis (gallinse filius albae)
 Quem decorat Pytho, quern Suada venustat amica,
 Quem pia religio, quern dia Modestia adornat,
 Omine felici cuncta incipit, omine fausto
 Perficit, et patriae servit vivitque fidelis
 Cella petulca domans, et opima trophea reportans." [4]

These and other laudatory productions prove the feelings of the influential writers of the day, and their sentiments regarding Drake. When the Golden Hind was too far decayed to receive repairs, a sufficient quantity of sound wood was preserved,, to be converted into a chair, which was presented to the university of Oxford, with the following appropriate verses written by the celebrated Cowley:

"To this great ship which round the globe has run,
 And match'd in race the chariot of the sun;
 This Pythagorean ship, (for it may claim,
 Without presumption, so deserv'd a name,)
 By knowledge once, and transformation now,
 In her new shape, this sacred port allow.
 Drake and his ship could not have wish'd from fate
 An happier station or more blest estate.
 For lo! a seat of endless rest is given
 To her in Oxford, and to him in heaven."

Honest old Purchas, too, must be allowed to give his commendation of Drake's daring and adventurous spirit. "The sun," he says, "followed him all the way, as if that most excellent and heavenly light had delighted himself in his society, and acknowledged him for his son, more truly than the Spaniards (whereof anon we shall heare) or that Phaeton of the poets, not able to compasse this compassing journey; once he was so good a scholar and learned the sun's instruction so well, that he followed him in a watery field still that his fiery circle, round about the earthy globe was carried with the moving winde, new starres, islands, seas attending and admiring the English colours; and first of any General loosed the girdle of the world, and encompassing her in his fortunate arms, enjoyed her love. But I lose myself while I find him, and yet excellent names, I know not how, compel men to stand awhile and gaze with admiration, if not with adoration." [5]

Among other verses in praise of the circumnavigator were the following, set up for the occasion upon the main mast of the Golden Hind, and said to be written by some of the scholars of Winchester School.

"Plus ultra, Herculeis inscribas, Drace, columnis,
    Et magno dicas Hercule major ero.

On Herc'les pillars, Drake, thou may'st
    Plus ultra, write full well,
And say, I will, in greatness, that
    Great Hercules excel.

Drace, pererrati novit quem terminus orbis,
    Quemque semel mundi vidit uterque Polus,
Si taceant homines, facient te sidera notum;
    Sol nescit Comitis non memor esse sui.

Great Drake, whom well the world's end knows
    Which thou didst compass round,
And whom both poles of heaven once saw
    Which north and south do bound;

The stars bright will make thee known
    If men present were;
The sun however cannot forget
    His fellow traveller.

Digna ratis quae stet radiantibus inclyta stellis;
    Supremo coeli vertice digna ratis.

Among the radiant stars to stand
    Thy ship well worthy were;
Well worthy on the highest top
    Of heav'n a place to bear." [6]

"But these things," says Camden, "may seem too light, and to proceed from an idle brain, and not beseeming the gravity of an historian." [7] This grave historian, however, in his "Britannia," has gravely given the vulgar error (prevalent, perhaps, in his time) of the Barnacle Goose. Speaking of the shire of Buchan, in Scotland, he says, "It is hardly worthwhile to mention the *clayks,* a sort of geese, which are believed by some, with great admiration, to grow upon trees on this coast, and in other places; and, when they are ripe, to fall down into the sea, because neither their nests nor eggs can anywhere be found. But they who saw the ship in which Sir Francis Drake sailed round the world, when it was laid up in the river Thames, could testify that little birds bred in the old rotten keels of ships, since a great number of such, without life and feathers, stuck close to the outside of the keel of that ship. Yet I should think that the generation of these birds was not from the logs of wood, but from the sea, termed by the poets, 'the parent of all things'." [8] Camden evidently was not acquainted with the fact of there being a barnacle *shell*, as well as a barnacle *goose*.

But the Golden Hind herself would appear to have become a resort of holiday people, the cabin being converted into a sort of banqueting house, as "We'll have our supper," (says Sir Petronell Flash, in the comedy called '*England Hoe*,' by Ben Jonson and others,) "We'll have our supper on board Sir Francis Drake's ship that hath compassed the world," - and sure enough they are there represented as follows:

Seagull. - "What's that, good Colonel?

Sir Petronell Flash. - This, Captain Seagull; We'll have our provided supper brought aboard Sir Francis Drake's ship that hath encompassed the world, where, with full cups and banquets, we will do sacrifice for a prosperous voyage. My mind gives me that some good Spirit of the waters should haunt the desert ribs of her, and be auspicious to all that honour her memory, and will, with like orgies, enter their voyages.

"Captain and Gentlemen, we'll begin a new ceremony, at the beginning of our voyage, which I believe will be followed by all future adventurers." [9]

But Drake was assailed from another quarter, in a less agreeable manner than in compliments from the Muses. He must have been aware, that among the indiscriminate captures he made afloat, some of them were the property of private individuals, and that, as soon as it should be discovered he had returned home, such individuals themselves, or through their agents, would attack him for indemnification; and so, after a short time, it happened. The Spanish Ambassador, Mendoza, was instructed to make representations to Queen Elizabeth of the enormities committed by Drake in his late voyage, and of the depredations on the inhabitants of the territories belonging to Spain, in America, which belonged exclusively to his nation; and he was therefore instructed to demand, in the name of his Sovereign, full restitution for the property so seized, and punishment of the offender. Don Bernardin de Mendoza carried his insolent demand to such a length, as to imply that the English had no right to navigate the Indian Ocean. To whom the Queen returned this spirited reply:

"That the Spaniards, by their ill treatment of her subjects, to whom they had prohibited commerce, contrary to the law of nations, had drawn these mischiefs upon themselves. That Drake should be forthcoming to answer according to law, if he were convicted by good evidence and testimony to have committed anything against law and right. That the goods in question were purposely laid by, that satisfaction might be made to the Spaniards, though the Queen had spent a greater sum of money than Drake had brought in, against those rebels whom the Spaniards had raised and encouraged against her, both in Ireland and England. Moreover, she understood not why her, or any other Prince's, subjects should be debarred from the Indies, which she could not persuade herself the Spaniards had any just title to, by the Bishop of Rome's donation (in whom she acknowledged no prerogative, much less authority, in such cases, so as to lay any tie upon Princes which owed him no obedience or observance, or, as it were, to infeoffe the Spaniard in that new world, and invest him with the possession thereof), nor yet by any other claim, than as they had touched here and there upon the coasts, built cottages, and given names to a river or a cape; which things cannot entitle them to a propriety. So that this donation of that which is another man's, which is of no validity in law, and this imaginary propriety, cannot hinder other princes from trading into those countries, and, without breach of the law of nations, from transporting colonies into those parts thereof where the Spaniards inhabit not (forasmuch as prescription without possession is little worth), neither from freely navigating that vast ocean, seeing the use of the sea and air is common to all. Neither can a title to the ocean belong to any people, or private persons; forasmuch as neither nature nor public use and custom permitted any possession thereof." [10]

A certain sum of money however was ordered to be paid by Drake to a person of the name of Pedro Lebura, whom the Ambassador presented as an accredited agent for certain individuals, who made good their claims on account of private property, but which it afterwards turned out was never paid to the proper owners; but was, by order of the King, employed against Elizabeth in paying the Spaniards serving in the Netherlands.

What the sum was does not appear; but there is a minute of the Lord High Treasurer of certain sums of money paid by Sir Francis Drake into the Royal Mint, of which the following is a copy extracted from the State Papers of Lord Burleigh.

Whether the money mentioned in the following account, as given by Purchas, be any part of the foregoing, under a different denomination, or separate, there are no means of knowing without reference to the closed up documents of the Lord Treasurer, at Hatfield House, but it may be as well to insert them here.

"Captain Drake carried from the coast of Peru, eight hundred sixtie-six thousand pieces of silver, which is eight hundred sixty-six kintals, at a hundred pound waight the kintal, and every kintal is worth twelve hundred duckets of Spaine, which is a million, thirty-nine thousand and two hundred duckets. Besides this, he carried away a hundred thousand pieces of gold, which is ten kintals, and every kintal is worth fifteen hundred duckets of Spain, which amounteth to a hundred and fiftie thousand duckets, besides that which he had in the ship that was not customed, which I do not know of; as well pearls, precious stones, and other things of great value, besides the money he had in coine." [12]

"A briefe note of all such silver bullion as was brought into the Tower by Sir Fras. Drake, Knight, and laid in the vaute under the Jewel-House, as also what hath been taken out, and what remaineth, (viz.) 26 Dec., 1585:

	Weight. lb.	oz.		lb.	oz.
In ingots of silver, being fine and coarse by tale, 650, which waieth in gross weight	22899	5	}		
More in small pieces called corento, which is coarse silver that hath been gathered in the mines without refining and melting thereof, weighing in gross weight .	512	6		23,411	11

	£.	s.	d.		£.	s.	d.
There hath been coyned, as by her Majesty's Warrant appeareth, for the Right Hon. Sir Christopher Hatton, knight, to the sum of	2,300	0	0				
Item, As by another Warrant of her Majesty, there hath been coyned for the Right Hon. Sir Fras. Walsingham, knight, to the sum of	4,000	0	0		39,925	15	9
Item, by another of her Majesty's Warrants there hath been coyned for the Right Hon. the Earl of Leicester, to the sum of .	4,000	0	0				
Item, there is refined and molten of the said silver into clean ingotts to the sum of	29,625	15	9				

Totall Sum taken out of the vaute is

	£.	s.	d.
More in gold bullion brought in by the said Sir Fras. Drake, knight, in cakes and ingotts of severall fines, weighing 101 lb. 1oz., which said gold is refined, molten and coyned into 30s. and 15s. pieces, the charges being deducted to the sum of	205	0	0

	lb.	oz.
There remaineth in coarse ingotts of silver in the vaute under the Jewel-House, by tale, 243, which are to be refined and molten, weighing in gross weight	8544	11¾
More remaineth in the said vaute, the small pieces called corento, which is coarse silver as above said, weighing in gross weight [11]	512	6

We see by this account of the Lord Treasurer, in what manner something above 10,000l. were disposed of, but there is no account how the balance of 29,625l. was accounted for, nor of the additional gold and silver brought in by the said Francis Drake, amounting to about 27,160l., and which taken together, amounts to the sum of 56,800l., or thereabouts. It is not clear, however, that any part of this was appropriated to meet the claim of the Spanish Agent, who nevertheless did, from some fund or other, receive and misapply a certain sum of money; nor does it appear that all or any part of it was restored to Drake. There is, however, an old volume, "The Merchant's Mappe of Commerce, 1638; by Lewes Roberts," now very little known, but highly esteemed at the time, by which is made known the amount of profit obtained by the adventurers who assisted in fitting out and joining Drake's expedition. The volume is dedicated to Sir Maurice Abbot, Governor of the East India Company, and Mr. Alderman Garraway, Governor of the Levant Company; of both which Companies Mr. Roberts was a member. He says,

"This voyage made profit to himself (Drake) and merchants of London, his partners and fellow-adventurers, according to an account made up at his return, all charges paid and discharged, which I have seen, subscribed under his own hand, 47*l*. for 1*l*.; so that he who adventured with him in this voyage 100*l*., had 4700*l*. for the same, by which may be gathered the benefit that redounded thereby; though accompanied with many rubbes, delaies and dangers." [13]

But that which does appear to us, of the present day, as most remarkable is this; that no inquiry, on Drake's arrival in England, should have taken place regarding the extraordinary trial and execution at Port St. Julian. The whole affair must have been well known at home from Captain Winter's ship, which deserted Drake in the Strait of Magelhaens, and if, during the five months he was excluded, as it were, from the court, and various attempts were made to disparage his fame, no case was got up against him on the score of this transaction, we may consider him to have been fully acquitted in public opinion of any impropriety in the proceedings regarding that unfortunate business. But it may be asked, who was the poor man that suffered? Had he no friends? He came to Plymouth when the Expedition was ready for sea; he knew no one but Drake; and this would lead to a supposition that their acquaintance had been made in Ireland; that Doughty had been one of Lord Essex's unfortunate adventurers, who were ruined; and that he had fled to Drake for advice, assistance, or employment. This is rendered the more probable, as he appears to have brought over with him a story that was current in Ireland respecting the poisoning of Essex, which some of that nobleman's friends supposed to have been perpetrated by some emissary of the Earl of Leicester, who was his bitterest enemy at Court; but the rumour was scouted by Essex himself, who was fully aware of the nature of his complaint. He died, and his friends procured a *post mortem* examination, which completely refuted any such charge as that of poison. On such a report, however, might easily be raised the absurd story of Leicester and Drake; and still more easily form matter for a scurrilous poem called "Leicester's Ghost," published six-and-forty years after the death of Drake; of which the following are two of its stanzas:

I doubted lest that Doughtie should bewray
My counsel, and with other party take;
Wherefore, the sooner him to rid away,
I sent him forth to sea, with Captain Drake,
Who knew how to entertain him for my sake.
    Before he went, his lot by me was cast;
    His death was plotted and perform'd in haste.

86

He hoped well; but I did so dispose
That he, at Fort St. Julian, lost his head,
Having no time permitted to disclose
The inward griefs, that in his heart were bred,
We need not fear the biting of the dead.
    Now let him go, transported to the seas,
    And tell my secret to th' Antipodes.

The following story, published by Prince in his "Worthies of Devon," is not more absurd than it is destitute of any foundation in fact; but the absurdity has not prevented it from repetition, and probably from obtaining a degree of credit, however improbable it must have been considered:

"About this time it was, that there fell out a contest between Sir Bernard Drake, and the immortal Sir Fras. Drake: chiefly occasioned by Sir Francis his assuming Sir Bernard's coat of arms, not being able to make out his descent from his family; a matter in those days, when the court of honour was in more honour, not so easily digested. The feud hereupon increased to that degree that Sir Bernard, being a person of a high spirit, gave Sir Francis a box on the ear; and that within the verge of the court. For which offence he incurred her Majesty's displeasure; and most probably it proved the occasion of the Queen's bestowing upon Sir Fras. Drake a new coat of everlasting honour to himself and posterity for ever; which hath relation to that glorious action of his, the circumnavigating the world, which is thus emblazoned by Guillim:

"Diamond, a fess wavy, between the two polestars, artic and antartic, pearl; as before.

"And what is more, his crest is a ship on a globe under ruff, held by a cable rope with a hand out of the clouds; in the rigging whereof is hung up by the heels a wivern gules, Sir Bernard's arms; but in no great honour, we may think, to that knight, though so designed to Sir Francis. Unto all which Sir Bernard boldly replied: 'That though her Majesty could give him a nobler, yet she could not give an antienter coat than his.'" [14]

"This relation, I had," says Prince, "from Sir John Drake, of Trill, knight and baronet, my honourable godfather."

This falsehood is scarcely worth a contradiction. To suppose that Drake would tamely submit to such an insult, without at once felling the offender to the ground, or that Elizabeth would soothe the wounded feelings of her newly created recreant knight by giving him a sugar-plum, would be to insult the memory of both. The arms were given immediately after the knighthood in 1581; over the globe is the motto *auxilio divino,* and underneath is *sic parvis magna.* The simple fact is, that Sir Francis asked his relation for the family arms, of which he was himself ignorant, and Sir Bernard testifies to the family relationship, and recognizes his right to the family bearings, for Sir Francis required these for the information of the gentlemen of the Heralds' College. This is the whole story.

Some time after Drake's return from his circumnavigation voyage, he received a letter from Mr. Davis, the Arctic Voyager, of whom Strype says, "I have one note more to make of one Davys, a mariner, sometime belonging to Sir Francis Drake, who being employed to find out a northwest passage into those seas in that part of the world, came back this year (in 1585), and upon his return, in a letter, acquainted the said Drake with some account of those seas, and how navigable they were. The letter shewing the first discovery of that passage, and wrote to so eminent a seaman, may deserve to be preserved, and is, as I take it from the original, to this tenor:"

"Right honourable, most dutifully craving pardon for this my rash boldness, I am hereby, according to my duty, to signify unto your honor that the north-west passage is a matter nothing doubtful; but at any time almost to be passed by a sea navigable, void of ice; the ice tolerable, the waters very deep. I have also found an isle of very great quantity, not in any globe or maps discovered, yielding a sufficient trade of furs and leather. Although this passage hath been supposed very improbable, yet, through God's mercy, I am in experience an eye witness to the contrary; yea, in the most desperate climates, which, by God's help, I will very shortly more at large reveal unto your honor, so soon as I can possibly take order for my mariners and shipping. Thus depending upon your honor's good favour, I most humbly commit you to God. This 3rd October.

"Your honor's for ever
"Most dutiful,
(Signed) "JOHN DAVIS."

Hence those straits in that passage were called Davis's Straits to this day. [15]

It would appear from this that Davis had been with Drake perhaps on the circumnavigation voyage, when the latter contemplated a passage from the Pacific to the Atlantic, and which was at the time and since so vigorously attempted in a contrary direction, by Frobisher, Davis, Baffin, Gilbert, and many others of "heroike courage, marine worthies, beyond all names of worthinesse," as Purchas describes.

Drake was always kind to his followers, and always ready to attend to their little concerns. The two following letters, among many others, afford examples of this.

"Mr. Doctor Caesar, this power man and dyvers others have indured to ther great charge myche wronge at this Powell's hands, as by good proffe they will make you know. You shall shew this bearer no favour but I will hold it donne to myself, and will be willyng in any thing to aqwyett it. From Charterhowse in som hast, this 12th February 1584.

"Your very lovinge friend,
FRA: DRAKE. [16]

"To the Worshippful my very
"lovinge friend Mr. Doctor Caesar,

88

"Judge of the Admiraltie."

"Good Mr. Doctor Caesar,
"This bearer, Roger Roffe, is like to have some cawse in question before you: it is supposed that he hath wronge, therefore I presume the rather to intreat your favour towards him, prayinge that for my sake you will shew yt in his behalf, being willinge, in that he will becom one of my companie to steed him in any honest cawse. And so with my right hertie commendations do bid you farewell. From your father's howse in Chepside, this 24 June, 1585.
"Your assured friend,
"FRA: DRAKE. [17]

"To the Worshipful my very
"lovinge friend, Mr. Doctor Caesar,
"Judge of the Admiraultie.
"With speede."

He now remained on shore for the next four or five years, but not without active employment. In 1582 he was mayor of Plymouth; but the records of that place contain but two entries of any transactions beyond the ordinary routine during his mayoralty; one, that he caused the compass to be put upon the Hoe; the other, that the order for wearing scarlet gowns was put in execution.

[1] Stow's Chronicles.
[2] Stow's Chronicles.
[3] Holinshed's Chronicles.
[4] Holinshed.
[5] Purchas, his Pilgrimes. Purchas was an honest and warm-hearted writer, but he did sometimes "lose himself;" his good opinion, however, is worth having. And on the same grounds are the numerous compliments in verse bestowed upon this voyage of Drake, which certainly had then no parallel.
[6] Camden.
[7] Ibid.
[8] Camden's Britannia.
[9] Old Play.
[10] Camden's Annals.
[11] Burleigh's State Papers.
[12] Purchas.
[13] Communicated by Mr. Bolton Corney, from whom much valuable information has been received.
[14] Prince's Worthies of Devon.
[15] Strype.
[16] Lansdowne MSS. British Museum.
[17] Ibid.

Chapter Six - Drake's Voyage to the West Indies - 1585-1586

The complete success of the circumnavigation voyage gave an additional spur, both to navy and army, to humble the arrogant pretensions of Spain, and punish the authors of the cruelties and unheard of miseries inflicted on our countrymen in their Indian possessions. Her Majesty was not less pleased with the result of the last voyage, and as a test of her approval she advanced Sir Francis Drake to the rank of Admiral; and signified her pleasure that he should put in preparation a fleet, which she destined for the West Indies. She had every motive for adopting this measure; she was well aware that the treaty she had just concluded with the United Netherlands would be considered by the King of Spain as little short of a declaration of war, and that she ought to be prepared accordingly. He had, in fact, already laid an embargo upon all the English ships, goods, and men, found within his territories, which was itself a hostile measure, and the first step to a declaration of war. Her Majesty was, moreover, fully aware that little chance could be entertained of restitution, or of obtaining any satisfaction for her subjects whose property had been seized, and therefore, she wisely adopted the only measure that could be taken, to indemnify themselves on the subjects of the King of Spain in the West Indies, from whence his chief reliance for supplies was derived. But the power of the King of Spain was not to be disregarded.

"The Queen and kingdom," says Strype, "had the greatest apprehensions from abroad of the King of Spain: with whom she could obtain no good understanding: and of whom especially it concerned her to beware, considering his power, which at that time was formidable; and thus set forth by our historian (Camden:) 'all the Princes of Italy were at his beck: the bishop of Rome was wholly addicted and engaged to him; the Cardinals were, as it were, his vassals; all the ablest persons, for matters both of war and peace, were his pensioners. In Germany, the house of Austria, a house extending and branching far and wide, and other houses allied unto the same by marriages, did, as it were, attend upon him and his service. His wealth also and his strength were so much increased, both by sea and land, since the late addition of Portugal and East India, that he was far more powerful and formidable than ever his father Charles V. was. And if he should once reduce the Netherlands under his power, there was nothing to hinder, but that the rest of the princes of Christendom must of necessity stoop to his greatness, unless it were prevented.' "This powerful prince then the Queen had to deal with. It was judged therefore the best course to favour the Netherlander, with whom he was now at war, and towards whom he had exercised great barbarities. It was now under deliberation concerning the doing of this weighty matter. The lord-treasurer had consulted with Hawkins, a brave seaman and treasurer of the Navy, upon this affair; and what means might be used in this undertaking, requiring to know his thoughts thereof. He soon after showed that statesman, in writing, the means to offend that king, and the reasons to maintain that faction." [1]

The reasons were strong enough, but the power of the enemy was not to be disregarded. He had, however, as it were, thrown down the gauntlet; his hostility to England had carried him so far as to lay an embargo on English ships, goods, and men, found in any port of his dominions. The Queen therefore saw plainly that nothing was left to meet this insolence but to authorize all such of her subjects as had suffered from this measure, and all others who might feel disposed to resent this hostile proceeding on the part of Spain, to be furnished with letters of marque and reprisal, with power to seize all ships and merchandise, wherever found, belonging to the subjects of the king of Spain. At the same time she ordered twenty-five sail of ships to be equipped to avenge the insults and wrongs she had received, to be employed under the command of Sir Francis Drake, whom she considered as the fittest officer in her dominions, from his experience and success in naval matters, to strike a blow against Spain.

But Drake, it appears, was beset by a volunteer, whose offer he could neither well reject, nor prudently accept. This was no less a person than the gallant and most accomplished Sir Philip Sydney, the friend and favourite of Queen Elizabeth, of whom one about the court said, "she was afraid (when he was about to leave her on another occasion) to lose the jewel of her times." In a life of this extraordinary gentleman, professed to be, and actually was, written by his friend, Sir Fulke Grevil, (Lord Brooke,) it is stated that this expedition was of Sir Philip's own projecting, "wherein he fashioned the whole body with purpose to become the head of it himself." - "I mean," says he, "the last employment but one, of Sir Francis Drake to the West Indies, which journey, as the scope of it was mixt both of sea and land service; so had it accordingly distinct officers and commanders, chosen by Sir Philip out of the ablest governors of those martial times." He then tells us, the project was contrived between themselves; it was, that he and Sir Francis should be equal commanders, when they had left England; that Sir Francis should bear the name for the preparations, and by the credit of Sir Philip, should have every thing abundantly supplied.

It was to be kept secret; as Sir Philip well knew it would be next to impossible to obtain the Queen's consent to his taking an employment so remote, and of so hazardous a nature; but when once it was ready, he presumed "the success would put envy and all her agents to silence." Sir Francis, on his part, found that Sir Philip's friends, with the influence of his excellent inward powers, would add both weight and fashion to his ambition; and consequently, "either with or without Sir Philip's company, yield unexpected ease and honour to him on this voyage." [2]

The preparations went on; every thing that Sir Francis required was at once procured. Sir Francis repairs to Plymouth; waits only the watchword from Sir Philip to put to sea. A letter arrives post "as if the whole fleet staid only for Sir Philip and a wind." He sets off for Plymouth, "was feasted the first night by Sir Francis, with a great deal of outward pomp and compliment." "Yet I, (says Lord Brooke,) being his loving and beloved Achates in this journey, observing the countenance of this gallant mariner, more than Sir Philip's leisure served him to do, acquainted him with my observation of the discountenance and depression which appeared in Sir Francis; as if our coming were both beyond his expectation and desire." [3]

It may be that the observation of Lord Brooke turned out to be correct, that Drake did not much relish such high company, and that, in fact, he was playing the game assigned to him. "For, (says his lordship,) within a few days after, a post steals up to the court, upon whose arrival an alarm is presently taken; messengers sent away to stay us, and, if we refused, to stay the whole fleet." It now indeed was sufficiently evident, that the Queen in her affection, almost parental, for Sir Philip Sydney, conveyed her royal mandate by a peer of the realm, "carrying with it in the one hand, grace, and in the other, thunder." [4] Of her grace he was certain, and of her thunder he had no reason to be afraid. It is impossible to read that beautiful letter of Sir Philip to the Queen, dissuading her from her understood resolution to marry the Duke of Anjou, without being strongly impressed with the real attachment and esteem which the Queen and Sydney mutually felt for each other. That letter, as Hume says, "is written with an unusual elegance of expression, as well as force of reasoning," - he might have added, with a delicacy of remonstrance, against such an union with a papist, softened by the most affectionate terms of regard, corresponding with the opening address, "For our most feared and beloved, most sweet and gracious Sovereign." [5]

How Drake contrived to settle this ticklish affair with the Queen does not appear. It is not improbable that he was, all the while, in communication with Sir Francis Walsingham, or some other person at court, and that he was desired to indulge the scheme of the romantic knight, until the expedition should be ready to depart. Everything in fact had been already settled, as to the officers and men, and the preparations were completed. It consisted of a fleet of one and twenty sail of ships, (some say twenty-five sail,) and pinnaces, on which were embarked two thousand seamen and soldiers, at Plymouth.

The principal officers were

Sir Francis Drake, Admiral or General. Thos. Fenner, His Captain.	Elizabeth Bonaventura.
Martin Frobisher, Vice-Admiral.	Primrose.
Francis Knollis, Rear-Admiral.	Gallion, Leicester.
To whom were added, Lieutenant-General Carleill, who had command of the troops, with one major, three corporals of the field, and ten captains under him.	Tyger.

The other sixteen ships were probably taken up as transports, but neither the tonnage, guns, nor men of any part of the expedition are mentioned.

This was evidently a combined expedition, of naval and military forces, strictly sent out on the public service, the first instance of a divided command, on which Drake had been employed; and though he was the chief, or General, of the expedition, yet the military part of the operations, to which it was in a great degree confined, necessarily devolved upon the superintending direction of the Lieutenant General Carleill (or Carlisle); and in point of fact, the whole account of their proceedings, as given in Hakluyt, is a copy from the narrative drawn up by one of his officers, Captain Walter Biggs, who died on the voyage; was completed by Lieutenant Cripps, who gave it to Lieutenant Cates, to be by him published, all three being officers of the army serving in the Lieutenant General's company.

On the 14th September, 1585, the expedition left Plymouth, and near to the coast of Spain fell in with divers French ships of small burthen, mostly laden with salt, one of which, having no person in her, the General took for the service, meaning at their return to pay the value of her, which he did; to this bark he gave the name of Drake. A few days after this, they fell in with a stout Spanish ship, having great store of dry Newfoundland fish on board, "commonly called with us *Poor John,*" a better sort it is to be hoped than Trinculo describes as "neither fish nor flesh, a kind of, not of the newest, *Poor John;*" but it is said to have been of great use to him during the voyage.

Coming before Bayonne, a message was sent to the Governor, to ask if there was war between Spain and England, and why our merchants were embargoed and arrested? Being satisfied on these points, and receiving from the Governor a present of bread, wine, oil, apples, grapes and marmalade, they took their leave, but scarcely could reach their ships, from the shore, before a storm arose which scattered the fleet.

Being again collected, they sent their pinnaces to see what might be done above the harbour of Vigo, where they succeeded in taking many boats and caravels laden with things of small value, one with "stuff of the high church or Cathedral of Vigo, among which was a cross of silver doubly gilt, having cost a great mass of money." The Spaniards declared that the property taken here amounted in value to thirty thousand ducats.

At Palma, in the Canary Islands, "by the naughtinesse of the landing place, well furnished with great ordnance," they thought fit to depart with "the receipt of many of their cannon shot, some into our ships, and some of them besides being in very deed full cannon high." [6] But their calling first at Bayonne, and then here, was imprudent, as it had enabled the Governor of the former to send a despatch to their several possessions, to warn them of the approach of English forces, the strength of which he greatly exaggerated. At Ferro they found the inhabitants were so poor, that they spared them, and proceeded to the Cape de Verde Islands, and anchored near Porta Praya, (which is called Playa by Gates,) where they put on shore a thousand men. Here they dallied for fourteen days, between the towns of St. Jago and Porta Praya, two of the most wretched Portuguese villages, mostly of miserable huts; the Governor (who, in our times, is usually a man of colour), the Bishop and the better sort having all run away into the mountains. All they could find as booty were two pieces of ordnance, one of iron and one of brass. The inhabitants met with one of their boys straggling, whom they killed, and mangled in a brutal manner; in revenge of which "we consumed with fire all the houses, as well in the country as in the town of St. Jago, the hospital excepted, which we left unconsumed." [7]

The Portuguese had also their revenge; for before the fleet was many days at sea, such a mortality took place among the people that there died from two to three hundred men before it ceased. They are described as having been marked with small spots like to those in the plague. They next proceeded to Dominica, which they reached in eighteen days. The island was at this time inhabited by a savage people (the Caribs), who were all naked, their skins painted, and in all respects a well-made, handsome and strong people, very civil and ready to assist, during their stay, in watering their fleet; that being done they then made sail for St. Christopher's, where they refreshed their men with what they could find, and spent their Christmas, but saw no inhabitants, and believed there were none on the island.

A council being held, it was decided they should next proceed to the great island of Hispaniola, "being allured thither by the glorious fame of the city of St. Domingo, being the ancientest and chief inhabited place in all the tract of country thereabouts." [8] On arriving there, they were informed that the Spaniards were in great force, particularly at this principal city. On new year's day, by the advice of a pilot they had taken in a frigate, they landed twelve hundred men at a convenient spot, about ten or twelve miles from the city. "Our General, after seeing all landed in safetie, returned to the fleet, bequeathing us to God and the good conduct of Maister Carleill our Lieutenant General; at which time, about eight of the clock we began to march." [9]

On approaching the town, about a hundred and fifty horsemen came out to oppose them, but were received by the invaders with so good a proportion of pikes and small shot, that they retreated hastily within the two sea-ward gates, both of which were manned and ordnance planted, besides troops placed in ambuscade by the road side. Carleill divided his force, of some twelve hundred men, into two parties, giving Captain Powell the command of one division. It was settled that they were to enter at both gates, at the same time, the General swearing to Powell "that with God's good favour they would not rest till they met in the market place." [10] Powell with his company pushed through one of the gates, and the General through the other, and they accordingly, after some fighting, gained the market-place, or square, in which was the great church. Here they quartered themselves, and by making trenches and planting ordnance, held the town for the space of a month, during which time not many accidents happened. One day, however, the General had occasion to send a message to the Spaniards by a Negro boy carrying a flag of truce; an officer of the King of Spain's galley meeting the boy, struck him through the body with a staff, and the poor fellow, having crawled back to the General, and told him what had happened, died on the spot. "The General being greatly passioned, commanded the provost martial to cause a couple of Fryars, who were among his prisoners, to be carried to the same place where the boy was stricken, accompanied with a sufficient guard of our soldiers, and there presently to be both hanged, despatching at the instant another poor Spanish prisoner, with the reason wherefore this execution was done; and with this message further, that until the party, who had thus murthered the General's messenger, were delivered into our hands, to receive condign punishment, there should no day passe, wherein there should not two prisoners be hanged, until they were all consumed, which were in our hands." [11] The murderer of the boy was brought to be delivered to the General; but it was thought a more honourable revenge to make them there perform the execution themselves, in his presence.

The ransom of the city was demanded, and, as the inhabitants were very slow in coming to terms, every morning the setting fire to the suburbs was put in practice for several days together, but the invaders found it "no small travail to ruin them, being very magnificently built of stone, with high lofts." Gates says, "for many successive days, 200 sailors from daybreak till nine o'clock, when the next began, did nothing but labour to fire these houses; yet we did not consume so much as one third part of the town; and so in the end, what wearied with firing, and what hastened by some other respects, we were glad to take, and they at length agreed to pay, a ransom of five and twenty thousand ducats." [12] Mr. Gates further informs us that in the gallery of their King's house, there is painted, on a very large escutcheon, the arms of the King of Spain, and in the lower part of the 'scutcheon a terrestrial globe, containing upon it the whole circuit of the sea, and the earth, whereon is a horse standing on his hind legs as in the act of leaping from it, with a scroll proceeding from his mouth, whereon was written, *Non sufficit Orbis.*" The invaders, who looked upon this "as a very notable mark and token of the unsatiable ambition of the Spanish king and nation, would not refrain from pointing it out to the Spaniards, who were sent to negotiate with them; nor from sarcastically enquiring what was meant by such a device? at which they would shake their heads and turn aside their faces, in some smiling sort, without answering any thing, as if ashamed thereof." [13]

Having found here, and supplied themselves with great store of strong wine, abundance of sweet oil, vinegar, olives, and such like provisions, some woollen, linen, and silk cloths, but little plate or silver, though of the latter they found some, they prepared for their departure.

From St. Domingo the expedition put to sea, and stood over to the mainland, keeping along the northern coast, till they came in sight of Cartagena, and entered the harbour about three miles westward of the town; to get into which it was necessary to pass along a narrow isthmus, not above fifty paces wide, with the sea on one side and the harbour on the other; and at the extremity was a stone wall built across it, with an opening just wide enough for the horsemen, or a carriage, to pass; arid this was barricadoed with wine butts filled with earth and placed on end. Against this part the assault was made, which Mr. Gates thus describes. "We soon found out the barricadoes of pipes or butts to be the meetest place for our assault, which, notwithstanding it was well furnished with pikes and shot, was, without staying, attempted by us: down went the butts of earth, and pell-mell came our swords and pikes together after our shot had first given their volley, even at the enemy's nose. Our pikes were somewhat longer than their's, and our bodies better armed, with which advantage our swords and pikes grew too hard for them, and they were driven to give place. In this furious entree, the Lieutenant-General slue with his owne hands the chief ensigne-bearer of the Spaniards, who fought very manfully to his live's end." [14]

He then tells us they rushed together into the town, and gave the enemy no time to breathe until they got to the market-place, when they were suffered to remain quiet and lodge in the town, and that they themselves would go into the country to their wives. During the fight, the Indians made use of poisoned arrows, so that the least scratch of the skin, "unless it were by great marveil," caused death.

They kept possession of Cartagena for six weeks, and pursued the same course to bring about a ransom as they had done at St. Domingo; and, "though upon discontentments and for want of agreeing in the first negotiations for a ransom, they touched the town in its outposts, and consumed much with fire," yet the other miseries of war were suspended; and Gates says, "there passed divers courtesies between us and the Spaniards, as feasting and using them with all kindness and favour." The Governor, the Bishop, and many other gentlemen of the better sort, visited the General and Lieutenant General. The only loss the English sustained, during their residence, was that of Captain Varney, who was killed by the discharge of some muskets from the bushes, when standing on the deck of a vessel he had boarded, when five or six others were mortally wounded, among whom was Captain Moon.

But the disease which they had brought with them, from the Cape de Verde Islands, never left them. They suffered greatly from sickness, which carried off numbers, and of those that survived very few ever recovered their strength, lost their memory, and became imbecile in mind: the name given to the disorder was the calenture, which is "a verie burning and pestilent ague." The permanence of this disease, and the great mortality, occasioned them to give up their intended enterprise against Nombre de Dios, arid from thence overland to Panama, "where we should have striken the stroke for the treasure, and full recompense of our tediouse travailes." And thus at Cartagena was taken their first resolution to return homewards; but, first of all, after a little firing of the town in consequence of some disagreement "touching the ransom," it was at last concluded, that one hundred and ten thousand ducats should be paid for the town. But as the priory or abbey, a quarter of a mile out of the town, was in possession of the English soldiers, a thousand crowns were exacted as the ransom of this.

At a consultation respecting this ransom, it was stated that they might at first have demanded a great deal more; but now the abovementioned sum was deemed sufficient, "inasmuch as we have taken our full pleasure, both in the uttermost, sacking and spoiling of all their household goods and merchandise, as also in that we have consumed and ruined a great part of their town with fire." [15] Then they also very properly considered that they had in the expedition a great number of poor men who had ventured their lives, had suffered much from sickness, had wasted their clothing, and what little provision their slender means had enabled them to lay in, with the best intention of punishing the Spaniard, "our greatest and most dangerous enemy, we cannot but have an inward regard to help toward their satisfaction of this their expectation; and, by procuring them some little benefit, to encourage them, and to nourish this ready and willing disposition both in them and in others, by their example, against any other time of like occasion." This was very kindly and properly considered; but the commanding and other officers did not stop here. "But because it may be supposed that therein we forgot not the private benefit of ourselves, and are thereby the rather moved to incline ourselves to this composition, we declare hereby, that what part or portion soever it be of this ransom for Cartagena, which should come unto us, we do freely give and bestow the same wholly upon the poor men who have remained with us in the voyage, meaning as well the sailor as the soldier, and wishing with all our hearts it were such or so much, as might seem a sufficient reward for their peaceful endeavour." [16]

On the 1st March the expedition left Cartagena, and on the 27th April reached Cape St. Antonio, the westernmost part of Cuba. Finding no fresh water there, they made for Matanzas; but the weather being boisterous, they were driven back to Cape St. Antonio. But their water was exhausted; and, after much search, they found only some pits of rain-water. "Here," says Gates, "I do wrong if I should forget the good example of the General, who, to encourage others, and to hasten the getting of water aboard, took no less pains than the meanest. Throughout the expedition, indeed, he had everywhere shown so vigilant a care and foresight in the good ordering of his fleet, accompanied with such wonderful travail of body, that doubtless, had he been the meanest person, as he was the chiefest, he had deserved the first place of honour. And no less happy do we account him for being associated with Master Carleill his lieutenant-general, by whose experience, prudent counsel and gallant performance, he achieved so many and happy enterprises, and by whom also he was very greatly assisted, in setting down the needful orders, laws and course of justice, and the due administration of the same upon all occasions." [17]

From hence they continued their course for the coast of Florida, keeping the shore in sight till, on the 28th May, they discovered a scaffold raised upon four high masts, as a look-out station towards the sea. Upon this, we are told, "Drake manned the pinnaces and landed, to see what place the enemy held there, no one in the armament having any knowledge of it." [18] Having gone up the river St. Augustine, they came to the fort of St. Juan de Pinos, newly erected by the Spaniards, and not yet completed. The Spaniards that were there took the alarm and abandoned the work, making the best of their way to the city or town of St. Augustine, where there was a garrison of 150 men. When the English, who had landed the next day to storm this fort, had reached it, and entered the place, they found nobody there. There were four-teen great pieces of brass ordnance placed on a platform, which was con-structed of large pine-trees, laid across, one on another, and some little earth between. The garrison, which, as we learned from a Frenchman, a fifer, and prisoner in the fort, consisted of 150 men, had retired in such haste, that they left behind them the treasure-chest, containing about 2000*l*. [19]

The same thing happened on the English marching for the city of St. Augus-tine, and on approaching it, they had a few shot fired at them by a party of Spaniards, who then ran away. Anthony Powell, the serjeant-major, pursued them, leaping upon one of the horses they had left behind; but having ad-vanced rashly beyond his company in pursuit, over ground covered with long grass, a Spaniard, laying wait for him, shot him through the head; and, before any of the party could come to rescue his body, it had been pierced with many wounds. The governor had withdrawn to St. Matheo, leaving the city without a single inhabitant. It was considered as wearing the appearance of being a prosperous settlement, having its council-house, church, and other edifices, and gardens all round about, all which were burnt and laid waste by the invaders, in revenge for the death of Capt. Powell. It was intended, on leaving this place, to visit another Spanish settlement, about twelve leagues farther on, called St. Helena, and attack and destroy it also; but they found the shoals too dangerous for them to attempt an entrance without a pilot, and under unfavourable circumstances of wind and weather. Abandoning therefore this design, they continued coasting along, proceeding in sight of the shore, in search of Sir Walter Raleigh's recently planted colony in Virgin-ia; which, by her Majesty's command, Sir Francis Drake was directed to in-spect, and to afford any assistance and encouragement he might be enabled to do. They found the shore inaccessible to their ships, like that of St. Helena, on account of the shoalness of the water. They therefore anchored in a wild exposed situation, two miles from the shore; from whence the General sent a message to Mr. Ralph Lane, the Governor, who was then at his fort at Roanoak, to offer him such supplies as his squadron would afford.

Mr. Lane, with some of his company, having waited on the General, re-quested him to grant to his little colony a fresh supply of men and provisions, with a small vessel and boats to attend them, in order that, should they be put to distress for want of relief, they might have the means at hand to embark for England; this request was immediately complied with by Sir Francis, and a ship selected for the use of the colony, fitted up and plentifully supplied with all manner of stores for a considerable period. While this however was in preparation, a storm arose which continued three days, and drove that ship, with some others, from their anchors to sea, which were never seen again till Drake's arrival in England, whither all of them had contrived to be driven instead of facing the storm.

Sir Francis then proposed to give them another of his ships; but the late accident, and a few former hardships which Mr. Lane and his colonists had undergone, had so preyed on their spirits, that they concluded Providence was not favourable to their design of establishing themselves on the shores of America; and considering, moreover, that the promised supplies from England had failed them, after consulting among themselves, they petitioned Sir Francis Drake to take them along with him home. The number that embarked was 103, being five short of those who originally landed, and who had died. [20] Mr. Lane is reported to have been the first to introduce tobacco into England, a name which this weed obtained from the island on which it was first found - *Tobago*.

"These men who were thus brought back were the first that I know of," says Camden, "that brought into England that Indian plant which they call tabacca and nicotia, or tobacco, which they used against crudities, being taught it by the Indians. Certainly from that time forward, it began to grow into great request, and to be sold at an high rate, which, in a short time, many men everywhere, some for wantonness, some for health sake, with insatiable desire and greediness, sucked in the stinking smoke thereof through an earthen pipe, which presently they blew out again at their nostrils: insomuch that tobacco-shops are now as ordinary in most towns, as tap-houses and taverns. So that the Englishmen's bodies (as one said wittily) which are so delighted with this plant, seem as 'twere to be degenerated into the nature of barbarians, since they are delighted, and think they may be cured, with the same things which the barbarians use." [21] Such, and more energetically expressed, were the feelings of King James, respecting this herb when he wrote the "Counterblast to Tobacco;" and such, it may be added, are the feelings of many people, regarding the too common practice of blowing out "stinking smoke" in public places and the public streets.

Thus ended this expedition of Sir Francis Drake, very unequal in profit or interest to his two former ones, where he was alone, the sole arbiter of his proceedings. The booty brought home was valued at 60,000*l.*; 240 pieces of brass and iron cannon, of which 200 were of brass; [22] and with the loss of about 750 men, who all, or most of them, died of calenture. Of these, four were captains of the army, two of the navy, four lieutenants of the army, and six masters, apparently of merchant ships. Of the money brought home, 20,000*l.*, as they had resolved in council, were divided among the soldiers and sailors, of which, "as I can judge," says Gates, "will redound some six pounds to the single share." [23] "And so, God be thanked," he continues, "both they (the colonists) and we in good safetie arrived at Portsmouth the eight-and-twentieth of July, 1586, to the great glory of God, and to no small honour to our Prince, our country, and ourselves."

Mr. Gates may be well assured of this, that the profit was small, whatever the honour may have been considered. He has, however, the *dictum* of a great naval critic in his favour. Sir William Monson says, "This fleet was the greatest of any nation but the Spaniards, that had ever been seen in those seas since the first discovery of them. And if it had been as well considered of, before their going from home, as it was happily performed by the valour of the undertakers, it had more annoyed the King of Spain than all other actions that ensued during the time of the war.

"But it seems our long peace made us uncapable of advice in war; for had we kept and defended these places, when in our possession, and provided to have been relieved and succoured out of England, we had diverted the war from this part of Europe; for at that time there was no comparison betwixt the strength of Spain and England by sea, by means whereof we might have better defended them, and with more ease encroached upon the rest of the Indies, than the king of Spain could have aided or succoured them." [24]

To which it might have been replied, "If we could not support the little colony of Virginia, unmolested by an enemy of any description, how should we have been able to support three or four populous districts, every human being in bitter hostility against us, not merely national and political but religious hostility, regarding us from the highest to the lowest with a hatred incapable of conciliation, and by the whole priesthood with an *odium plusquam theologicum?*"

True policy, at the time in question, would rather incline us to agree with what Queen Elizabeth said to her Parliament, than with Sir William Monson's suggestion on this head. "It may be thought simplicity in me, that, all this time of my reign, I have not sought to advance my territories, and enlarge my dominions; for opportunity hath served me to do it. I acknowledge my womanhood and weakness in that respect; but though it hath not been hard to obtain, yet I doubted how to keep the things so obtained: and I must say, my mind was never to invade my neighbours, or to usurp over any; I am contented to reign over my own, and to rule as a just Princess." [25]

"But," continues Sir William, "now we see, and find by experience, that those places which were then weak and unfortified, are since so fortified that it is to no purpose to us to annoy the king of Spain in his West Indies. And though this voyage proved both fortunate and victorious, yet considering it was rather an *awakening* than a *weakening* of him, it had been far better to have wholly declined than to have undertaken it upon such slender grounds, and with so inconsiderable forces." [26]

The real cause of failure appears to be the unfortunate landing of 1000 men at St. Jago, the delay there of fourteen days, and the fever they caught at this most filthy and miserable of all places; the subsequent delay at Dominica and St. Christopher, making it full thirteen weeks before they appeared at St. Domingo, and by which the Spaniards had ample time to prepare for them, and were prepared accordingly at Nombre de Dios, Panama, and other places, where the gold and silver of Peru and Mexico are usually deposited.

"About this time returned into England Sir Francis Drake, a man of rare knowledge in navigation, and verie fortunat in the event of his enterprises, after manie feats of good service accomplished in forren countries (as at Baióne, Hispaniola, St. Domingo, Carthagena, &c.), to the admiration of all people amongest whom he came, and contrarie to the expectation of the Spaniards, upon supposal of places impregnable, grew so confident that they seemed lightly to esteeme anie proposed force of the enemie, and therefore doubted no kind of annoiance. Howbeit they were as safe as he that hangeth by the leaves of a tree in the end of autumne, when the leaves begin to fall. For they were so terrified at the sight of sacke and spoile, as also doubting a totall wast by fire and swoord, that they were glad to yeeld to composition." [27]

[1] Strype Camden.
[2] Life of Sir Philip Sydney.
[3] Lord Brooke's Life of Sir Philip Sydney.
[4] Ibid.
[5] Cabala.
[6] Cates.
[7] Cates, in Hakluyt.
[8] Gates, in Hakluyt.
[9] Ibid.
[10] Ibid.
[11] Cates.
[12] Cates Hakluyt.
[13] Cates.
[14] Cates.
[15] Cates.
[16] Cates.
[17] Gates.
[18] Ibid.
[19] Cates.
[20] Hakluyt.
[21] Camden.
[22] Ibid.
[23] Cates.
[24] Monson's Tracts.
[25] Harleian Miscellany.
[26] Monson's Tracts.
[27] Holinshed.

Chapter Seven - Expedition to Cadiz, 1587

In the course of the present year, 1587, the intentions of Spain with regard to England could no longer be concealed. Under the guise of an earnest desire of Philip, to come to an amicable adjustment of the differences that had too long subsisted between the two nations, every preparation was secretly making for an invasion of England, with an overwhelming force. In the meantime Catholic priests were employed as spies, both in Great Britain and the continent, to ascertain the feelings of the Queen and her ministers and of foreign powers regarding war; and also as to the extent and state of the warlike preparations of England. They had besides what they called seminary priests in England, whose business was to seduce the people from their allegiance to the Queen and the established religion, and to entice them into the body of the Catholic church. The Queen, on her part, was well informed of the designs of Spain, and measures were taken to counteract them. These designs, as to the invasion of England, are said to have been first discovered in consequence of a letter written by Philip to the Pope, asking the blessing of his Holiness on the intended project, a copy of which Mr. Secretary Walsingham procured from a Venetian priest, whom he retained at Rome as a spy. It was obtained in this manner: the original letter was stolen out of the Pope's cabinet by a gentleman of the bed-chamber, who took the keys out of the pocket of his Holiness while he slept.

One favourite object of Philip was to get possession of the person of Queen Elizabeth, and to deliver her into the hands of the Pope, who would no doubt consign her over to the inquisition. [1] This he conceived would give a death-blow to heresy in England, and be the means of establishing universal orthodoxy. As the power and protection of Elizabeth were the chief safeguards of the Protestants, "he hoped," says Hume, "by the destruction of that power, if he could subdue that Princess, to acquire the eternal renown of re-uniting the whole Christian world in the Roman Catholic communion." [2] Having hitherto failed in his project, it was reported "that the King of Spain gave great charge to the commander of the Expedition and to all the captains that in no wise they should harm the person of the Queen; but, upon taking her, use the same with reverence; looking well to the safe custody of her. And further, that the said commander should, so speedily as he might, take order for the conveyance of her person to Rome, to the purpose that his Holiness, the Pope, should dispose thereof as it should please him." [3]

A person of the name of Allen, a papist priest and an English traitor, circulated the Pope's bull of excommunication of the Queen, dethroning her, and absolving her subjects from allegiance, and granting plenary indulgence for her murder; and went even to the Duke of Parma to preach the meritorious doctrine of putting to death heretical sovereigns; but the Duke was a gentleman by birth, family, and education, (Farnese) and openly declared his respect for Elizabeth. [4]

It appears, however, that Philip was fully persuaded by the priests and his courtiers of the certain success of an invasion of Great Britain. He was told that England, by a long peace, had lost all military discipline and experience both in the army and navy; that the Catholic population which abounded therein would be ready to a man to join his forces on their landing; and that a single battle by sea, and another at land, would decide her fate. In the meantime, however, the ambassador of Spain affected to express a strong desire on the part of his sovereign to maintain a state of peace; but when he discovered that their plans were detected, and that England was also preparing her forces, he assumed a more haughty tone, and put forward such demands, in the name of Philip, as he well knew never would be complied with: That the Queen should withdraw her protection from the Netherlands; replace the ships and treasure seized unlawfully by Drake; restore the abbeys and monasteries destroyed by Henry VIII., and acknowledge the supremacy of the Pope.

Historians tell us that all these insolent demands were made to Elizabeth in the following Latin hexameters:

"Te veto ne pergas bello defendere Belgas;
Quae Dracus eripuit nunc restituantur oportet;
Quas Pater evertuit jubeo te condere cellas;
Religio Papae fac restituatur ad unguem."

Translation by Doctor Fuller:

"These to you are our commands -
Send no help to the Netherlands;
Of the treasure tooke by Drake
Restitution you must make;
And those abbeys build anew
Which your father overthrew;
If for any peace you hope
In every point restore the Pope."

The Queen is said to have given *extempore* the following reply:

"Ad Graecas, bone Rex, fient mandata Kalendas."
Imitation:
"Worthy King, know, this your will
At latter Lammas we'll fulfil."

Whether this insolent demand was actually made in the above dictatorial language, as a compliment to her acknowledged talent in the knowledge of various languages, is not material; it contains briefly, pointedly, and unceremoniously, what Spain aimed at. In fact, "Queen Elizabeth," as Hume says, "wrote and translated several books; and she was familiarly acquainted with the Greek as well as Latin tongue. It is pretended that she made an extemporary reply in Greek to the University of Cambridge, who had addressed her in that language. It is certain that she made answer in Latin without premeditation, and in a very spirited manner, to the Polish Ambassador, who had been wanting in respect to her. When she had finished, she turned about to her courtiers, and said, 'God's death, my lords!' (for she was much addicted to swearing) 'I have been forced this day to scour up my old Latin that hath long lain rusting.' [5] Her old master, Roger Ascham, says, "It is your shame (I speak to you all, you young gentlemen of England), that one maid should go beyond ye all in excellency of learning, and knowledge of divers tongues. Point out six of the best given gentlemen of this court, and all they together shew not so much good-will, spend not so much time, bestow not so many hours daily, orderly and constantly, for the increase of learning and knowledge, as doth the Queen's Majesty herself. Yea, I believe, that besides her perfect readiness in Latin, Italian, French and Spanish, she readeth here now, at Windsor, more Greek every day than some prebendary of this church doth Latin in a whole week." [6]

The first step to be taken in this emergency was to ascertain, by personal inspection, the actual state of the enemy's preparations in the ports on the coast of Spain and Portugal; to intercept any supplies of men, stores, or ammunition, that the Duke of Parma might dispatch from the Low Countries; to lay waste the harbours of Spain and Portugal, on the western coast; and destroy all the shipping that could be met with at sea conveying stores and provisions, or to attack them in port. For such a purpose, no one was considered so fitting as Drake. He was sent for, and, always ready to undertake any service which the Queen might command, he did not hesitate for a moment to accept that which her Majesty was pleased to commit to his charge, and forthwith to put in train such measures for equipping such a fleet as might be suitable for the occasion. The Queen told him he should have four of her best ships, and she doubted not her good city of London would cheerfully furnish the rest. The ships thus appropriated were

Ships.	Commanders.
The Elizabeth Bonaventure	Sir Francis Drake.
Lyon	Capt. Wm. Burroughs.
Rainbow	Capt. Bellingham.
Dreadnought	Capt. Thos. Fenner.

This squadron, increased by twenty ships supplied by the Londoners chiefly - some accounts say, twenty-four - was ordered by Drake to assemble at Plymouth, to which port he repaired to hasten their equipment. The chief adventure in this voyage (besides those four ships of her Majesty) was made, as the Queen had anticipated, by her good city of London, whose owners are said to have "sought their own private gain more than the advancement of the service; neither were they deceived in their expectation." Lord Charles Howard, Earl of Effingham, being appointed Lord High Admiral of England in 1585, then in expectation that Spain intended before long to carry her design of an invasion into execution, put himself in communication with Drake, who appears, by the following letter of 2nd April, 1587, to be ready to proceed, arid that the London fleet had just joined the expedition; and in fact that he was then under sail.

SIR FRANCIS DRAKE TO SIR FRANCIS WALSINGHAM.

April 2d., 1587.

RIGHTE HONORABLE,

THIS last nyght past came unto us the Ryall Marchant, with 4 of the rest of the London flett, the wynd would permett them no sooner. We have since ther comyng agreed uppon all condycyons between us and them, and have found them so well affected, and so willing in all our good proceedings, as we all persuad ourselves there was never more lykely in any flett, or a more loving agreement, then we hope the one of the other. I thanck God I fynd no man but as all members of one body, to stand for our gracyous Quene and country agaynst anty-Christ and his members.

I thanck God these gentellmen of great place, as Captayne Burrowghes, [7] Captayne Vennard, and Captayne Bellengham, which are partakers with mee in this servis, I fynd very dyscrett, honest, and most suffycyent.

Yf your honor did now see the flett under sayell, and knew with what resollucyon men's myndes dow enter into this accyon, as your Honor would rejoyce to see them, so you would judge a small fforce would not devyde them.

I assure your honor uppon my credytt ther are manye suffycyent men in this accyon, yeat ther hath dyvers start from us within this tow dayes past, and we all thinck by som practys of some adversaryes to the accyon, by letters written; they are most maryners, we have soldyers in ther place.

I have written to the Justysses for the sending of som of those that are ronne awaye in our countries, to send them to the gayell, and ther to be punyshed by the dyscresyon of the judges which are now in the Serqwett here with us.

I have written more largely to my Lord Admerall in this matter, for yf ther should be no punyshment in so greate a matter, in this so dangerous a tynie, it may dow mych hurt to her Majestie's servis.

I assure your Honor here hath byne no tyme lost, nether with the grace of God shall be in any other place. I have uppon my owne credytt supplied such vittuall as we have spent, and augmented as moch as I could gett, for that we are very unwylling to retorne arrantlesse.

Lett me beseeche your honor to hold a good opynyon, not of myself only, but of all the reste servytors in this accyon, as we stand nothing doubtfull of your honor, but yf ther be any yll affected, as ther hath not wanted in other accyons, and it is lykely this will not go free, that by your honorable good meanes, whether it be to her Majestic or unto your Honor, that the partyes may be knowen. Yf we deserve yll, lett us be punyshed; yf we dyscharge our dutyes in doing our best yt is a hard measure to be reported yll by those which will ether keep their fynger out of the fyer, or too well affect to the alteratyon of our Goverment, which I hope in God they shall never live to see.

The wynd commaunds me away, our shipe is under sayell, God graunt we may so live in his feare, as the enemey may have cawse to say that God doth fight for her Majestic as well abrod as at home, and geve her long and happye lyfe, and ever victory agaynst God's enemyes and her Majestie's.

God geve your honor parfect helth in bodye, and all yours, and let me beseeche your honor to pray unto God for us that he will direct us the right way, then shall we not doubt our enemyes, for they are the sonnes of men. Haste, from abourd her Majestie's good shipe the Ellyzabethe Bonaventure, this 2th. Aprell, 1587.

By hym that will allwayes be commanded by you, and never leave to pray to God for you and all yours,

FRA: DRAKE. [8]

To the Right Honourable
Sir ffrancis Walsingham, Knight,
    Principal Secretary to Her Majestie and of Her Majestie's Moste Honorable Pryvie Counsell at the Courte.
    With speede.

Drake accordingly left Plymouth on the day his letter was written, and on the 16th of the same month, in the latitude of 40°, fell in with two ships of Middleburgh, which had come from Cadiz, and by them was informed, that there was great store of warlike provision at Cadiz, which they were busily employed in embarking, and nearly ready, and under orders to take the first opportunity to proceed to Lisbon. Upon this information, the General, with all possible speed, urged on his fleet, and directed his course for Cadiz with the view of cutting off the said supplies and shipping before they got out of the port. On the 19th of April, he entered with his fleet into the harbour of Cadiz, where he was immediately assailed over against the town by five galleys, which, after a short combat, he compelled to retire under the guns of the Castle. There were lying in the road sixty ships and divers other small vessels, under the protection of the fortress; there were, moreover, about twenty French ships and some small Spanish vessels, that could pass the shoals, and therefore made the best of their way into Porto Real. On Drake's squadron coming in, they sunk, with their shot, a large ship of Ragusa of about 1000 tons, furnished with forty pieces of brass cannon, and very richly laden. There came out two galleys more from St. Maryport, and two from Porto Real, which fired freely at the General's ships; but all in vain, and they were compelled to get away with the blows they received, well beaten for their pains.

Before night, Drake had taken, burnt and Destroyed about a hundred sail of ships, and become complete master of the road, in despite of the large galleys so vaunted by the Spaniards, which were glad to retire under the guns of the fort. Among the number of ships taken or destroyed was one new ship of extraordinary size (being in burthen above 1200 tons), belonging to the Marquis of Santa Croce (Santa Cruz), who was at that time High Admiral of Spain. There were also five other great ships of Biscay, of which, four were burnt because they were only partly laden, and were taking in the king's stores and provisions of victuals, for the furnishing his fleet at Lisbon; the fifth, being a ship of about 1000 tons burthen, laden with iron spikes, nails, iron hoops, horseshoes, and other like necessaries, bound for the West Indies, was fired in like manner and burnt. The squadron also took a ship of 250 tons, laden with wines for the King's provision, which was carried out to sea for the use of the squadron, and her cargo discharged into the several ships, and then she was also set on fire. Moreover, there were taken three fly-boats of three hundred tons each, laden with biscuit, whereof one of them was half unladen by the squadron in the harbour, and there fired; and the other two were taken into the fleet and carried to sea. Drake also caused ten other ships, which were laden with wine, raisins, figs, oils, wheat and such like, to be burnt. In short, the whole number of ships and barks then burnt, sunk, and brought away, amounted to, at the least, about ten thousand tons of shipping.

There were still left, and in sight of the squadron at Porto Real, about forty ships, besides those that fled from Cadiz.

It is reported that the squadron found but little ease during their abode before Cadiz, by reason of the continual firing from the protected galleys, the fortress and the shore; where, at every point most convenient, they had planted new pieces of ordnance continually to annoy the invaders; besides the inconvenience which was suffered from their ships, which, when they could defend no longer, they set on fire, and sent them adrift into the squadron, when, on the turn of the tide, it required no little exertion to keep clear of the devouring element. "This, nevertheless," says one of the narrators, "was a pleasant sight for us to behold, because we were thereby eased of a great labour, which lay upon us day and night, in discharging the victuals and other provisions of the enemye. Thus by the assistance of the Almightye, and the invincible courage and industry of our General, this strange and happy enterprize was achieved in one day and two nights, to the great astonishment of the King of Spain's officers, and bred such a chagrin in the heart of the Marquis of Santa Cruz, the High Admiral of Spain, that he never enjoyed a good day after, but within five months died (as may justly be supposed) of extreme griefe and sorrow." His death was a great disappointment to the King and the officers serving in the Armada, which he was appointed to command, for he was esteemed a good and brave officer.

"Thus having performed this notable piece of service, the General with his squadron came out of the road of Cadiz, on Friday morning, the 21st of the said month of April, with very small loss on his side, so small as not worth the mentioning.

"After his departure, ten of the great galleys that were in the road came out, as it were in pretence of making some exercise with their ordnance, at which time the wind grew scant; whereupon the English cast about again and stood in with the shore, and came to an anchor within a league of the town; where the said galleys, for all their former bragging, at length suffered the squadron to ride quietly." The squadron had already had some little experience of a galley fight, a favourite kind of ship of the Spaniards, who were accustomed to rely more on their prowess, than on any other class of their ships of war; but Drake assures us that the four ships only of Her Majesty which he then commanded, would make very little account of galleys, if the four were alone and not busied in taking care of others that were attached to them. Their galleys could never be better placed, nor have a fitter opportunity for their advantage in fight against other ships, than on the present occasion; but they were still forced to retire, while the English ships were riding at anchor in a narrow gut, the place yielding no better position, and compelled to maintain the same until the ships taken were discharged and burnt, which could not conveniently be done but upon the flood, at which time they might drive clear of the fleet.

Thus being victualled with bread and wine, at the enemies' cost, for several months (besides the provisions that were brought from home), the General despatched Captain Crosse to England with his letters, giving him further in charge to declare unto her Majesty all the particulars of this their first enterprise.

Of the letters here mentioned the following is a copy of that to Sir Francis Walsingham, taken from the. original in the State Paper Office.

27th April, 1587.

SIR F. DRAKE TO SIR F. WALSINGHAM.

RIGHT HONORABLE,

THEISE are to geive to understande that on the seconde of this moneth we departede out of the Sound of Plymouth. We had sighte of the Cape Venester the 5th. We were encountrede with a violente storme, duringe the space of five daies, by which meanes our fleete was putt a sender and a greate leake sprange uppon the Dreadnoughte: the 16th we mette all together at the Rocke. & the 19th we arrivede into the roade of Gales (Cadiz) in Spaigne, where we founde sondrie greate shippes, some laden, some halfe laden, and some readie to be laden with the King's provisions for Englande. We staied there untill the 21st, in which meane tyme we sanke a Biskanie of 12 C (1200) tonnes, burnte a shippe of theMarques of Santa Cruse of 15 C (1500) tonnes and 31 shippes more, of 1000: 800: 600: 400, to 200 tonnes the peice, and carried awaie fower with us laden with provision, and departede thence at our pleasure with as moch honor as we coulde wishe, iiotwithstandinge that duringe the tyme of our aboade there we were bothe oftentymes foughte withall by 12 of the Kinges gallies (of whome we sanke two) and allwaies repulsed the reste, and were (withoute ceassinge) vehementlie shotte at from the shoare, but to our little hurte, God be thankede. Yeat at our departure we were curteouslie written unto by one Don Pedro, generall of those gallies. I assure your Honor the like preparacion was never hearde of, nor knowen, as the Kinge of Spaigne hathe and dailie makethe to invade Englande. He is allied with mightie Prynces and Dukes in the Straits, of whome (besides the forces in his owne domynyons) he is to have greate aide shortlie: and his provisions of breade and wynes are so greate as will suffice 40,000 men a wholle yeere, which if they be not ympeached before they joyne, will be verie perillous. Oure intente therefore is (by God's helpe) to intercepte their meetinges by all possible meanes we maye, which I hope shall have such goode successe as shall tende to the advauncemente of God's glorie, the savetie of her Highnes' royall person, the quyett of her countrie, and the annoyance of the enemye. This service which by God's sufferance we have done, will (withoute doute) breade some alteracyon of their pretences, howbeit all possible preparacions for defence are verye expediente to be made. Thus moch touchinge our proceedinges, and farther entente in this actyon, I have thoughte meete to signifie unto your Honor, & would also more larger discourse, but that wante of leisure causeth me to leave the same to the reporte of this bearer. And so in verie greate haste, with remembraunce of my humble duetie, doe take my leave of your Honor. From aboarde her Highnes' good shippe the Elizabethe Bonaventure, the 27th of April 1587.

Your Honor's
redye allwayes
to be commaunded,   FRA: DRAKE. [9]

I leave the report of dyvers partycullers to the bearer hereof, and pray pardon for not writtyng with my owne hand. I am overcom with busynesses.

Your Honor's ever redy,

FRA: DRAKE.

The Right Hon.
    Sir Fras. Walsingham.

But there is another mutilated letter of Drake of the 21st May, from Cape Saker, (Sagres, near Cape St. Vincent,) being one of the many papers of the Cottonian Collection of MSS. that were burned in the fire that occurred at Ashburnham House. The upper part of the letter now inserted is destroyed. [10]

21 May, 1587.

[Top part burnt.]   with the other w

I thank God

My good Lord, I am very unw(illing [11] to) coraplayne, especiallye by writtyng; Borrowghes hath not carried hymself (in this) accyon so well as I wyshe he had don (for) his owne sak, and in his persistynge hath cometted a dubbell offence (not) only agaynst me, but it towcheth further; I dysmest hym of his place: Captayne Parker, yf your honor reqwyre it, will advertise your honor of muche of the matter. I humbly take my leave of your honor. From som what to estwards of Cape Saker (Sagres) this 21 May 1587.

Your Lordship's ever redye
to be commanded,

Fra: Drake [12]

The Right Hon.
    Lord Burleigh.

This brief letter alludes to a transaction of an important nature, on which the discussion was necessarily deferred to the conclusion of the voyage, as the ship, the Lion, in which Captain Burroughs was, and once commanded, was in a state of mutiny, and carried away by the mutineers to England. The correspondence is therefore reserved for the end of this chapter.

After the departure of Captain Crosse, the General shaped his course towards Cape Sacre (Sagres), and in the way thither captured, at various times, ships, barks, and caravels, amounting nearly to an hundred, laden with hoops, galley-oars, pipe-staves, and other provisions of the King of Spain, for the furnishing of his forces intended against England, all of which were burned, having dealt favourably with their crews, and sent them on shore. He also spoiled and burnt all the fishery boats and nets in proceeding along, to their great detriment, and, as may well be supposed, to the utter overthrow of the rich Tunny fishing for the same year. On arriving at Cape Sacre (Sagres) the General went on shore; and the better to enjoy the benefit of the place, and to ride in the harbour undisturbed, the castle was assailed, and three other strong-holds, some of which were taken by force and some by surrender.

Hence the squadron proceeded before the haven of Lisbon, anchoring near unto Cascais, where the Marquis of Santa Cruz was then lying with his galleys, who, seeing the fleet chasr his ships on shore, and take and carry off his barks and caravels, was content to leave the ships of Drake unmolested, and quietly to tarry and likewise to depart, without having even fired a single shot at them. The historians of this voyage generally state, that when the General sent a message to the marquis to say that he was there ready to exchange certain shot with him, the marquis refused his challenge, returning for answer, that he was not at that time ready to meet him, nor had any such commission to do so from his king. This statement, made in most of the narratives, cannot be true; for Drake, in the following letter of 17th May, expressly says, that he sent a message to the marquis to inquire only if he was disposed to redeem any of his master's subjects, whom he had as prisoners.

17 May, 1587.

SIR FRANCIS DRAKE TO SIR F. WALSINGHAM.

SENCE the departyng of Captayne Crosse, Right Honorable, ther hath happened betweene the Spanyards, Portyngalls, and ourselves, dyvers combatts, in the which it hathe pleased God that we have taken forty shipes, barks, carvelles, and dyvers other vesselles, more than a hundreth, most laden; som with oorse for gallyes, planke, and tymber, for shippes and penaces, howpes and pype-staves for casks, with many other provytions for this great armey. I assuer your honor the howpes and pype-staves were above 16 or 17 C tonn (1600 or 1700) in wayght, which cannott be lesse than 25 or 30 thousand tonn if it had bynn made in caske redy for lyqwyer; all which I comaunded to be consumed into smoke and asshes by fyer, which will be unto the King no small waste of his provycyons, besyds the want of his barks. The netts which we have consumed will cawse the people to curse ther governours to ther fface.

The Porttyngalles I have allwayes comaunded to be used well, and sent them ashoore without the wantyng of any ther aparrell, and have mad them to know that it was unto me a great greffe that I was dryven to hurtt of these to the vallew of one ryall of platt, but that I found them imployed for the Spanyards servesses which we hold to be our morttall enemyes, and gave som Porttyngallers som mony in their pursses, and put them aland in dyvers places, upon which usage, yf we staye here any tyme, the Spanyards which are here in Porttyngall, yf they com under our hands, will become all Porttyngalles, and play as Petter dyd, forsweer ther master, rather then to be sold as slaves. I asshure your honor this hath breed a great fear in the Spaynard.

I spake with the Marquyes of Santa Cruse, at Cast Calles (Cascayes) nere Lysbona, by messenger, wher he was abourd his gallyes, to know whether he would redeme any of his Master's subjectts, which I had som fear of, for suche of my Mystryes' people as he had under his government. The Marqwes sent me word, that as he was a gentleman he had nonne, and that I should asshuer my-selfe that yf he had had any he would shurly have sent them me; which I knew was not so, for that I had trew entellegence by Ynglyshemen and Porttyngalles that the Marquyes had dyvers Ynglyshemen bothe in his gallyes and prysons; but in trewth I thinck the Marquyes durst not release our Ynglyshmen before he have order from his King, and lyberttye from the persecuttyng clergey.

I sent lykwyse to the Generall of the K gallyes at Calles, and to all such Governors as I convenyently myght for the redemyng of ther Spaniards they all aunsered me kyndly, but som had bowght a plow of oxen, others had taken a farme, and the rest had maryed wyffes; the former preyed to be held excused, and the latter could send us no Ynglyshmen, whereupon it is agreed by us all, her Majestic's captaynes and masters, that all such Spanyards, as yt shall please God to send under our hands, that they shall be sold unto the Mowres, and the mony reserved for the redemyng of such of our contryemen as may be redemed therwith.

For the reveng of these things, what forces the contry is abell to make, we shall be sueer to have browght uppon us, as ffar as they may, with all the devyces and trappes they cann devyse; I thancke them much they have stayed so long, and when they com they shall be but the sonnes of morttall men, and for the most part enemyes to the truthe and upholders of balles to Dagon's imag, which hath alredye ffallen before the arke of our God, with his hands, armes, and head stroken of.

As long as it shall please God to geve us provycyons to eat and drincke, and that our shipes and wynd and wether will permett us, you shall surly hyer of us nere this Cape of St. Vencent; wher we dow and will exspecte daylly what her Majestic and your honors will farther comaund.

God make us all thanckfull that her Majestic sent out these ffewe shipes in tyme.

If ther were here six more of her Majestie's good shippes of the second sort, we should be the better abell to kepe ther forces from joynyng, and happelly take or impeache his fletts from all places in the next monthe, and so after which is the chefest terms of their retornes home, which I judge in my power opynyon will bring this great monarchye to those condycyons which ar meett.

There must be a begynnyng of any great matter, but the contenevving unto the end untyll it be thoroughly ffynyshed yeldes the trew glory. Yf Hanybull had ffollowed his victoryes, it is thowght of many he had never byne taken by Sepyo.

God mak us all thanckfull agayne and agayne that we have, althowghe it be lettell, mad a begennyng upon the cost of Spayne. If we can thorowghly beleve that this which we dow is in the defence of our relygyon and contrye, no doubt but our mercyfull God for his Christ, our Savyour's sake, is abell, and will geve us victory, althowghe our sennes be reed. God geve us grace we may feare hym, and daylly to call upon hym, so shall nether Sattan, nor his menesters prevayell agaynst us; although God permett yow to be towched in body, yeat the Lord will hold his mynd pure. Lett me be pardoned of your honor agayne and agayne for my over myche boldnes, it is the conffecyon of my owne concyence, my dutty in all humbellnes to your honor, my good lady your yocke partener and all yours, beseching you all to pray unto God hartelly for us, as we dow daylly for all you. Hast, from her Majestie's good shipe the Ellyzabethe Bonaventure, now rydyng at Cape Saker, this 17th May, 1587.

Your honor's most redy to be comanded,

FRA: DRAKE. [13]

The Right Hon: Sir Fras. Walsingham.
With all speede.

The statement alluded to further says, "Our General being thus refused a meeting by the Marques, and seeing no more good to be clone in this place, having destroyed every kind of craft near the mouth of the Tagus, thought it expedient to spend no longer time upon this coast; and therefore, with the approbation of the next officer in command, and to the great satisfaction of the merchant adventurers, who were not at all pleased with the destruction of so much valuable property before Calais and Cascais, he shaped his course for the Isles of Azores, and, in making for the Isle of St. Michael, and coming within twenty or thirty leagues thereof, it was his good fortune to fall in with a Portuguese carrak called Saint Philip, being the same ship which, in the voyage outward, had carried back the three princes of Japan, who had visited Europe, into the Indies. This carrak, without any great resistance, was captured, and the people thereof were transferred into certain of the merchant vessels well furnished with victuals, and sent away courteously home into their own country. This was the first carrak that ever was taken on a return voyage from the East Indies; and her fate was considered by the Portuguese as an evil omen, because the ship bore the King's own name." It may be suspected that the loss of the valuable cargo she was freighted with was considered a far greater loss than the name she bore.

The wealth of this prize seemed so great unto the whole company, (as in truth it was), that they assured themselves every man would receive a sufficient reward for all his trouble and expenses; and thereupon they all resolved to return home, without further delay in looking for prizes, in which they were gratified by the approbation of the General, who was fully aware of the very great value of the prize he had captured. He therefore ordered his squadron to bear up for England, which they all most cheerfully obeyed, and happily arrived in Plymouth the same summer, with their whole fleet of merchant ships, and this rich booty, to their own profit and due commendation, and to the great admiration of the whole kingdom, and the extreme care and anxiety of her Majesty's government to secure that "rich booty" for future appropriation, as we shall presently see.

"And here, by the way, it is to be noted that the taking of this carrak wrought two extraordinary effects in England: first, that it taught others that carraks were no such non-descripts but that they might easily enough be taken (as since indeed it hath turned out in the taking of the Madre de Dios, and firing and sinking of others); and secondly, in acquainting the English nation, and the merchants more particularly, with the detail of the exceedinggreat riches and wealth of the East Indies; whereby the Portuguese, and their neighbours of Holland, have long been encouraged, both being men as skilful in navigation, and of no less courage than the Portugals, to share with them in the traffic to the East Indies, where their power is nothing so great as heretofore hath been supposed."

It was not however till the year 1600, that Queen Elizabeth granted a charter to certain merchants of the City of London to trade to the East Indies, with certain exclusive privileges, under the title of "The Governor and Company of Merchants of London, trading to the East Indies," which has continued ever since.

The enormous wealth brought into England by this carrak was deemed of so much importance, that the Lords of Her Majesty's Privy Council appointed Commissioners to go down forthwith to Plymouth, for purposes which are best explained in the following documents:

1 July, 1587.

"A letter to Sir John Gilbert and Sir Frances Godolphin, Knighte. That whereas the Queen's Majestic had made choice of certaine speciall commissioners to be sent down to Plimmouth, there to view such commodities as have been brought in by Sir Francis Drake, and to take order for the conveyance of such of them as shall be thought fitt to be brought hither, and disposing the rest in those partes, for the better execucion of which service her Majestic thoughte meete that the two above named should also joyne with them: Whereupon their Lordships directed them to call the said parties to their assistance, by vertue of their Instructions, which they were willed to communicate unto them. Their Lordships required them according to Her Majestie's pleasure they should be aydinge and assistinge unto the said commissioners as two speciallie chosen and appointed to be of their number in the due execucion of the contents of their said Instructions." [14]

2 July, 1587.

"A letter to Sir Francis Drake: That the Queen's Majestic had thought meete that certaine Commissioners should be appointed to repaire downe unto him, with direccions for the viewing of such commodities as he had brought in, and taking order for the safe conveiance of such parte of the same as shall be thought fitt to be brought hether, and otherwise, as he shoud more particularlie understand uppon view of their instruccions, which they were required to comunicate unto him for his better direccion and concurrencie with them in the service." [15]

Here follow the Instructions given by the Lord of Her Majestie's Privy Counsell, to four Commissioners.

"You shall at your first repaire and deliverie of our letters unto Sir Fraunces Drake, acquaint him with the contents of theise your Instruccions.

"You shall require to see the billes of ladinge of the severall merchandize and commodities that are in the prizes taken by him.

"And being by meanes hereof acquainted with the several kindes and quantities of the said commodities, you shall then consider what is fitted to be conveied hether by land, what by sea; and what to be wanted there in those partes.

113

"You shall consider how that which you shall find meete to be brought up hether by land or by sea, may be conveied with safetie.

"You shall cause all such coffers and boxes as you maie judge or know to have in them anie gold, silver, jewelles, or other like precious things, to be opened before Sir Fraunces Drake and yourselves.

"You shall take an Inventorie of the severall thinges that you maie so finde in the said coffers or boxes, which Inventorie shall be subscribed by Sir Fraunces Drake and yourselves joyntlie.

"You shall for your better assistance in the execution of these directions call unto you Sir John Gilbert and Sir Fraunces Godolphin Knight, unto whom we have written especiallie to repaire unto you for such purpose." [16]

"Apud Thebaldes, 9 August, 1587.

"Letters to Sir John Gilbert, Sir Fraunces Godolphin, Sir Fraunces Drake, Knights, andto John Hawkins, Esq.

"That when theyr, we are advertised from them of a fleet of 120 shippes discovered on the seas not far from the isles of Scilly. Their Lordships thancke them for their care in spedely advertysinge the same, and in warninge given to the Lieutenants for puttinge of men in a readynes, enjoyninge them to call unto them Sir Richard Greenfield, and with his advice to contynewe their care for the defence of the Carrick lately taken by Sir Fraunces Drake, which it is to be suspected that fleet would assayl." [17]

After the destruction of so great a number of ships at Cadiz and Lisbon, it is not easy to conceive whence the 120 sail had proceeded, or on what grounds they calculated to intercept a ship in the beginning of August, which had safely anchored in Plymouth before the end of June, and the whole cargo of which was .in the Thames before the end of August, as appears by the following letter to the Lord Mayor. It may be added that the great Carrack, when freed from her lading, was sent up to Saltash, and there by accident took fire and was consumed.

"1 Sep. 1587.

Apud Otelands. E. of Warwicke. Mr. Secretary Walsingham.
L. Admirall. Sir Am: Poulett. L. Chamberlaine. Mr. J. Wolley.

"A letter to the Lord Mayor signifying Her Majestie's pleasure to have the goods brought in by Sir Francis Drake in the Spanish Caracke, which were sent in divers vessels to the River of Thames, to be unladen and putt in some place fitt and convenient for the receipt thereof in Leaden Hall, until Her Majestie's pleasure was further knowne. - And that diligent care might be had for the safe custodie thereof that nothing might be missing at such time as it should be required at their hands which should take the charge thereof." [18] What the amount of all this wealth was, and how disposed of, the Burleigh MSS., had they been available, would probably have told us. .

With this voyage and its result Sir William Monson, very unusual on his part, has no fault to find; he says, "This voyage proceeded prosperously, and without exception; for there was both honour and wealth gained, and the enemy was greatly endamaged." It is probable, had he known the case of Captain Burroughs, which has been touched upon in this chapter, and will now be concluded, as far as the MS. documents go, he might have had some stringent remarks on naval discipline to offer; there appears to be abundant scope for them. The first two letters following were received by Drake, when off Cape St. Vincent, on his return from Cadiz.

30 April, 1587.

FROM CAPTAIN BURROUGHS TO SIR FRANCIS DRAKE.

MY VERY GOOD ADMIRALL,

FOR that hitherto in all this voyadg since our coming forthe (albeit there have bin often assemblies of the Captains of this fleete aboord of you, called by a flag of counsell, which I have judged had bin chiefly for such purpose) I could never perceive any matter of counsell or advice touching the accion, & service for her Majestic, with the fleete nowe under your chardge, to be effectually propounded, & debated, as in reason I judge there owght to have bin, as well for the better ordering of the affaires, busynes & attempts, as also for your owne securitye (for when you shoulde deale by advice and counsell of suche as are appointed for your assistaunce, & such other of experience as may be woorthye to be called thereunto, howsoever the succes fall out, yt shall be the better for your dischardge). But at all and every suche assemblye you have either shewid briefly your purpose what you wolde doe, as a matter resolved in yourself and of yourselfe, for oughte that I know, unlesse you have called unto you suche as happelye will soothe you in any thinge you shall saye, & so concluded the matter with his or theire consents before hande, in such sorte as no reason made by any other, not fullye agreeing with your owne resolucion, coolde be accepted to take any place wherein we (I speake chiefly for myne owne parte) have servid but as witnesses to the woordes you have delivered; Or els you have used us well by entertaining us with your good cheare, & so most tymes after our staye with you most part of the daye, we have departed as wise as we came, without any consultacion or counsell holden. This manor of assemblies (albeit it maye please you to terme them either counsells or courts) are farre from the purpose & not suche as in reason they ought to be. You also neglected giving instructions to the Fleet in tyme and sorte as they ought to have had, and as yt owght to be, for which I have bin sorye, & wolde gladlye yt had byn otherwise. But I have founde you alwaies so wedded to your owne opinion & will, that you rather disliked and shewed as that it were offencive unto you that any shoold gyve you advice in anything (at least I speake it for myself) for which cawse I have refrained often to speake that which otherwise I woold, and in reason in dischardge of the duetye. I owe to Her Majestie and the place I serve in, I ought to have don: which place you make no accompte of, nor make any difference between it & the other Captains, naye you deale not so with me as you doe to other, your affection maye leade you therein, & to love and use any man better then you doe me ys no cawse of reason whye I

115

shulde dislike it, for myself, or any man, maye be likewise affected to one man, more then another, but I looke to be well used by you, in respect of, and according to, my place, which I fynde not. I have servid in place as I doe no we, viz Admirall at the sea, unto the no we L. Admirall of Englande; yt pleased his Lordship to use me well; and accompted of me according to the place for the tyme. I have served Her Majestic as her Admirall at the Seas, as you are nowe (& doe thinke that I shold not have bin appointed for this service, & in this place, with suche woordes from Her Highness, except I had bin thought meet to take chardge of suche a Fleet, yf you should miscarye).

I have had instructions (for comission) for divers services comitted to my chardge, with as large and ample woordes in effect as you have nowe. ffor, as I take it, the substaunce of the skope that is geven you is this, ffor that by informacion the King of Spaine is prepairing a great army by sea: parte at Lisbone, & other in Andellozia, and within the Strayts, all which was judged shuld meete at Lisbone, & the same to come for England or some parte of Her Majestie's dominions, Her Majestie's pleasure is, by advice of Her Highnes' Counsell, that you, with these ships nowe under your chardge, shuld come hyther to this Cape, & upon this coast, & seeke, by all the best meanes you can, to impeache theire purpose, and stop their meting at Lisbone, if it myght be, whereof the manor howe, is referred to your discreation. This is the effect of your Instructions (as I remember) and suche like in effect I have received, divers which I can shew.

Nowe that you should conster these woordes to go whether you will, and to attempt and do what you lyst, I thinke the woordes will not beare you owt in it. And therefore I praye you (for youur owne good) advize yourself well in theise matters you purpose to attempt, which may not well be maintained by the woordes of your Instructions.

The chief cawse that moovid me to write you thus muche, is, for that it pleased you yesterdaye, to tell me that you purposed to lande at the Cape, for surprising the Castell of Cape Saker or the Ablye to the eastwards of it, (or both). I heard speaches and debaiting of suche matter intended by you, by divers as they weare standinge in troopes upon the decke, before the steridg of your ship, before you told it me, and I heard the lyke ther amongst them also after you had told it me. I coold not perceive any of them to lyke there should be any landing upon this Coast nere those places, neyther for taking the Castell or Ablye, nor yet for freshe water, for that there is no watring place nerer then half a myle from the water syde, which is but a poole, to the which the waye is badd: I doe not finde by your Instructions, any advice to lande, but I remember a speciall caviat and advice geven you to the contrarye by the Lord High Admirall.

Nowe to land at this place for the attaining of 3 or 4 peces of ordinance that maye be in the castell, & perhaps as manye in the ablye, yf you should atchive, your purpose, as yesterdaye it was reasoned & alledged amongst them, What have you of it? No matter of substance! neither shall any man be bettrid by it, but a satisfying of your mynde that you maye saye, Thus I have don upon the King of Spaine's land. But Sir, I wolde have you to consider, that though you have a good mynde to attempte the thinge in hope of good successe, yet you maye mysse of your purpose, for (some) of your owne Captaines that shoulde serve for the lande have said, that yf they were in eyther of those 2 places (being suche as they are reported) with one hundreth of good men they woulde not dowbt to keepe you out with all the force you can make.

And shall we thincke that the people of this contrye are so symple that upon suche advertisements of us as they have, & our being continuallye in theire sight thus many daies as we have bin, that they will not seeke to provide for those places, & for the Coast hereabowt as well as they can? Surelye I doe not thinke so of them, & therefore the getting of them maye be dowbtfull, and so maye it be dowbted of your safe landing & safe retorning backe to the ships, without great losse of men, or overthrowe by the power that maye be raised in the lande, which God keepe you from.

Besydes, you knowe what galleis we lefte at Gaels, & of 20 more that are come from Gibralter, let us thinke that the gonnors under the King have a care for keeping of his Coasts, and whye maye there not be part, or the most part of those gallies sent to lye upon this coast, to wayet oportunytye to take the advantadge upon us (as this night divers of my company said they sawe 3 betweene us and shore, even at the verye instant as the gale began) you knowe they may be uppon the coast nere at hande, where they maye see us, or have intelligence where we are, and what we doe from tyme to tyme, and yet we not to see them, nor have any knowledg of theire being, so maye they wayet for your landing, & cut you off, and indanger the fleete (yf it be calme and the ships at anker, where they cannot travers to make playe with them) yea, they may treble us, and doe some mischief to our fleet being calme as of late it hath bin, yf we keepe so nere the shore, scaterid, as yesterdaye, & in former tyme we did, albeit we attempt not to lande.

Moreover, to land men, requireth a land wind, or calme wether & smothe water, that the ships may be brought at anker nere the shore; when men are landed, yt is uncertaine when they shall retorne; yf in the meane the winde sholde chop off into the sea uppon the sodden, what then, do you thinke it mete that the ships shold remaine at ancker, & put all in hazard to be lost and cast away?

Consider, I praye you, effectually of theise points, for I have don so, and thereuppon am resolved in opinion that it is not meete nor convenient that you attempte to lande hereabowt: which I thought good to advertise rather by writing which you may keepe to yourself, or manyfest it at your pleasure (for I have done it as I will answere to everye pointe therof) then to have sayd so muche openlye, or in hearinge of some, which happellye might have bin to your dislikinge. I praye you to take this in good parte as I meane it, for I protest before God, I doe it to none other ende, but in dischardg of my duety towardes Her Majestie and the service, and of good will and well meaninge towardes you.

Aboorde the Lyon in sight of Cape St. Vincent this Sondaye morne the 30th of Aprill: 1587.

Yours at commaunde,

(Signed) W: B: [19]

To the Right Worshipfull
    Sir ffrauncis Drake, Knyght,
        Her Majestie's Adinirall of the Fleet here present at the Seas. Aboord the Elsabeth Bonaventer.

Whether Drake made any reply or not to this foolish letter does not appear, but it may be inferred from the following, that he had let him know what he thought of it.

2d Maye, 1587.

SIR,

I AM sorye that you make suche construction of my lettre. I protest I did it only in dischardge of my duetye, and for the better performance of Her Majestie's service; yf you shall willinglye accept it soe, yt is that wherof I shall be very glad, and you shall finde as muche good will and forwardnes in me, for the execution of Her Majestie's service in this accion, as shall become that place and credit that Her Majesty, and her Highnes' counsell, have thought me woorthye of, and myself as readye to followe your directions, as at any tyme I have don, or any man shall doe. And for furder satisfying of you I will doe such furder matter, as theise gentlemen shall relate unto you. [*]

Abooard the Lyon, this Tewsdaye the 2d of Maye, 1587.

Yours to Comande,
(Signed) W. B. [20]

To the Rt. Worshipfull
    Sir Francis Drake, knyght,
        Her Majestie's Admirall of the fleet here present at the seas. Aboord the Elsabeth Bonaventer.

[*] That we to burne, or deliver hym the coppye of my lettre."

Drake does not appear to have taken any further notice of these letters while the Golden Lyon remained on the station. He might not indeed have had the opportunity, as at the time of his supercession of Burroughs, the ship was in a state of mutiny, though he says he had no knowledge of it till 27th May. Besides, the crew ran away with the ship to England, carrying Burroughs in her; otherwise he might have answered him in the same way that Lord St. Vincent did Sir John Orde, when the latter interfered with and lectured his Lordship, on the appointment of Lord Nelson to the command of the Mediterranean squadron, questioning his authority in very intemperate and indecorous language. His Lordship sent him home with the following laconic epistle:

SIR,

I HAVE acknowledged your letter dated off Cadiz, 31st August, expressed in terms of insubordination that, even in these times, I did not conceive could have come from an officer of your rank.

I am yours,
ST. VINCENT.

To whom Drake (on his arrival in England) made the charge, to which the following is Burroughs' answer, does not appear. There is nothing in the Lansdowne MSS. beyond what follows; sufficient however to show his conduct was highly reprehensible. Yet he was employed in the armada as Captain of the galley Bonavolio, 250 men, but is not once mentioned in any of the proceedings, nor did he obtain either honours or promotion; nor does it appear he was ever again employed. The case is here given, as far as the want of documents will allow, as an illustration of the state of discipline in the navy some 250 years ago, and because it appears to have escaped the notice of every biographer of Drake, whether contemporary or modern.

1587.

"*Objection.* - Sir Francis Drake allegeth agaynste me, William Boroughe, that I am in faulte and guyltie for the Golden Lyon's cominge awaye from him at the sea, without his conserite; which faulte hee, his associats, and followers, thincke worthye to be punished by deathe, which they urge and prosecute as they maye.

"*Answer.* - My answer is: That I am not guiltie any manner of waye; for procuringe the comynge awaye of that shippe in suche sorte, but the grounde and cause therof was the companye of the shippe, which did mutenye agaynste the Captain and Master, whereof I had noe knowledge or suspition untill it burste oute on the 27th of Maye, in the forenoone, at what tyme I was uppon the Decke with Captain Marchant, and then one of the quarter Masters delyvered to the saide Captain a wry tinge made in the name of the whole companye, wherein they declared what weakiies and feebleness they weare fallen into, thrughe the spare and badde dyette they had (It was farder alleaged by som of them that there was small store of victualls lefte in the shippe, and forty-six men then sicke) and therefore with the faier winde that blewe they woolde not alter the coorse, but beare awaye for Englande; whereunto the Captain answered, that he woolde not goe for Englande, but plie back to the Generall; and therefore chardged them in Her Majestie's name to bring the tacks aboorde and takle the sails as the Master commanded, which they refused. Whereuppon both he and the Master used perswations, all which woolde not prevayle to alter theire purpose determyned. Whereuppon the saide Captayne requyred to be set aboorde Her Majestie's pynnes, the Spye, that was neere at hande. When he was in the boate by the Shippes side, I spake unto the companye, and tolde them that they had entered into a matter that myght hazard their lives, and therefore wisshed them to be better advised, and prayed them to staye till they had spoken with the Admyrall, and made him acquainted with their wantes and greefes. They answered they woolde not staye to speake with him, for they had had many faier promyses, but founde nothinge performed; and if they sholde go backe unto him he woolde shifte them out of that Shippe, and use them with tyranye, and therefore they woolde (go) home, and rather stande to the Queene's Mercye for their lives, or be hanged at home, amongst their freindes, then to stande to the Admyrall's courtesey, or perishe at the seas for wante of victualls."

"*Captain Marchant in faulte.* - Their Captaine, Mr. Marchante, used no resistance by force and violence to withstande theire purpose (which he ought to have donrie) and so did I the laste yeere in the same shippe, when the companye did mutyne for abridgynge their victualls in resonable order for prolonging the voyage, whereby the service myght be the better performed, and thereby I appeased them. If I had byne in that place of authoritie, and not used resistance by vyolence to the uttermoste of my power, then had my faulte byen greate and suche punnyshemente as is urged myghte (and I doubte sholde) have byne layde upon me: But I was then as a prysoner in that shippe, dismyssed from all rule and authoritye by the Admyrall, and the companye charged uppon payne of deathe soe to accepte of me and not otherwyse, and the authoritie of govermente was wholye committed to the said Captain Marchant, who had remayned soe from the 2nd of Maye, that I was displaced, till then. All which tyme I stoode ever in doubte of my lyfe, and did expecte daylie when the Admyrall would have executed upon me his bludthirstie desier as he did uppon Dowtey.

"Now seeing it was soe, and that by the providence of God this meane was wroughte to save me from that myscheif, what reason had I to strive against them for comynge away? If the shippe had staide by the Admyrall I had assuredly byn put to deathe, for Sir Francis hath often saide, since he came home, that nothinge soe muche repentithe him as that he did not cut me of whilste I remayned by him. And what passed againste me, after the Lyon's departure, was partlye declared by his own mouthe out of his own booke which he did reade the 25th July, at Tyballs. He panneled a jurie, and uppon their verdicte (by his lawe, and himselfe the judge) pronounced sentence of deathe againste me, the Master of the shippe, the boatswane and other, and made full accompte that, at his retorne home, the same judgement sholde have ben executed uppon us, but if he had gotten us at sea he woolde have performed it there.

"Sir Francis Drake in urginge this matter soe vehemently againste me, beinge able sufficiently to cleere myself from beinge previe or abettynge to the comynge awaye of the Lyon, doth altogether forget, ho we he demeaned himself towards his Master and Admyrall, Mr. John Hawkins, at the Porte (of) St. John de Loo, in the Weste Indyes, when, contrary to his sayde Admyrall's comaunde, he came awaye and lefte his sayde Master in greate extremytie; whereuppon he was forced to set at shoare in that contrye to seek their adventure, 100 of his men; which matter if it had byn soe followed agaynste him (for that he colde rioe wayes exchuse it) might iustly have procured that to himselfe which nowe most uniustly, blodely, and malitiously, by all devises whatsoever, he hath soughte and still seekethe, agaynste me."

"Articles objected, with the answears to the same, touching the voyadge with the Lyon of Her Majestic.

"1. Not a man in the gunner's roome that was of any skill or knowledge.

"*Answer.* - They weare suche as the master gunner provided and made choice of, and suche as Sir Francis lefte in the shippe."

"2. The company of the ship, fishermen and symple fellowes of small valew, and easily to be ledd.

"They were the same that Sir Francis caryed in that shipp with hym from Quinsborow, and suche other as he appointed to her at Plymouth, saving ten sufficient men that I brought with me and added to them."

"3. That Mr. Borowes was so afraid of the shot as he coold not tell where to ride with the ship.

"That I had no suche feare of the shott it maye apeare by the places where the Lyon roade in the baye of Gaels, after our first anckoring the evening we came in, for at all times whensoever the Admirall and fleet removed from the shot of the shore and gallies, the Lyon anchored and remained betweene them and the shott, till at length when they had brought a piece of ordinance out of the towne and placed it upon a cliff against the ship, with which they strooke of the gunner's legge and hit the ship under water." (When he goes on to say that they warped off.)

"4. That if Sir Francis Drake had been advised by Mr. Borough, there had bin no service don, and they should have come home as they went forthe.

"Touchinge the attempt at Gales, I was never against it; but was allwaies desirous that we might have had conference with suche as knew the place, &c. &c."

"5. That the most of the companye's sicknes of the Lyon came by feare they had of the galleis rather than otherwise.

"I never perceived any feare in the companye of the Lyon of the galleis, albeit it may be ther were some suche in corners which I sawe not, &c. &c."

"6. That the companye of the ship might have bin perswaded to have stayed, if Mr. Boroughs would have travailed in it."

He states that after that Captain Marchant and the master had done what they could, "he did reason with the company" - (see the other statement in full on this point, which is here briefly reported).

"7. That they were of opinion that the mutiny of the mariners grew by the devise of Mr. Boroughes, although he wold not be sene in it, rather then otherwise.

"That I was the worker of the mutinye, or privye unto any part of their doings therein, before it burst out by the companye generallye, when I was upon the decke with Captaine Merchant, amongst them, it shall never be provid, or founde trewe; and this I saye farther, as no man can justlye chardge me with it, or with having any intelligence or knowledge thereof, till yt burst owt as aforesaid. So I protest before the Lorde God, who knoweth the secreats of all harts, and as I hope to be saved by the bloode of Christ, that I did neyther knowe, thincke, or imagine of any suche matter of theire mutiny, till it brake owt.

(Signed) "W. BOROUGH." [21]

Whether any and what further steps were taken in this case, none of the collections examined, either in the British Museum or in the State Paper Office, could satisfy the enquiry. Perhaps the Burleigh Papers at Hatfield, as in the case of the Caracke, might supply the deficiency. It is indeed much to be regretted, that a nation like England should have no suitable building appropriated solely for the reception of her historical and other valuable documents, which, at present, in many cases, are so scattered and separated in different depositories, the British Museum, the State Paper Office, the Tower of London, and private collections, that a complete set of documents for the illustration of any particular question is rarely to be found in one place.

[1] Strype.
[2] Hume.
[3] Strype.
[4] Camden.
[5] Hume.
[6] Hume.
[7] He had great cause to alter his opinion of this officer, as will presently be shown.
[8] MS. State Paper Office.
[9] MS. State Paper Office.
[10] Sir Henry Ellis says, "We have various letters of Drake, but unfortunately several of them are mutilated, having been placed in that part of the library, when in Ashburnham House, upon which the fire of 1731 feasted."
[11] Within the parentheses supplied.
[12] Cottonian MSS., British Museum.
[13] MS. State Paper Office.
[14] Council Register. H. M. Privy Council Office.
[15] Ibid.
[16] Council Register.
[17] Council Register.
[18] The Ministers at Oatlands. - Council Register.
[19] Burghley Papers. Lansdowne MSS., British Museum.
[20] Lansdowne MSS., British Museum.
[21] Lansdowne MSS., British Museum.

Chapter Eight - The Spanish Armada, Called the Invincible 1588. *Part First.*

The effect of the last expedition, which Drake somewhat facetiously called "singeing the King of Spain's beard," was to defeat any attempt for the invasion of England, as had been intended that year, and for which they had considered themselves fully prepared, whilst England certainly was not. But the multitude of transport-shipping, of stores and provisions, and other necessaries and equipments, for the supply of a large naval and military force, that were collected in their ports, having been destroyed by Drake, it required another year to replace them. In the meantime, the Prince of Parma in behalf of Philip, and certain commissioners on the part of Elizabeth, were continuing to discuss, in the Netherlands, the farce of negociating for a treaty of peace, generally considered as a mere pretence on both sides, begun, as was said, by a device of the Queen of England, to divert the hostile preparations of Spain, and continued by the Spaniard for the sake of concealment, in order to take England by surprise, unawares and unprovided. So says Camden, striving, as it seemed, on both sides, "to sew the Foxe's skin to the Lion's." [1]

But long before the commission was dissolved, there was neither concealment of intention nor diversion from preparations on the part of Spain. It was publicly known that, encouraged by the Pope, Philip had avowed his determination to make the conquest of England, by which the true church of God and the Roman Catholic religion would then be restored, and heresy abolished. That the cause was just and meritorious, the Queen being already excommunicate, and contumacious against the church of Rome; that she supported the King's rebel subjects in the Netherlands, annoyed the Spaniards by constant depredations, surprised and sacked their towns in Spain and America, and, not long before, had put to death the Queen of Scotland, violating thereby the Majesty of all Sovereign Princes.

But if any concealment were intended, the activity of the late Spanish Ambassador, Bernardin Mendoza, formerly at the court of London, and now at Paris, and his inveterate hatred of Elizabeth for having got rid of him, prevented any such measure. By means of the press at his disposal, he disseminated every species of falsehood and invective against England; and anticipated the overthrow of that kingdom, by the immense forces of Philip then in preparation, and the weakness of the enemy in her naval and military establishments; and withal the disaffection of her subjects. There happened however at this time to be resident in London an English Catholic Missionary (or seminary) priest, who took the trouble to write a letter to Mendoza, in order to disabuse him and his partizans of the erroneous opinions they were propagating respecting England; giving him at the same time what he conceived to be the more proper conduct for Spain to pursue in her invasion of England. This priest, in the interest of Spain, suggests that the hopes of a foreign invasion of England depended less on a large army to be transported, than on a strong catholic party in England, ready to join the foreign forces on landing; he advises to act more politically than by the excommunication of the Sovereign, the Pope's usurped power to absolve subjects from their allegiance, and to dispose of kingdoms by violence, blood, slaughter, and conquest; and, above all, to conceal their intentions till the time came for striking the blow effectually: "For," says the writer, "when such things are published without reserve, they only induce the Queen to strengthen her kingdom, by calling out the military, and to guard those parts of the coast where a landing is feasible. Besides," he adds, "every nobleman, knight, and gentleman of fortune, immediately took the alarm, and thought it time, for their own and the public safety, by arming their servants and dependents." [2]

This *honest* priest is said to have been afterwards executed for treason, committed during the time that the Armada was on its way to England.

Not only Mendoza and his partizans, but all the priests, politicians, and poets of Spain, were sedulously employing their pens in joyful effusions of her glorious success and triumph, of which it would be little short of impiety to entertain a doubt, and which the grand armament in preparation for the invasion of England would certainly achieve. The following lines, the translation of part of an infamous Ode, on the intended Armada, show to what a pitch the bitterness of bigotry, of hellish superstition and national hatred, a Spanish Roman Catholic could work himself up. Addressing England, he says,

"How art thou doom'd to everlasting shame
　For her accursed sake,
　Who, for the distaff, dares to take
　The sword and sceptre in her bastard hand!
　She-wolf libidinous, and fierce for blood!
　Thou strumpet offspring of th' adult' rous bed,
　Soon may avenging heaven hurl down
　Its lightning-vengeance on thy impious head!"

GONZARA, on the "Spanish Armada."

Other effusions were poured forth, thus prematurely, in songs of triumph, mixed with denunciations of vengeance; but all of them full of prophetic confidence in the success of the intended invasion; and in anticipation of the glories that were destined for Spain, by the subjugation of England, the capture of her Queen, and stability of the supremacy of the Pope. Others again were so sanguine of success as to treat their anticipations in a playful or ludicrous manner. Thus a little childish ballad, said to be found in the Life of Lopé de Vega, by the late Lord Holland (which it is not), is amusing enough; [3] a little girl, speaking to her playfellow, says,

"Mi hermano Bartolo
　Se va a Ingalaterra,
　A matar al Draque
　Y a prender la Reyna,
　Y a los Luteranos
　De la Bandamessa:
　Tiene de traerme
　A mi de la guerra,
　Un Luteranico
　Con una cadena.
　Y una Luterana,
　A Señora aguela."

Thus closely and ingeniously translated:

"My brother Don John
　To England is gone,
　To kill the Drake
　And the Queen to take,
　And the heretics all to destroy:
　And he will give me
　When he comes back
　A Lutheran boy
　With a chain round his neck;
　And our lady grandmamma shall have,
　To wait upon her, a Lutheran slave."

In short, the same enthusiasm, that prevailed in Spain the preceding year, did not appear in the least to have been diminished by the destructive operations of Drake, or the delusive negotiations in the Netherlands. The Spaniards, in fact, were again prepared, in the spring of the present year, to make the attempt; and when the equipment of the Armada was nearly completed, Alphonso Perez de Gusman, Duke of Medina Sidonia, was appointed to the chief command, and John Martinez Recaldé, an experienced seaman, to the second in command under him. The Duke of Paliano and the Marquis of Santa Croce were originally designed to fill these offices, but they both died before the preparations were completed; and it was said that the marquis received his death-blow from Drake, at Cascais, the preceding year; at least he fell sick almost immediately after, and never recovered.

When ready to put to sea, the Duke of Medina Sidonia received his instructions; the outline of which was, that in order to avoid falling in with the English fleet, he should keep as near to the coast of France as wind and weather would permit, and proceed as far as the neighbourhood of Calais, where he might expect to meet the Duke of Parma, with a fleet of small vessels and 40,000 men; and, if not arrived, to come to anchor in a place of safety thereabouts, and wait his joining; when the whole were to stand over and enter the Thames, directing their course for London, which it was presumed would be taken by a sudden assault, or fall after a single battle that is to say, provided they were permitted quietly to proceed so high up the river, which was not very probable. In laying down this plan of operations, they were not aware that Lord Henry Seymour had taken his station, with a fleet of sixty English and Dutch ships, to prevent the Duke of Parma from coming out of harbour.

The Duke of Sidonia, however, on his arrival in the Groyne, to which the fleet had been driven for refuge by stress of weather, was induced to deviate from the King's Instructions, in consequence of false information received from the master of an English barque, that the English fleet were lying inactive in Plymouth Sound, and not making any preparations to meet such an armament. Relying on this information, the General, Don Diego de Valdez, an able and experienced seaman, on whose opinion the greatest reliance was placed, and who in fact was the chief adviser of the original plan, prevailed on the Duke to alter that plan, and to proceed direct to Plymouth and attack the British fleet unprepared in that port, which, once destroyed, would lay all England open to their victorious arms.

Here again they made a great mistake; England was now fully prepared to receive them. The Queen had selected Charles Lord Howard of Effingham, Lord High Admiral of England, to the chief command, of whose meritorious conduct she had a very great persuasion, by the sweetness of his temper, and his bravery; she knew that, at the same time, he was not eminently skilled in sea affairs; but that he was wary and provident, industrious and active, and of great authority and esteem among the officers of her navy. Sir Francis Drake was next sent for, and received from the Queen his commission as

Vice-Admiral, next in command to Lord Charles Howard; and Lord Henry Seymour, second son of the Duke of Somerset, was already in command of a squadron of ships, English and Netherlanders, to watch and prevent the Prince of Parma from putting to sea with his forces to join the expected Armada.

Her Majesty was not disappointed in the activity displayed by her two commanders, Lord Charles Howard and Sir Francis Drake. Lord Charles immediately hoisted his flag in the Ark Royal, and having obtained information of the movements of the enemy, he writes the following letter to Sir Francis Walsingham.

9th March, 1587-8.

LORD C. HOWARD TO SIR FRANCIS WALSINGHAM.

SIR,

As I had maed up my other letter, Capten Fourbysher dowthe advertyse me that he spake with 2 shyps that chame presently from Lysbone, who declared unto him that for certenty the King of Spaynse flyte dowthe parte from Lysbon unto the Groyne, the 15 of this monthe by ther acounte. Sir, ther is non that comse from Spayne but bryngse this advertysment, and yf it be trew I am afrayd it wyll not be helped when the tyme sarvethe. Surly this charge that heer Majestic is at is ether to muche or to lyttell, and the stay that is maed of Sir Francys Drake going owt I am afrayd will bred graet parell, and yf the King of Spayne dow send forses ether into this Relme, Irland, or Scotland, the Queene's Majestic shall say, the Duke of Parme is tretyng of a pece, and therfor it is not pryncly downc of his master to dow so in the tyme of Trete, but what is that to the pourpos yf we have by that a Casado. And yf her Majestie chanot show the King's hande his sarvant's hande wyll be but a bad warant, yf they have ther wyshe. Sir, for my selfe I am detarmyned to end my lyfe in it, and the matter is not graet: I protest my graetest care is for heer Majestie's honor and surte. I send you a letter that now as I wryght, I receved from a man of myne, wyche afyrmeth the lyk. And so, Sir, I tak my leave from aboarde the Ark Rawly, (Royal) the 9 Ma. at 12 o'clock at nyght.

Your very lovyng frend,
C. HOWARD. [4]

To The Righte Honorable my verie
lovinge freinde Sir ffrances Walsingham, Knighte:
Principall Secretare unto Her Majestie.

Drake was equally ready, and proceeded to Plymouth, where he hoisted his flag in the Revenge. But before proceeding further, we may now take a cursory view of the respective armaments of the two nations.

LIST OF THE SHIPS OF THE BRITISH NAVY, THEIR FORCE, AND THEIR RESPECTIVE COMMANDERS.

	Names of the Ships.	Names of the Captains.	Tons.	Seamen.	Guns.	Remarks.
1	The Ark Royal	Lord Charles Howard	800	425	55	Lord High Admiral
2	Elizabeth Bonaventure	Earl of Cumberland	600	250	34	
3	Rainbow	Lord Henry Seymour	500	250	40	
4	Golden Lion	Lord Thomas Howard	500	250	38	
5	White Bear	Lord Edmund Sheffield	1000	500	40	
6	Vanguard	Sir William Winter	500	250	40	
7	Revenge	Sir Francis Drake	500	250	40	Vice-Admiral
8	Elizabeth Jonas	Sir Robert Southwell	500	500	56	
9	Victory	Sir John Hawkins	800	400	42	Rear-Admiral
10	Antelope	Sir Henry Palmer	400	160	30	
11	Triumph	Sir Martin Frobisher	1100	500	42	
12	Dreadnought	Sir George Beston	400	200	32	
13	Mary Rose	Edward Fenton	600	250	36	
14	Nonpareil	Thomas Fenner	500	250	38	
15	Hope	Robert Cross	600	250	48	
16	Galley, Bonavolia	William Boroughs	—	250	—	

No.	Ship	Captain			
17	Swiftsure	Edward Fenner	400	200	42
18	Swallow	Richard Hawkins	360	160	8
19	Foresight	Christopher Baker	300	160	37
20	Aid	William Fenner	250	120	18
21	Bull	Jeremy Turner	200	100	—
22	Tiger	John Bostock	200	100	22
23	Tramontana	Luke Ward	120	70	21
24	Scout	Henry Ashley	120	70	10
25	Achates	Henry Rigges	100	60	13
26	Charles	John Roberts	70	40	16
27	Moon	Alex. Clifford	60	40	9
28	Advice	John Harris	50	40	9
29	Spy	Ambrose Ward	50	40	9
30	Martin	Walter Gower	50	35	7
31	Sun	Richard Buckley	40	30	5
32	Signet	John Shrive	30	20	—
33	Brigantine	Thomas Scot	—	35	—
34	George-a-Hoye	Richard Hodges	120	24	—
34	Ships of the Navy.		11820	6279	837

This list, it must be observed, is confined to the Queen's ships; and it embraces the whole navy at that time, short of some six or seven others. But the whole English fleet was made up to nearly two hundred sail, furnished by the city of London and several ports on the coast, being of every possible burthen from three hundred tons to thirty.

The abstract of the several squadrons may be stated as under:

No. of Ships.		Tons.	Mariners.
34	Her Majesty's Ships under the Lord High Admiral	11850	6279
10	Serving by tonnage with the Lord High Admiral	750	239
32	Serving with Sir F. Drake	5120	2348
38	Fitted out by the City	6130	2710
20	Coasters with the Lord High Admiral	1930	993
23	Coasters with the Lord Henry Seymour	2248	1073
18	Volunteers with the Lord High Admiral	1716	859
15	Victuallers	——	810
7	Vessels not mentioned in the King's-library list	——	474
197		29744	15785[5]

No. of Ships.		Tons.	Guns.	Mariners.	Soldiers.
12	Squadron of Portuguese Galleons under the Generalisimo	7739	389	1242	3086
14	Fleet of Biscay, Captain General Don Juan Martinez de Recaldé	5861	302	906	2117
16	Fleet of Castile, General Don Diego de Valdez	8054	474	1793	2924
11	Andalusian Squadron, General Don Pedro de Valdez	8692	315	776	2359
14	Squadron of Guypuscoa, Don Mighel de Oquendo	7192	296	608	2120
10	Eastern fleet or Levantiscas, Don Martin Ventendona	8632	319	844	2792
23	Fleet called Urcas or Hulks, Don Juan Lopez de Medina	10860	466	950	4170
24	Pataches and Zabras, Don Antonio de Mendoza	2090	204	746	1103
4	Galiasses of Naples, Don Hugo de Moncada	—	200	477	744
4	The Galleys of Portugal, Don Diego de Mendrana	—	200	424	440
132		59120	3165	8766	21855

Besides 2088 Galley Slaves.

The comparison then of the two forces will stand thus:

	Ships.	Tons.	Guns.	Mariners.
English	197	29744	837	15785
Spaniards	132	59120	3165	8766 21855 soldiers
				30621 men
	45 more E.	29376 more S.	2328 more S.	14836 more S.

So that the Spaniards had double the force of the English, except in the *number* of ships, and in guns nearly four times the force. The only *cannon* of 60lb. shot, being 19 pieces in the whole of the English fleet, and 28 pieces of *demi-cannon* of 33lb. shot. The rest of their armament consisted of culverins, demi-culverins, sakers, mynions, falcons, and other small pieces.

How the merchant ships were armed does not appear; but, looking at their tonnage, two-thirds of them at least would have been of but little, if any, service; and, indeed, must have required uncommon vigilance to keep them out of harm's way.

Even the best of the Queen's ships, placed along side one of the first class of Spaniards, would have been like a sloop of war by the side of a first-rate. Their high forecastles, so well named, bearing one or two tiers of guns, and their high poops equally acting as castles, made it next to impossible to board them, as the musketry from thence would pick the men off on reaching the main deck; besides, it was an article in the general Instructions of the Spanish fleet, that every ship should be supplied with a chest or cask full of stones to hurl down upon the boarders. The odds therefore were fearful against the English, - but the English heart and English seamanship made ample amends for other deficiencies. The odds, however, were formidable. Spain at this time possessed the first navy in Europe, and her numerous and well-disciplined army was inferior to none. In addition to their large ships, bearing castles on their poops and their bows, their galleons and galiasses, they had a fleet of hulks stored with provisions and ammunition, and every kind of article that could be required for establishing themselves on shore. So certain were they of success, that there were in the fleet upwards of a hundred (some say 180) monks or friars and Jesuits, *ad propagandam fidem* among the English heretics, to be drilled by English papist traitors said to be among them; every device was adopted to give a sacred or religious character to the invasion; twelve of their ships were named after the twelve Apostles: and such was the prevailing enthusiasm, that every noble family in Spain had a son, or brother, or nephew, that entered the fleet as volunteers.

Nor was the enthusiastic spirit of the sons and relatives of the English nobility and gentry less distinguished, in a better cause. Numbers of them joined the auxiliary ships, which poured in to re-inforce the fleet from all quarters. The City of London requested they might send fifteen stout ships, with 5000 men, to the fleet. They actually supplied 38 ships, and 10,000 men, of whom 2700 were seamen.

Nothing indeed could exceed the general feeling of love and duty towards the Queen. This noble lady, with a dignity of spirit equal to the wisdom of her measures, gave a most striking example of patriotism and devotion to her country and cause, in placing herself at the head of her troops, and taking her stand at Tilbury fort, to arrest the progress of the enemy, should they dare to approach her capital. The speech she delivered on the occasion affords a memorable example of a great and noble mind.

The Queen's speech in the camp of Tilbury was in these words:- "My loving people, we have been persuaded by some that are careful of our safety, to take heed how we commit ourselves to armed multitudes, for fear of treachery; but assure you, I do not desire to live to distrust my faithful and loving people. Let tyrants fear: I have always so behaved myself, that, under God, I have placed my chiefest strength and safeguard in the loyal hearts and goodwill of my subjects. And therefore I am come amongst you at this time, not as for my recreation or sport, but being resolved, in the midst and heat of the battle, to live or die amongst you all; to lay down, for my God, and for my kingdom, and for my people, my honour and my blood, even in the dust. I know I have but the body of a weak and feeble woman, but I have the heart of a King, and of a King of England too; and think foul scorn that Parma or Spain, or any prince of Europe, should dare to invade the borders of my realms: to which, rather than any dishonour should grow by me, I myself will take up arms: I myself will be your general, judge, and rewarder of every one of your virtues in the field. I know already, by your forwardness, that you have deserved rewards and crowns; and we do assure you, on the word of a prince, they shall be duly paid you. In the mean time my lieutenant-general shall be in my stead, than whom never prince commanded a more noble and worthy subject; not doubting by your obedience to my general, by your concord in the camp, and your valour in the field, we shall shortly have a famous victory over those enemies of my God, of my kingdom, and of my people."

The number of troops that attended the Queen at Tilbury were

22,000 foot, and 1000 horse

34,000 foot, and 2000 horse, for the Queen's Guard under Lord Hunsdon.

20,000 soldiers stationed along the coast.

Early in March the Lord High Admiral, having made his arrangements, hoisted his flag, as already stated, on board the Ark Royal, and proceeded to visit the stations on which his fleet was placed, beginning with that of Lord H. Seymour in the Downs, appropriated to watch Dunkirk, where the Duke of Parma was preparing his armament to join the Armada; from whence it was his intention to proceed to Plymouth, where Drake was preparing the Western Squadron.

30 March, 1588.

SIR FRANCIS DRAKE TO THE LORDS OF THE COUNCIL.

RIGHTE HONORABLE AND MY VERIE GOOD LORDES,

Understandinge by your good Lordships' letters her Majestie's goode inclynacion for the speedye sendinge of theise forces here unto the seas, for the defence of the enemye, and that, of her Majestie's greate favor, and your Lordships' good opynyon, you have made choice of me (althoughe the least of manye) to be as an actor in so greate a cause, I am moste humblie to beseeche my moste gracious Soveraigne and your good Lordships to heare my poore opynyon with favor, and so to judge of it accordinge to your greate wisdomes.

If her Majestic and your Lordships thincke that the King of Spaigne meanethe any invasyon in Englande, then doubtlesse his force is and will be greate in

Spaigne, and thereon he will make his groundworke, or foundation, whereby the prynce of Parma maye have the better entraunce, which in myne owne judgemente is most to be feared: but if there maye be suche a staye or stoppe made, by any meanes of this ffleete, in Spaigne, that they maye not come throughe the seas as conquerors (which I assure myselfe they thincke to doe) then shall the Prince of Parma have suche a checke therebye as were meete.

To prevente this I thincke it goode that theise forces here shoulde be made as stronge as to your Honors' wisdomes shall be thoughte convenyente, and that for two speciall causes: ffirste, for that they are like to strike the firste blowe, and secondlie, it will putt greate and goode hartes into her Majestie's lovinge subjectes bothe abroade and at home, ffor that they will be perswaded in conscyence that the Lord of all strengthes will putt into her Majestic and her people coraige & boldnes not to feare any invasyon in her owne countrie, but to seeke God's enemyes and her Majesties' where they maye be founde: fFor the Lorde is on our side, whereby we may assure ourselves our nombers are greater than theirs. I muste crave pardon of your good Lordships againe and againe, for my conscience hath caused me to putt my pen to the paper, and as God in his goodnes hathe putt my hande to the ploughe, so in his mercy he will never suffer me to turne backe from the truthe.

My verie good Lords, next, under God's mightie proteccion, the advantaige and gaine of tyme and place, will be the onlie and cheife meane for our goode, wherein I most humblie beseeche your good Lordships to persever as you have began, for that with feiftie saile of shippinge we shall doe more good uppon their owne coaste, then a greate manye more will doe here at home, and the sooner we are gone the better we shall be able to ympeache them. There is come home, synce the sending awaie of my laste messenger one bark(whome I sente out as an Espiall), who confyrmeth those intelligences whereof I have advertized your Lordships by him; and that divers of those Biskaines are abroade uppon that coaste, wearinge Englishe flagges, whereof there are made in Lisbone three hundreth, with the redde Crosse, which is a great presumptcons proceedinge of the hautynes & pride of the Spaynierde, and not to be tollerated by any true naturall Englishe harte.

I have herein enclosed sente this note unto your Lordships, to consider of our proporcions in powlder, shotte, and other munycion, under the hande of the surveyor's clerke of the ordynaunce: the which proporcion in powlder and shotte for our greate ordynaunce in her Majestie's shippes is but for one daie and halfe's servyce, if it be begonne and contynewed as the service maye requyer; and but five lastes of powlder for 24 sails of the marchaunte shippes, which will scante be suffytient for one daie's service, and divers occasyons maye be offred.

Good my Lords, I beseeche you to consider deeplie of this, for it importeth but the losse of all.

I have staied this messenger somewhat the longer for the hearinge of this Ducheman who came latelie out of Lisbone, and hath delivered theise advertisements herein enclosed under his hande the 28th of this Marche before myselfe and divers Justices.

I have sente unto your good Lordships the note of such powlder and munytyon as are delivered unto us, for this great service, which in truthe I judge to be just a thirde parte of that which is needefull: ffor if we should wante it when we shall have moste neede thereof it will be too late to sende to the Tower for it. I assure your Honors it neither is or shall be spente in vaine. And thus restinge at your Honors' farther direccion, I humblie take my leave of your good Lordships.

From Plymowth this xxxth of Marche, 1588.

Your good Lordships'

verie readie to be commaunded,

FRA: DRAKE. [6]

To the righte Honorable & my verie
   goode Lordes the Lordes of Her Majestie's
   Most Honorable Previe Counsell.

13 April, 1588.

SIR FRANCIS DRAKE TO THE QUEEN.

MOST GRACYOUS SOVERAIGNE,

I have receaved from Mr. Secreatary som particuller notes and withall a comandment, to awnswere them unto your Majestic.

The first is that your Majestic would willyngly be satysfyed from me how the forces nowe in Lysborne myght best be dystressed.

Trewly this poynt is hardly to be awnswered as yeat, for tow specyall cawses, the fyrst, for that our intelligences are as yeat uncertayne. The second, is the resolucyon, of our owne people, which I shall better understand when I have them at sea. The last insample at Calles is not of dyvers yeat forgotten, for one such flying nowe, as Borrowghes dyd then, will put the wholle in perille ffor that the enemyes strengthe is ri5w so great gathred together and redy to invade; but yf your Majestic will geve present order for our preceding to the sea, and send to the strengthning of this fleett here, fower more of your Majestie's good shippes, and those 16 saill of shipes with ther penaces which ar preparing in London, then shall your Majestic stand assured, with God's assistance, that yf the flett come out of Lysborne as long as we have vittuall to leve withall, uppon that cost, they shall be fowght with, and I hope, throwghe the goodnes of our mercyfull God, in suche sort as shall hynder his qwyett passage into Yngland, for I assure your Majestic, I have not in my lyffe time knowen better men and possessed with gallanter mynds then your Majestie's people are for the most parte, which are here gathred together, vollontaryllye to put ther hands and hartts to the fynyshing of this great peice of work, wherin we ar all perswaded that God, the gever of all victoryes, will in mercye lowke uppon your most excellent Majestie, and us your power subjects, who for the defence of your Majestie, our relygyon, and natyve country, have resolutly vowed the hassard of our lyves.

The advantage of tyme and place in all marciall accyons is half a victory, which being lost is irrecoverable, wherefore, if your Majestie will comaund me away with those shipes which ar here alredye, and the rest to follow with all possible expedycyon, I hold it in my power opynyon the surest and best cowrse, and that they bring with them vittualls suffycyent for themselves and us, to the intent the service be not utterly 'lost for want thereof: Whereof I most humbly beseche your most excellent Majestie to have such consideracyon as the wayghtenes of the cawse reqwyrethe. For an Ynglyshman being farre from his country and seing a present wante of vittuall to insue, and perseaving no beneffytt to be lowked for, but only blowes, will hardlye be browght to staye.

I have order but for tow monthes vittualles begynning the 24th of Aprell, whereof one wholl monthe may be spent before we com there, the other monthes vittuall will be thowght, with the least to bring us back agayne; here may the wholl service and honor be lost for the sparing of a fewe crownes.

Towching my power opynyon how strong your Majesties fleett should be to encounter this great force of the enemey, God encreac your most excellent Majestie's forces, both by sea and land, dayly: for this I surly thincke ther was never any force so stronge as ther is now redye or makynge readye agaynst your Majestie and trewe relygyon, but that the Lord of all strengthes is stronger and will defend the trewth of his word, for his owne name's sake, unto the which God be all glory geven. Thus all humble duty, I contynewally will pray to the Allmyghtye to blesse and geve you victorye over all his, and your enemeyes. From Plymothe this 13 of Aprell 1588.

Your Majesties most loyall

FRA: DRAKE. [7]

To The Queene's
Moste excellente Majestie.

Another letter, of the 28th April, acquaints Her Majesty of the intelligence he had gained, that the merchant ships of foreign nations had been detained in the several ports of Spain, and had been embargoed; he mentions also the reports he had received of the great preparations of the enemy; that he considers the embargo as a token of their intention of coming out; and suggests that her forces should go out and meet them at a distance from England; after this preamble he thus proceeds:

That if a goode peace for your Majestic be not forthwith concluded (which I as moche as anie man desirethe) then theise greate preparacions of the Spayneyerde maie be speedelie prevented as moche as in your Majestic liethe, by sendinge your forces to encounter them somewhat farre off, and more neere their owne coaste, which will be the better cheape for your Majestie and people, and muche the deerer for the enemye.

Thus muche (as duetie byndethe me), I have thought goode to signifie unto your Majestie, for that it importethe but the hazerde or losse of all: The promise of peace from the Prince of Parma and these mightie preparacions in Spaigne agree not well together: Undoubtedlie I thincke theise advertisements true; ffor that I cannot heare by anye man of warre, or otherwise, that anie shippe is permytted to departe Spaigne, which is a vehemente presumpcion that they holde their purposed pretences: And for farther testymonie of theise reports I have sente this bearer, a Captaine of one of your Majestie's shippes, who (if it shall please your Highnes to permytte him) can deliver some thinges touchinge the same.

Thus restinge allwaies most bounden unto your Majestie for your gracious and favourable speeches used of me, both to Mr. Secretarie and others, (which I desier God no longer to lette me live then I will be readye to doe your Majestic all the duetifull service I possiblie maie,) I will contynewallie praye to God to blesse your Majestie with all happie victories.

From Plymouthe this 28th of Aprill, 1588.

Your Majestie's most loiall,

FRA: DRAKE. [8]

On the 23rd May, the Lord High Admiral announces his arrival at Plymouth [not addressed, but apparently to Lord Burleigh; this letter has suffered so much from fire, and otherwise defaced, as to make part of it nearly unintelligible]. He says that Drake came out to meet him with sixty sail of ships very well appointed; announcing moreover his intention to proceed to sea, and stand off and on, between the coasts of England and Spain, to watch the coming of the Spanish forces.

* * * * Althoughe there be not much worthie the writinge unto your Lordship, [____] understande howe that uppon Tuesdaie, the 1st of this instant, the winde servinge exceedinglie at the Downes, assigninge unto my Lord Henry Seymour [____] shipes appointed to stale with him in the narrow seas [____] partinge companye the same daye thwarte of Dover, and [____] a pleasante gale of winde all the waie, came and arrived here at Plymmouthe this daie, about 8 of the clocke this morninge, whence Sir Francis Drake came forthe with sixty sayle very well appointed to meete me, and soe, casting aboute, put with me into the haven againe, where I meane to staie theise twoe daies to water the fleete, and then, God willinge, to take the opportunitye, of the first winde towarde the coaste of Spaine, with intentione to lye on and of, betwixte Englande and that coaste, to watche the comminge of the Spanishe forces, which I doubte not if God send us the good hap to meete withall, but that in like sorte he will send us as good succes, to conquer and overthrowe them. Unto whome I commend your good Lordship, and soe bid the same moste heartilie well to fare: from this porte of Plymmouth 23th of Maie, 1588.

Your Lordship most assured to command,

C. HOWARD. [9]

Good lord, bear with me that I do not wryghte with my owne hand. I am but newly landed, and have much business. * * *

According to the intention stated in the foregoing letter, the Lord High Admiral, with the western squadron, put to sea, and reached within a short distance of the coast of Spain, when a strong southerly wind drove them back to Plymouth. Here he found a letter waiting for him, dated 9th June, from Sir Francis Walsingham, written by command of the Queen, signifying Her Majesty's pleasure, that he should not go so far from the English coast, and assigning her obvious reasons for such an order, - that the coasts of England would be left unprotected. In his reply, dated 15th, he says, "it was deeply debated by those whom the world doth judge to be men of the greatest experience, that this realme hath, which are these: Sir Francis Drake, Mr. Hawkins, Mr. Frobisher, and Mr. Thomas Fenner; and I hope Her Majesty will not thinke we went so rashlie to worke, or without a principal, or choice care and respect of the safetie of this realme. And," he adds, "if we found they did but linger on their own coast, or put into the isles of Bayonne or the Groyne, then we thought, in all men's judgments that be of experience here, it had bin most fit to have sought some good waie: and the surest we could devise (by the good protection of God) to have defeated them." And he further gives Her Majesty to understand, that if the fleet are to stand off and on betwixt England and Spain, the south-west wind, which might carry the Spaniards to Scotland or Ireland, would throw him to leeward; that on the contrary, if his fleet was high up in the Channel, the Spaniards might come for the Isle of Wight, "which, for my parte, if they coome to England, they will attempt when we are cleane out of the waie of any service against them. But I must and will obey."

On the 23d June, Lord C. Howard addresses another letter to Sir Francis Walsingham, chiefly to let him know that he was about to get under way; that the foul weather that forced him in, no doubt dispersed the Spanish fleet; and advises that Her Majesty trust no more to Judas's kisses, assuring herself there is no trusting to the French King nor to the Duke of Parma. "Let her defend herself like a noble and mighty Prince; and trust to her sword and not to their word, and then she need not to fear, for her good God will defend her." He distrusts the Duke of Guise, and means to pay a visit to the coast of France.

23 June, 1588.

LORD HOWARD TO MR. SECRETARY WALSINGHAM.

SIR,

This Sonday about 7 of the cloke at nyght I recevid your letter of the 22 of this present, and the advertysments with them, wyche I dow most hartely thank you for: but I parceave by your letter there shuld another letter come from my Lordse to Mr. Dorell, and also a warante that the poursyfant shuld brynge, wyche shuld be open for me, but he nether browght the Lordse letter nor any suche warrant. Sir, I pray you pardon me that I dow not send yow the namse of the townse devyded, suche as be wyllyng, and suche as be not. Sir F. Drake bathe the newse of them, now at this ower is full ocupyed, as I am also. Our watche chame to us this last nyght about 12 of the cloke, and we wyll not ete nor slype tell it be abourd us. We must not lose an ower of tyme. You shall see by a letter that I have sent Heer Majestic what advertysment I have. I meen to way presently and set sayle: this foull wether that was on Thursday, that forsed us in surty, disparsed the Spanyshe flyt: it shall goo hard but I wyll fynd them out. Let Heer Majestic trust no mor to Judises kyses; for let heer asure heerself ther is no trust to F. K. (French king) nor Duke of Parme. Let heer defend heerself lyke a noble and mightie Prynce: and trust to heer sworde and not to ther word, and then she ned not to feer, for heer good God wyll defend her.

Sir, I have a pryvy intelligence, by a sure fello, that the flyt of Spayne dowthe meen to come to the cost of France, and ther to receve in the Duke of Guyse, and great forses: and it is very lykly to be trew. I meen, God wyllyng, to vyset the cost of France, and to send in small penyses to discover all the cost alongst.

If I heer of them, I hope, ar it be long after, you shall heer newse. God Mr. Secretary, let the narro sees be well strantened (strengthened). "What charge is ill spent now for service? Let the Hoyse of Harwyge (Harwich) goo with all speed agayne to my Lord H. Semor, for they be of great sarvyse.

Sir, for these thyngs heer I pray take order with Mr. Dorell, for I have no lesur to thynk of them. I pray you, Sir, delyver my letter unto Heer Majestic with my humble duty, and so in hast I bid you farwell.

Abourd the Arke, this Sonday, at 12 of the clok at nyght. Your assured levying frend,

C. HOWARD. [10]

(No date, but supposed June 23d, 1588.)

Sir, God wyllyng, I wyll com sayll within this three houers.
To my very lovyng frend,
    Mr. Secretary Walsyngham.

---

[1] Camden.
[2] The long letter of thirty-two pages which this refers to, is to be found in the Harleian Miscellany and Lord Somers' Tracts. It never reached Mendoza, who, if it had, would have disregarded it.
[3] Naval Chronicle.
[4] MS. State Paper Office.
[5] Lediard's Naval History. The Author, after consulting the best authorities and several manuscripts, does not hesitate to say that these and the following lists are the most complete and perfect that have hitherto appeared of these two fleets. They nearly agree with an average of demi-official returns.
[6] MS. State Paper Office.
[7] MS. State Paper Office.
[8] MS. State Paper Office.
[9] MSS. Cottonian Collection, British Museum.
[10] MS. State Paper Office.

Chapter Eight - The Spanish Armada, Called The Invincible. 1588. *Part Second.*

The day was now approaching when the great contest was to be decided between two of the most powerful fleets that had hitherto ever met in hostile array; the palm to be contended for, on the one hand, was the preservation of an empire, the crown, religion, and independence; on the other, conquest, bigotry, and slavery. On the 19th day of July, the Lord High Admiral having received certain information from one Fleming, the master of a pinnace, that the Spanish fleet was in the Channel, near the Lizard Point, lost not a moment in towing out the British fleet from the port of Plymouth, the wind blowing in stiffly; but the alacrity and the industry, assisted and encouraged by the Admiral in person, overcame all difficulty.

The following anecdote may or may not be true, but the authority on which it rests is noted. The labour on that day, as above stated by the Lord Admiral, in warping out the ships, makes it very improbable.

"It is traditionally reported, that when the news reached the British Navy of the sudden appearance of the Armada off the Lizard, the principal commanders were on shore at Plymouth playing bowls, on the Hoe; and it is added that Drake insisted on the match being played out, saying, that 'There would be plenty of time to win the game, and beat the Spaniards too.'" [1]

On the following day, the 20th, the Spanish fleet were discovered with their lofty turrets, like so many floating castles; their line extending its wings about seven miles, in the shape of a half-moon, proceeding very slowly, though with full sail, "The winds," says Camden, "being as it were tired with carrying them, and the ocean seeming to groan under the weight of their heavy burdens." [2]

21st July. - The Lord High Admiral, on their passing, sent out his pinnace, named the Disdain, in advance, challenged the Duke of Sidonia to give the defiance by firing off her ordnance, as a declaration of war, when his own flag-ship, the Ark Royal, "thundered thick and furiously upon a large ship which he thought to be the Spanish Admiral, but was that of Alphonso de Leyva. At the same time Drake, Hawkins and Frobisher played stoutly upon the rear division of the fleet, commanded by General Juan de Recalde, whose ship and others, being much shattered, made shift to get away to the main body, under the Duke of Medina Sidonia." A Spanish narrative says she was disabled, her rigging cut up, and two shot lodging in her foremast: that the flag-ship took in her sails, and waited to receive her into the line; that the Duke now collected his scattered fleet, not being able to do more on this occasion, as the enemy had gained the wind. "Their (the English) vessels," he says, "were well fought, and under such good management, that they did with them what they pleased." [3] The fight having continued two hours, and forty sail of the English fleet, the last out of the harbour, not having yet joined, the Admiral thought good not to press them further this day.

The following letter from Lord Charles Howard describes the fight very briefly; and is one of the many, both from him and Drake, so mutilated, as to make it impossible to give it in a perfect state.

21st July, 1588.

LORD C. HOWARD TO SIR F. WALSINGHAM.

SIR,

I will not trouble you with anie longe letter. We are at this present otherwise occupied then with writinge. Uppon Fridaie at Plymouthe I receaved intelligence that there were a greate number of ships descried of the Lisarde. Wheruppon, althoughe the winde was verie skante, we firste warped out of harbor that nyghte, and uppon Saterdaie turned out verie hardly, the wind beinge at southe weste, and aboute 3 of the clock in the afternope descried the Spanishe fleete, and [__ __] did what we could to worke for the wind, which [__ ___] morninge we had recovered discryinge theire [___ _] consiste of 120 saile: Whereof there are 4 g[___] and many ships of greate burthen. At nine of the [___] we gave them feighte, which contynewed untill [_____] feighte. We made som of them to beare roome to stop their leaks. Notwithstandinge we durste not adventure to put in amongste them theire fleete being soe stronge. But there shall nothinge be eather neglected or unhasarded that may worke theire over-throws.

Sir, the Captaines in her Majestie's ships have behaved themselves moste bravely and like men hitherto, and I doubte not will contynewe to their greate comendacion. And soe recomendinge oure good successe to your godlie praiers, I bid you hartelie farewell. From aboard the Arke, thwarte of Plymouthe; the 21 of Julie 1588. Youre verie lovinge freind,

C. HOWARD. [4]

(Postscript.) Sir, the sowtherly wynde that browght us bak from the cost of Spayne browght them out, God blessed us with tornynge us bak. Sir, for the love of God and our country, let us have with sume sped some graet shote sent us of all bignes, for this sarvis wyll contenew long, and sume powder with it.

The Righte Honorable
  my verie lovinge friende,
    Sir Francis Walsingham, knight. [5]

On the same day Sir Francis Drake writes to Lord Henry Seymour to ap-prize him of the arrival of the enemy on the coast; that a few common shot had passed, and that they seemed to be determined to sell their lives with blows. He tells him he is commanded by the Admiral to desire that the ships under his charge should be held in the best possible order.

21st July, 1588.

SIR FRANCIS DRAKE TO LORD HENRY SEYMOUR.

RIGHT HONORABLE AND MY VERIE GOOD LORD,

I am comaunded by my good Lord, the Lord Admiral, to send you the Carvaile in haste with this letter, geivinge your Lordship to understand that the armye of Spaigne arrived uppon our coaste the 20th of this presente, the 21th we had them in chase; and so cominge upp unto them there hath passed some comen shotte betweene some of our fleete and some of theirs; and as farre as we per-ceive they are determined to sell their lives with blowes. Whereuppon his Lord-ship hath commaunded me to write unto your Lordship and Sir William Wynter, that those shippes servinge under your charge should be putte into the best and strongest manner you male, and readie to assiste his Lordship for the better in-countering of them in those parts where you nowe are. In the meane tyme what his Lordship and the rest here following him maie doe, shall be suerelie per-formede. His Lordship hathe comaunded me to write his hartie commendacions to your Lordship and Sir William Wynter. I doe salute your Lordship, Sir William

Wynter, Sir Henry Pallmer, and all the rest of those honorable gentlemen serving under you with the like. Beseeching God of his mercie to geive her Majestic our gratious Soveraigne alwaies victorie against her enemyes. Written abord her Majesties good shipp the Revenge of Steart, this 21th (July), late in the evening, 1588.

Your good Lordship's

poore freend readie to be comaunded,

(Signed)   FRA: DRAKE.

This letter, my honorable good Lord, is sent in haste; the ffleete of Spanyards is somewhat about a hundreth sailes; many great shipes, but trewly I thinck not half of them men of warre, haste, your Lordship's assured,

FRA. DRAKE.

To the Right Honorable
  the Lord Henry Seymour,
  Admirall of her Majesties Navie in the narrowe Seas, or, in absence, to Sir William Wynter, knyght, geive theise with speed - hast, hast, hast. [6]

In the evening of this day, a vast ship of Biscay, bearing the flag of Oquendo, having the King's Treasurer on board, took fire, designedly as was said, by some gunpowder laid for that purpose by a Dutch gunner, who had received some ill-treatment. The flame was however happily extinguished by some vessels coming to her relief, but not before the two decks and the poop blew up; no mention is made of the Dutch gunner in the Spanish narrative. Another accident happened this evening. There was a large galleon, commanded by Don Pedro de Valdez, which in tacking fell foul of another and sprung her fore-mast, and was left behind; the night being dark, with the sea running so high, in consequence of which no succour could come to her. Diego de Florez represented to the Duke the danger of lying to for this ship, arid as the main body of the Armada was getting much a-head, he would find himself, in the morning, with only half of his ships; and that the enemy, being so near at hand, the safety of the whole was not to be hazarded for a single ship; in short that in staying by her, the object of the expedition would be sacrificed. [7] This ship thus abandoned was taken possession of by Drake. Our chroniclers make a great deal too much of this affair, and, no doubt, more than is strictly true; but the following is the most circumstantial:-
"The next day following Sir Francis Drake, espying this lagging gallon, sent forth a pinnace to command them to yield, otherwise his bullets should force them without further favour; but Valdez, to seeme valorous, answered, that they were foure hundred and fifty strong; that himself was *Don Pedro,* and stood on his honour, and thereupon propounded certain conditions. But the Knight sent his reply, that he had not leizure to parley; if he would yield, presently doe it; if not, he should well prove that Drake was no dastard; whereupon *Pedro,* hearing that it was the *fiery Drake* (ever terrible to the

141

Spaniards) who had him in chase, with 40 of his followers, came on board Sir Francis his ship; where, first giving him the *congé,* he protested that he, and all his, were resolved to die in defence, had they not falne under his power, whose valour and felicty was so great that *Mars* and *Neptune* seemed to attend him in his attempts, and whose generous minde towards the vanquished had often been experienced, even of his greatest foes. Sir Francis, requiting his Spanish compliments with honourable English courtesies, placed him at his owne table, and lodged him in his owne cabbin. The residue of that company were sent into Plymouth, where they remained eighteene months 'til their ransoms were paid; but Sir Francis his souldiers had well paid themselves with the spoile of the shippe, wherein were fifty-five thousand ducats in gold, which they shared merrily among them." [8] The ship was sent into Dartmouth.

But Drake on this night nearly got into a scrape. He was ordered to carry a light. Observing five large ships hovering near the fleet to which, having suspected to be enemies, he gave chase, forgetting the light, which caused his detachment to remain behind, while the Admiral pursued the Armada; but no harm ensued. [9]

22nd July. On this day there was no fighting. In the course of it the Duke formed the Armada into two divisions, he taking the van, and Don Alonzo de Leyva the rear. "The Duke," says the narrative, "summoned to him all the *Sargentos Mayores,* and ordered them to proceed in a patache, so that each ship should keep the position assigned to her, in the new order of sailing; and he further gave them written orders, directing, that in case any ship did not observe the order, and quitted her post, the captain should forthwith be hanged, the Sargentos Mayores taking the provosts with them for that purpose; and for the better execution of the order, they were distributed, three in the van and three in the rear division. On the same day the captain of the flag-ship of Oquendo reported to the Duke that she was sinking, on which he ordered that the crew and the Treasurer's money should be taken out of her, and the ship sunk." [10]

The first order was obeyed, the second not, but she was turned adrift, and boarded by Lord Thomas Howard and Captain Hawkins, who found her decks fallen in, her steerage ruined, the stern blown out, and about fifty poor wretches burnt in a most miserable manner. The stench and the horrible sight made them speedily return to the Admiral, who ordered a small bark to take possession of her, and in that shattered condition she was carried into Weymouth. [11]

23rd July. On this day there was what may be called a second fight, brought on by the two fleets each endeavouring to obtain the weather gage, in the course of which there was no little confusion, as might be expected from fleets constituted as they were, and more especially from the great number of merchant ships in that of England. It appears that some of the London ships, being surrounded by Spaniards, were rescued by a brave attack of a few of her Majesty's ships, while the Spaniards boldly reinforced the squad-ron of Recaldé, which was suffering much by a spirited attack of the English rear division. After this a running fight took place, the two Admirals crossing each other, and each sustaining the fire of their opponents.

According to the "Narrative," all the galleons and galleasses were engaged this day. The enemy, he says, came united against the Duke's flag-ship whilst she was advancing to the assistance of Recaldé and de Leyva; that the English flag-ship passed with the whole of their fleet, each ship giving her fire to our flag-ship, when four or five of their largest ships came to her support. He says, that frequent attempts were made to board our ships, but they were so light and well managed that there was little hope of succeeding. [12]

"The great guns," says Camden, "rattled like so many peals of thunder; but the shot from the high-built Spanish ships flew for the most part over the heads of the English without doing any execution, owing to their high fore-castles, and their inability to depress their guns. One Mr. Cook (or Cope) was the only Englishman that died bravely in the midst of his enemies, command-ing his own ship. The reason was, that the English ships were moved and managed with such agility, giving their broadsides to the larger and more unwieldy of the enemy, and sheering off again just as they pleased, while the Spanish heavy ships lay as so many butts for the English to fire at." [13]

It was suggested to the Lord High Admiral, with more zeal than discretion, that they should board the Spaniards, which would have been a most ruinous proceeding, considering the size of their ships, the enormous advantage of their high forecastles and high poops, the number of troops each had on board, and that their ships of war were four to one of our war-ships. He, very prudently, acted more on the defensive, than on obtaining very decisive re-sults at the risk of ruining the only fleet that England possessed; knowing that if, by any imprudent step, that fleet should be defeated, the great object of the enemy would be gained, and her army landed on the British shores. It was, therefore, his policy to keep his fleet, as much as possible, between that of the enemy and the shore.

24th. On the 24th there was a cessation on both sides. The Lord High Ad-miral took the opportunity of dividing his fleet into four squadrons, - the first under himself; the second under Sir Francis Drake; the third under Hawkins; and the fourth under Frobisher. He also sent some of the smaller vessels to the neighbouring ports for a supply of powder and ammunition.

25th. This being the day of St. James (which the "Narrative" calls St. Do-mingo), a galleon of Portugal, the St. Anne, not being able to keep up with the fleet, was taken by some of the English ships, and Don Alonzo de Leyva, with Don Diego Felles Enriques, attempted to rescue her with three galleasses, but were so warmly received by the Lord Admiral himself, and the Lord Thomas Howard of the Golden Lion, who, by reason of the calm, had their ships towed along with boats, and succeeded with much ado in carrying off the galleon, but not without considerable loss; and it is observed that from this time none of the galleasses ever ventured to engage.

In the next place the Lord Admiral with some others made an attack upon the Spanish Admiral, cut the rigging of her main mast, and killed several of her men. But five or six of the larger ships coming up to her rescue, and a great portion of their fleet advancing, the Lord Admiral desisted, as the "Narrative" says, much damaged.

The "Narrative" further states, that the English flag-ship was in so much danger that she was towed by eleven launches, striking her standard, and firing guns as signals of distress. On seeing this, the Spanish Admiral and a great part of the fleet made towards her; but the English, also standing towards their Admiral for his support, and the wind springing up, the launches were cut off, and the Spanish fleet pursued its voyage. The writer says: "We made certain this day of being able to board the English ships, which was the only means of obtaining any decisive advantage." [14] On this day the Duke dispatched an officer to Dunkirk, being the third, to apprize the Duke of Parma of their position (off the Isle of Wight), and to urge his immediate coming out, and to send some shot for four, six, and ten-pounders, of which much had been expended in the late engagements. The following day (26th) another message was sent to the Duke of Parma, requesting he would send forty small vessels to the Armada, to be employed against the enemy; "the heaviness of our ships, compared with the lightness of theirs, rendering it impossible in any manner to bring them to close action; and to represent to him of how much importance it was he should join the Armada the day of its appearing in sight of Dunkirk." In the evening, he says, a breeze sprang up, with which the Armada began to shape its course for Calais. [15]

26th July. On this day it was calm, the fleets in sight of each other. The Duke repeated by another messenger to the Duke of Parma his urgent desire that he would send forty small vessels, to be employed against the enemy; acquainting him that "the heaviness of his ships, compared to the lightness of the English, rendered it impossible in any manner to bring them to close action." [16] The Lord High Admiral this day bestowed the honour of knighthood on Lord Thomas Howard, Lord Sheffield, Roger Townsend, Captain John Hawkins, and Captain Martin Frobisher, in consideration of their gallant behaviour. And it was decided, in Council, that no further attempt should be made on the enemy, until they came into the Straits of Calais, where Lord Henry Seymour and Sir William Winter would there reinforce them. The following day (27th), in the afternoon, the Armada anchored off Calais, by the advice of the pilots, lest they should be carried away by the current into the North Sea; and an officer was again sent off to the Duke of Parma, to join them there, and stating at the same time the impossibility of their remaining long in that position without much risk to the whole Armada.

28th July. "Early this morning Captain Don Rodrigo Fello arrived from Dunkirk. He reported that the Duke of Parma was at Bruges, where he had

144

waited upon him, and that although the Duke had expressed much satisfaction at hearing of the arrival of the Armada, yet, on Saturday, at 6 P.M., when the Captain left Dunkirk, the Duke had not arrived there; neither were they beginning to embark the troops, nor the stores or provisions, the whole of which were still on shore." [17] It is pretty clear that the Duke had no relish to engage in the invasion. - This day the Lord Admiral was joined by Lord Henry Seymour; and now he had a hundred and forty sail, all stout ships, and good sailors. They anchored not far from the Spanish fleet; and at night the Lord Admiral (as is said by the Queen's especial command) singled out eight of his worst ships, charged with pitch, tar, resin, and other combustibles, and loaded all their guns with bullets, chain-shot, and other destructive materials; "and thus equipped sent them before the wind and with the tide, a little after midnight, into the midst of the Spanish fleet. Their approach was no sooner discovered, when their prodigious blaze threw the whole fleet into the utmost consternation. A clamour was immediately made of "Cut your cables, and get up your anchors," which was hastily done in the midst of the greatest confusion. A large galleasse, having lost her rudder, was tossed about for some time, and finally driven on the sands before Calais; here she was attacked by the Admiral's longboat and some others, against whom, in defending himself, the Captain Moncada was killed by a shot in the head; and the soldiers and rowers, to the number of 400, were either drowned or put to the sword. The ship and guns, after the English had set free three hundred galley-slaves, which were on board, and taken out fifty thousand ducats of gold, fell as a wreck to M. Gourd on, governor of Calais.

The letter of Sir Francis Drake, which follows, alludes, it is presumed (though the date is incorrect, 29th instead of 27th), to the confusion into which the enemy had been thrown, and hopes that the Prince of Parma and Duke of Sidonia will not shake hands for a few days, but he gives no description whatever of what had happened.

29 July, 1588.

SIR FRANCIS DRAKE TO SIR FRANCIS WALSINGHAM.

RIGHT HONORABLE,

THIS bearer cam a bourd the ship I was in, in a wonderffull good tyme, and browght with hym as good knowlege as we could wyshe: his carffullness therin is worthye recompence, for that God hathe geven us so good a daye in forcyng the enemey so far to leeward, as I hope in God the prince of Parma and the Duke of Sedonya shall not shake hands this ffewe dayes. And whensoever they shall meett, I beleve nether of them will greatly reioyce of this dayes Servis. The towne of Callys hathe scene som parte therof, whose mayer her Majestic is beholding unto: Busynes comands me to end. God bless her Majestic our Gracyous Soveraygne and geve us all grace to leve in his feare. I assure your Honor this dayes servis hath much apald the enemey, and no dowbt but incouraged our armey. From a bourd her Majestie's "good ship the Revenge, this 29th July 1588.

Your Honor's most redy to be comanded,

FRA: DRAKE.

Ther must be great care taken to send us monycyon and Vittuall whether soever the enemey goeth.

To the Righte Honorable
Sir Francis Walsingham, knighte.
Haste, haste, poste haste for Her Majesties service. [18]

It is stated in the "Narrative" that the Duke of Sidonia had his suspicions of the intention of the enemy to employ fire-ships, and that he had given the necessary orders for vigilance, and that, when they approached, he gave orders for weighing their anchors, and, when the fire-ships had passed, to resume their stations. But it was too late: the fears of a great number of his fleet had led to their dispersion, and several of them got among the shoals on the coast of Flanders. In short, it now became clear that their game was up; their retreating fleet was closely pursued, many of their galleons and other large ships attacked, taken or sunk, and the whole fleet in the greatest distress. One of the heaviest blows they received was the total failure of the Prince of Parma.

29th July. There was much fighting on this day on the Flemish coast; several of their ships, three of the largest, are stated in the "Narrative" to be the most damaged; they were now quite disabled and unserviceable, with most of their crew killed or wounded. [19] In the midst of their distressed situation, in which it appears from all the reports that they behaved most nobly, the Duke of Sidonia was desirous of turning, with the whole of the Armada that could be collected, against the enemy, in order still to maintain his position in the Channel; "but the pilots declared it to be impossible against the wind and tide, and that the Armada must proceed into the North Sea, or it would be driven on the shoals. It thus became unavoidable to quit the Channel; almost all the ships of the Armada, which had been relied upon, were now in a very bad condition, and unable to make resistance, both from the effects of the action they had sustained, and from the want of shot for the use of their guns." [20]

30th July. On the 30th the Lord High Admiral was still in pursuit of the flying Armada; but perceiving the ships drifting toward the shoals of Zealand, he did not think proper to press them. At this time "the pilots on board the flag-ship, who were best acquainted with the coast, declared to the Duke that it was impossible to save a single vessel of the whole Armada; but with the north-west wind, then blowing, the whole must inevitably go upon the shoals on the coast of Zealand; and that God only could prevent it. In this hopeless situation, without any human means to escape, and when the Armada was only in six fathoms and a half, it pleased God to change the wind to west-south-west, and the Armada was enabled to make way to the northward, without the loss of a ship." [21] In this miserable situation, the Duke called a council of the Admirals and superior officers, and put to them the question, "Whether it were most expedient to go back into the English Channel, or to return by the North Sea to Spain, since there were no advices from the Duke

146

of Parma of his being able shortly to come out. All the members agreed that they ought to go back into the Channel, if the weather allowed them to do so; but if not, that, yielding to the weather, they should return by the North Sea to Spain; considering that the Armada was in want of all the most necessary articles, and that those ships, which had hitherto withstood the enemy, were now disabled." [22]

31st July. "The Armada continued its course with the wind fresh from the south-west, and much sea; and the enemy's fleet followed us." [23] This day Drake addressed a letter to be submitted to the Queen, claiming Don Pedro de Valdez, and some others, as his prisoners; and doubts not but that ere long they will so handle the matter with the Duke of Sidonia, as he shall wish himself at St. Marie Port among his orange-trees.

31st July, 1588.

SIR FRANCIS DRAKE TO LORD WALSINGHAM.

MOST HONORABLE,

I AM comaunded to send these presoners ashore by my Lord Admerall, which had, ere this, byne long done, but that I thowght ther being here myght have done something, which is not thowght meett now.

Lett me beseche your Honor that they may be presented unto her Majestic, either by your honor, or my honorable good Lord, my Lord Chancellor, or both of you. The one, Don Pedro, is a man of greate estymacyon with the King of Spayne, and thowght next in this armye to the Duke of Sedonya. If they shoulde be geven from me unto any other, it would be som gref to my friends. Yf her Majestic will have them, God defend but I shoulde thinck it happye.

We have the armey of Spayne before us, and mynd with the Grace of God to wressell a poull with hym.

Ther was never any thing pleased me better than the seeing the enemey flying with a Sotherly wynd to the Northwards. God grant you have a good eye to the Duke of Parma, for with the Grace of God, yf we live, I dowbt it not, but ere it be long so to handell the matter with the Duke of Sedonya, as he shall wish hymselff at Saint Marie Port among his orynge trees.

God gyve us grace to depend upon him, so shall we not dowbt victory; for our cawse is good.

Humbly taking my leave, this last of July, 1588.

Your Honor's faythfully
to be commanded ever,

FRA: DRAKE.

To the Most Hon.
Sir Fras. Walsingham, knight, &c.

P.S. I crave pardon of your Honor for my haste, for that I had to watch this last nyght uppon the enemey.

Your's ever
FRA: DRAKE. [24]

To the Most Honorable
Sir Fras. Walsingham.
With speed. -

On the 1st August is a letter addressed by Lord Henry Seymour to the Queen, in which he says,

1st August, 1588.

LORD SEYMOUR TO HER MAJESTY.
[Extract.]

The 29th of the sayd month, being resolved, the day before, my Lord Admiral should gyve the first charge, Sir Francis Drake the next, and myself the third, yt fell out, that the galliass distressed altered my Lord's former determination, as I suppose, by prosecuting the destruction of her, which was done within one ower after.

In the meane time, Sir Francis Drake gave the first charge uppon the Spanish Admiral, being accompaned with the Triumph, the Victory, and others.

Myself, with the Vanguard, the Antelop, and others, charged upon sayle being somewhat broken and distressed; 3 of their great shipps, among which my ship shot one of them through 6 times, being within less than musket shot. After the long fight, which continued almost 6 owers, and ended, between 4 and 5, in the afternoon, until Tuesday, at 7 in the evening, we continued by them; and your Majty's 8 fleet followed the Spaniards along the Channel, until we came athwart the Brill, where I was commanded by my Lord Admiral, with your Majesties fleete under my charge, to returne back, for the defense of your Majestys coasts, if anything be attempted by the Duke of Parma; and therein have obeyed his Lordship, much against my will, expecting your Majestys further pleasure. [25]

2nd August. The Armada continued their course, and the English followed at a distance. "On the 2nd August," the "Spanish Narrative" says, "the enemy's fleet still followed the Armada in the morning, but they turned towards the coast of England, and we lost sight of them." He then says, "we continued our course until we got through the Channel of the Sea of Norway; not being possible to return to the English Channel, though it has been our desire to do so to the present day, the 20th August (the 10th by our reckoning), on which day, having doubled the Islands of Scotland, we are steering for Spain with the wind east-north-east." [26]

And so concludes the Diary.

On the 7th August, Lord Howard writes to Sir F. Walsingham, giving his opinion as to the course taken by the Armada.

August 7th, 1588.

LORD C. HOWARD TO SIR F. WALSINGHAM.

SIR,

IN our laste feighte with the enemye, before Gravelinge, the 29th of Julie, we sonke three of their ships, and made some to go neare with the shore, soe leake, as they were not able to live at sea. After that feighte, notwithstanding that our powder and shot was wel neare all spente, we set on a brag countenance and gave them chase, as though we had wanted nothinge, untill we had cleared our owne coaste, and som parte of Scotland of them; and then, as well to refreshe our ships with victuals whereof moste stoode in wonderful neede, as alsoe in respecte of our want of powder and shot, we made for the Frith, and sente certaine pinesses to dog the fleete untill they sholde be paste the Isles of Scotlande which I verelie beleave, they are loste at theire stearnes, or this. We are pers waded that they eather are paste aboute Irelande, and so dooe what they can to recover theire owne coaste, oneless that they are gon for some parte of Denmarke. I have herewith sent unto you a breife abstraete of such accidents as have happened, which hereafter at better leisure I will explaine by more particular relations. In the meane tyme I bid you hartelie farrewell.

From aboarde the Ark, the 7th of Auguste, 1588.

Your verie lovinge friende

C. HOWARD.

The Right Honorable
Sir Fra. Walsingham, knight.

Good Mr. Secretarie, lett not Her Majestic be too haste in desolvying her forses by sea and land: and I pray you send me with speed what advertysements you have of Dunkerk, for I long to dow some exployt on their shippinge. If the Dukes forses be retyred into the land I dowt not but to dow good. I must thank your favourable yousing of my brother Hoby. He telleth me how forwarde you weer to forder all thyngs for our wants. I wold some weer of your mynde: If we had had that wych had been soe, England and her Majestie had had the gretest honor that ever any nasion had: but God be thanked it is well.

On the 8th August Drake also addresses a short letter to the Queen, on the same subject, and on the 10th a more detailed one to Sir F. Walsingham, stating the distressed state of the Spaniards, and his opinion that they have not so few as five thousand men less than when they first appeared off Plymouth.

8th August, 1588.

SIR FRANCIS DRAKE TO THE QUEEN.

THE absence of my Lord Admirall, most gratious Soveraigne, hath emboldened me to putt my penne to the paper. On Fridaye last, uppon good consideration, we lefte the army of Spaigne so farre to the northewarde, as they could neither recover England nr Scotlande; and within three daies after we were entertayned with a greate storme, considering the tyme of the yere; the which storme, in manye of our judgements, hath not a litle annoyed the enemie's armye.

If the wind hinder it not, I thinck they are forced to Denmark; and that for divers causes; certaine it is that manie of theire people were sicke, and not a fewe killed; ther shippes, sailes, ropes, and wasts, needeth greate reperations, for that they had all felte of your Majesties force.

If your Majestic thoughte it meete, it were [_____] amisse you sent presentlie to Denmark to understand the truth, and to deall with their king according to your Majesties great wisdome.

I have not written this whereby your Majestic should deminish any of your forces. Your Highnes' enemies are manie; yeat God hath, and will heare your Majestie's praier, putting your hand to the plough, for the defence of his truth, as youre Majestie hath begunne. God for his Christ's sak, blesse your sacred Majestie, now and ever.

Written aboard your Majestie's verie good shipp the Reveng, this 8th August, 1588.

Your Majestie's faithfullest vassall,

FRA. DRAKE. [27]

10th August, 1588.

SIR FRANCIS DRAKE TO SIR FRANCIS WALSINGHAM.

MOST HONORABLE,

THE armye of Spaigne I thincke certainlye to be putt either into Norwaye or Denmarke; ther are dyvers causes which moveth me so to thincke. The firste we understood by dyvers prisoners which we have taken, that jenerallye throwgh all ther hoole fleet ther was no on shipp free of sycke people. Secoundlie, their shipps, masts, sayles, and ropes were verve much decayed and spoyled by our greate shot. Thyrdlye, at Callys, by ffyer we forced them to cut manye of their cables, wherby they lost manye of their anckors, which of necessytye they muste seke to supplye. Further, yf they had had none of these former great causes of distrese, yet the wynds and storme with the wynde westerlye as yt was, hath forced them theither; and I asure myselfe that whensoever her Majestic shall here of their aryvall in anye of these coastes, that her Heighnes shall be advertised bothe of their greate distrese and of no smalle losse amongst them: for I asure your honor her Majestie's good shipps felt muche of that storme, and loste manye of their boats and pynaces, with some anckors and caibles; yet were we fayer by our own shoare, and the wynde ryght of the land; some amongst us wyll not lett to saye that they are in Scotland. I cannot thincke so, for that we had no wynd wherby they were able to recover anye parte of the mayne lande of Scotland, without yt were some of the out isles, which are no meet places to releve their so manye great wants. Nor waye, or the out isles of Scotlande, can releve them but with water and a ffew cowes, or bad beof, and some smalle quantitie of goats and henes, which ys to them as nothinge; and yet these bade relefes are to be had but in few places, and their roads daungerous. The onely thinge which ys to be lookt for ys. that if they should goe to the Kinge of Denmarke, and there have hys frendshipp and healpe for all their releifcs, non can better helpe their wants in all these partes tru-n he, for that he ys a Prynce of greate shippinge, and cane best supplye hys wants, which nowe the Duke of Medyna the Sedonya standeth in nede of, as great anckors, caibles, mastes, roopes, and vitualles, and what the Kinge of Spaigiio's whole crownes will doe, in cold counteryes, for maryncrs and men, I leave to your good Lordship, which can best judge thereof. We lefte a pynace of her Majesties, the Advise, and a fyne carvell of my owen to attende the fleet of Spaigne when we lefte them; but what ys become of them, that great storme, or whether they maye be stayed in anye other country, as they maye, I knowe not. My power oppynion ys, that yt were moste meet to sende a good shipp, and some fyne barke, with some verie sufficient personne to dele effectualy from her Majestic with the Kinge of Denmarke, as he shall fynde the cause to requyer; and to send the trew report backe with all speede possyble, that they maye be the beter prevented: for no doubt, but that which they are able to dooe they wyll presentlye put yt in execusyon, the wynter wyll overtake them else in those partes. Yf they staye in the sounde thys wynter I hope manye of the

Spanyards wyll seke Spaigne by lande. The Prynce of Parma, I take him to be as a beare robbed of her whealpes; and, no doubte, but beinge so great a soldiour as he ys, that he will presentlye, if he maye, undertake some great matter, for hys reste wyll stande now thereuppon.

Yt ys for certayne that the Duke of Sedonia standeth somewhat jelious of hyrn, and the Spanyards begynne to hate hym, their honour being towcht so nere, manye of their lyves spent. I asure your Honor not so lyttle as fyve thowsande men lesse then when firste we sawe them nere Plymoth, dyvers of their shipps soncke and taken, and they have nothinge to saye for themselves in excuse but that they came to the place apoynted which was at Callys, and there stayed the Duke of Parma's commynge above 24 howers, yea, and untyll they were fyred thence. So this ys my power conclusyon, if we maye recover near Dunkerke this nyght or to morrowe mornynge, so as their power may see us retorned from the chase, and readye to encounter them yf they once sallye, that the next newes you shall here will be the one to mutenye againste the other; which, when yt shall come to passe, or whether they mutenye or no, let us all, with one consent, bothe hygh and looe, magnyfye and prayse our most gratious and mercyful God for hys infynyt and unspeackable goodnes towards us; which I protest to your good Lordship that my belefe ys that our most gratious Soveraigne, her power subjects, and the Church of God, hath opened the heavens in dyvers places, and perced the eares of our most mercyfull Father; unto whome, in Christe Jesus, be all honor and glorye, so be yt. Amen, Amen.

"Wrytten with much haste, for that we are readye to sett sayle to prevent the Duke of Parma, this southerlye wynde, yf yt please God, for trewlye my power oppynion ys that we should have a greate eye unto hym.

From her Majestic 's verye good shipp the Eevenge, the 10th of Auguste, 1588.
Your Honor's faythfully to be
Commanded always,

FRA. DRAKE.

To the Righte Honorable
Sir Francis Walsingham, knight.

P.S. For that we wer very neere to sett saile, I most humbly beseech your Honor to pardon my pen, for that I am forced to writ the very copy of that letter which I have sent to my Lord Chanceller. Sence the writteng hereof I have spoken with an Ynglishman, which cam from Dunckerck yesterday, who sayeth, uppon his lyfe ther is no feare of the flett; yeat would I willinglye see it.
Your Honour's ever,

FRA. DRAKE. [28]

The next letter, of the 11th of August, seems to have been written for no other purpose than to certify to the Queen, that the Lord High Admiral has bravely done his duty, and has become a very apt scholar; it would appear that it was written at the desire of Lord Charles.

11th August, 1588.

SIR FRANCIS DRAKE TO SIR F. WALSINGHAM.

MOST HONORABLE,

THE soden sending for of my very good Lord, my Lord Admerall, hath cawsed me to screbell these fewe lynes, fyrst, most humbly beseching your honor to delyver this letter unto her Majestic as a testyfycatyon of my Lord Admerall's most honorable usage of me in this accyon, wher it hath pleased his good Lordship to except of that which I have somtymes spoken, and commended that lettell servis which I was abell, much better then ether of them bothe I was abell to deserve, - wherein yf I have not performed as much as was lowked for, yeat I perswade my self his good Lordship will confesse I have byne dutiffull. Towching any other cawsses that ether hath byne done, or is to be done, lett me pray pardon of your honor, for I assure your Honor that my Lord Admerall hath so suffycyently instructed hymself dayly, as I faythfully beleve his good Lordship will throwghly satisfye her Majestic and your Honor what is now best to be done; thus humbly takyng my leave, I besech God to bless the work of her Majestie's hands allways. Written abourd her Majestie's good ship the Reveng, at mydnyght, this 11th August, 1588.

Your Honor's faythfully
to be comanded,
FRA. DRAKE. [29]

To the Right Honorable
Sir Francis Walsingham, knight.

[1] Tytler's Raleigh, Edin. edit., 1835.
[2] Camden.
[3] "A Narrative of the Voyages of the Royal Armada, from the Port of Corunna, under the command of the Duke of Medina Sidonia, with an account of the events which took place during the said voyage." This manuscript, in the Spanish language, was sent to a gentleman of the Admiralty, from the archives of Madrid, after the conclusion of the revolutionary war. It is evidently a journal kept by an officer of the Duke of Medina's flag-ship, and it may safely be pronounced a modest and honest narrative.
[4] MS. State Paper Office.
[5] MS. State Paper Office. Many Letters of Lord Howard and Sir Francis Drake are so tattered, and the writing so obliterated and in parts so illegible, that it is impossible to follow the meaning.
[6] MS. State Paper Office.
[7] Spanish MS, Narrative.
[8] Speed's Historie of Create Britaine.
[9] Harleian Miscellany.
[10] Spanish MS. Narrative.
[11] Camden - Lediard.
[12] Spanish Narrative.
[13] Camden.
[14] Spanish MS. Narrative.
[15] Spanish MS. Narrative.
[16] Idem.
[17] Spanish MS. Narrative.
[18] MS. State-Paper Office.
[19] Spanish MS. Narrative.
[20] Ibid.
[21] Spanish MS. Narrative.
[22] Idem.
[23] Idem.
[24] MS. State-Paper Office.
[25] MS. State-Paper Office.
[26] Spanish MS. Narrative.
[27] MS. State-Paper Office.
[28] MS. State-Paper Office.
[29] MS. State-Paper Office

Chapter Eight - The Spanish Armada, Called The Invincible, 1588. *Part Third.*

The disasters and distress of the Armada in its passage along the western coast of Ireland were most deplorable. The loss of officers and men by shipwreck and sickness, and the destruction of their ships, exceeded in a great degree all their misfortunes and discomfiture in the English Channel and the North Sea. By an account taken apparently with great care, after a minute examination of various parties in different parts of the coast of Ireland, it appears that : exclusive of those who were slain in fight, arid died of sickness and famine.

		Ships.	Men.
On the west coast of Ireland there were wrecked and destroyed		17	5394
In the British Channel and the North Sea it was estimated		15	4791
	Total	32	10,185

But it is said, apparently on good authority, that the utmost number of ships that reached the Spanish ports did not exceed sixty, and these generally in a very shattered condition. Stow makes the loss much greater; and Harris and Hakluyt say: "Of one hundred and four and thirty sail, that came out of Lisbon, only three and fifty returned to Spain. Of the four galiasses of Naples, but one; the like of the four largest galleons of Portugal; of the one and ninety galleons and great hulks, from divers provinces, only three and thirty returned. In a word, they lost eighty-one ships in this expedition, and upwards of thirteen thousand five hundred soldiers." [1]

It may easily be conceived how severe the shock must have been to Philip, on receiving the melancholy intelligence of the defeat and disasters of his *Invincible* Armada; and, with it, the destruction of those delusive hopes he had been led to entertain of the conquest of England, and the extirpation of her heretical church. He is said, however, to have borne his disappointment like a true Christian, by humbling himself on his knees, and returning thanks to God that it was no worse. He could not, however, overlook the conduct of those, who had caused his orders for the fleet to be disregarded, the Duke of Medina Sidonia in particular, against whom his anger was so much excited - that he gave orders he should never again appear at court; but the duchess, who was a beautiful lady, and a great favourite with the king, prevailed on his Majesty to rescind the order, and again to receive him into favour. As for Don Diego de Valdez, who was the person to mislead the Duke, he was sentenced to be imprisoned in the castle of Saint Andrea, where Sir William Monson says, "He was never seen nor heard of after, as was told me by his page, who was my fellow prisoner at Lisbon." The other de Valdez, (Don Pedro) remained a prisoner in England between two and three years, and was only released on a ransom of about 3000*l*.

153

But how different was the conduct of the conclave of the Vatican from that of the King! His Holiness the Pope, the cardinals and priests, monks, and Jesuits, were exasperated beyond bounds, not perhaps so much at the defeat of the Armada, which they had pronounced Invincible, as the falsification of their sinister prophecies regarding England, and the detection of the lies which they had caused to be circulated throughout Europe.

The conduct of one person, however, was utterly unintelligible. The defeat of the Armada was known in Paris immediately after the dispersion of the fleet by the fire-ships off Calais; yet after it was so known, Mendoza, the late ambassador to London, kept his printing-press at work to disseminate lies against the Queen, the Lord High Admiral, and Sir Francis Drake. He was admonished by one of his own friends, one of the same religious persuasion with himself, of the impropriety and impolicy of his conduct. "I marvel, good Sir," (he says,) "to see a man of so noble a lineage, and no less endued with gifts of nature than others, should have your ears so opened to hear the rumours and lies which the scoffing arid gibing flatterers do write you; and I wonder not so much in that you credit them, as at the speed wherewith your honour doth write them. Your honour writeth to Spain that it is a matter most true that the Lord High Admiral was come, running away with twenty-five or twenty-six ships, unto London, and that he had lost his flag-ship; and that Drake was taken prisoner; and that this was written for a matter most certain by persons of credit from London." [2]

Though Drake very rarely gave himself the trouble to answer personal abuse, yet, on the present occasion, his anger got the better of his usual habit, and he published a letter, which proves that he was no less able to vanquish a libeller with his pen than an enemy with his sword. But let Stow introduce this admirable letter of Drake:-

"But however coolly Philip might take the disastrous account of his Armada, his ambassador in France, Don Bernardin Mendoza, and his tool, one Capella, were industrious enough to spread false reports in print, claiming a victory for Spain. So blindly did his impudence and indignation carry him, that he dispersed his lies in French, Italian, and Spanish, pretending he had received advices from London, that the Queen's High Admiral had been taken by the Spanish Admiral, and that he saved himself in a boat, and that Drake was either taken or slain; that the Catholics, perceiving her navy to be spoiled, had made a mutiny, which induced the Queen to take the field in person, and that it is affirmed, as true, that no ship nor boat of the Spaniards had been carried into England, except the ship of Don Pedro de Valdez." [3]

Mendoza was, in fact, known to be the regular channel for the circulation of falsehoods throughout Europe. "This fabulous gazette of Don Bernardin was reprinted in England, and exposed under the title of 'A pack of Spanish Lies,' sent abroad into the world, translated out of the original, and now ripp'd up, unfolded, and, by just examination, condemned, as containing false, corrupt, and detestable wares, worthy to be damn'd and burnt." [4]

"It is not easy," (continues Stow,) "to conceive that a man in the high station of Ambassador should be the means of circulating through the Continent of Europe these base lies which he so well knew to be such. But they drew from Drake a letter full of truth, and with the spirit of honest indignation completely refuted the falsehoods of the swaggering Spaniard." [5]

"They were not ashamed," says Drake, "to publish in sundry languages in print, great victories in words, which they pretended to have obtained against this realm, and spread the same in a most false sort over all parts of France, Italy, and elsewhere; when, shortly after, it was happily manifested in very deed to all nations, how their navy, which they termed invincible, consisting of one hundred and forty sail of ships, not only of their own kingdom, but strengthened with the greatest Argosies, Portugal carracks, Florentines, and large hulks of other countries, were, by thirty of Her Majesty's own ships of war, and a few of our merchants, by the wise, valiant, and advantageous conduct of the Lord Charles Howard, High Admiral of England, beaten and shuffled together even from the Lizard in Cornwall, first to Portland, where they shamefully left Don Pedro de Valdez, with his mighty ship; from Portland to Calais, where they lost Hugh de Moncado, with the galleys of which he was captain; and from Calais, driven with squibs from their anchors, were chased out of the sight of England round about Scotland and Ireland; where, for the sympathy of their religion, hoping to find succour and assistance, a great part of them were crushed against the rocks, and those other that landed, being very many in number, were, notwithstanding, broken, slain, and taken; and so sent from village to village, coupled in halters to be shipped into England, where Her Majesty, of her princely and invincible disposition disdaining to put them to death, and scorning either to retain, or entertain them, they were all sent back again to their countries to witness and recount the worthy achievement of their invincible and dreadful navy. Of which the number of soldiers, the fearful burthen of their ships, the commanders' names of every squadron, with all other, their magazines of provisions, were put in print, as an army and navy irresistible and disdaining prevention; with all which their great terrible ostentation they did not, in all their sailing round about England, so much as sink or take one ship, bark, pinnace, or cockboat of ours, or even burn so much as one sheepcote on this land." [6]

Whether we look upon this letter as a most favourable specimen of the talent of the writer displayed in its composition, or the truth and spirit in which he indignantly repudiates the calumnies of his and his country's enemies, it is most deservedly entitled to the encomiums which have been bestowed on it by persons eminently qualified to pronounce judgment.

"If the knowledge of a writer, with respect to the subject which employs his pen, ought to render his relation more credible; or if the quality of an author can add any weight to his productions, this will not fail of being esteemed as well as believed. To speak the truth plainly, there is not perhaps in our own, or in any other language, within so narrow a compass, so full, so perspicuous, and so spirited a relation of a transaction, glorious as this was, extant in any history. Indeed, what wonder, if the defeat of the Spaniards be as finely painted by the pen, as it was gallantly achieved by the sword, of Sir Francis Drake." [7]

A report was also published in England, perhaps no better founded than those of Spain, that the Spanish nobles and officers of the Armada had made a special division among themselves of all the noblemen's estates in England by their names, and had to a certain extent quartered the kingdom among themselves; and had decided that the rich merchants' houses in London, which were put into a register, should be given as plunder to the soldiers and sailors.

This will not appear the less credible when it is recollected that, in our days, a foe more inveterate than Philip of Spain, with means more formidable, and hatred more intense, threatened to invade our shores, whose insatiable myrmidons had partitioned out, precisely in the same way, the estates of the nobility and gentry of England as their spoil, and equally disappointed as were the Spanish heroes of their expected prey.

While the loss was so great, which the nobility and gentry of Spain had sustained by the destruction of so large a portion of the Armada, in the several conflicts that had taken place, that there was scarcely a family in Spain but went into mourning, England everywhere resounded with acclamations of joy, in which all the Protestant nations of Europe participated. Poets and painters employed their respective talents in giving celebrity to the joyful issue of the late contest. Among the former, the learned and pious Theodorus Beza, one of the first and most active champions of the Reformation, composed the following ode on the occasion.

> Straverat innumeris Hispanus Classibus aequor,
>   Regnis juncturus sceptra Britanna suis.
> Tanti hujus rogitas quae motûs causa? Superbos
>   Impulit Ambitio, vexit Avaritia.
> Quàm bene te, Ambitio, mersit vanissima ventus:
>   Et tumidae tumidos vos superastis aquae!
> Quàm bene Reptores orbis totîus Iberos
>   Mersit inexhausti justa vorago maris!
> At tu, cui venti, cui totum militat aequor,
>   Regina, O mundi totius una decūs:
> Sic regnare Deo perge, Ambitione remota,
>   Prodiga sic opibus perge juvare pios;
> Ut te Angli longùm, longùm Anglis ipsa fruaris,
>   Quàm dilecta Bonis, tam metuenda Malis.
>
> Spain's king with navies the sea bestrew'd
>   T'augment with English crown his Spanish sway.'
> Ask ye what caus'd this proud attempt? 'twas lewd
>   Ambition drove, and Av'rice led the way.

'Tis well: Ambition's windy puff lies drown'd
　　By winds; and swelling hearts by swelling waves.
'Tis well: those Spaniards who the world's vast round
　　Devour'd, devouring sea most justly craves:
But thou, O Queen, for whom winds, seas do war;
　　O thou sole glory of this world's wide mass;
So reign to God, still from ambition far,
　　So still with bounteous aids the good embrace,
That thou do England, long, long may England thee enjoy;
Thou terrour of all bad, thou every good man's joy.

Nor was the Queen backward in acknowledging, in the most public and solemn manner, her gratitude to Almighty God for the signal victory she had gained, by his providence, over an enemy that had threatened destruction to the whole kingdom, to the established religion, and to herself personally.

"At a council held at Greenwich the third of November, 1588, at which all the great officers of state were present, a letter to the Archbishop of Canterbury, lettinge his lordship to understande that Her Majestie's expresse pleasure and comandment was, that order should be given by his Lordship in all the dioceses under his Lordship's province, to the severall bishoppes, curates, and mynisters, to appoint some speciall daye wherein all the realme might concur in givinge publique and generall thanckes unto God with all devocion and inward affection of hearte and humblenesse, for his gratyous favor extended towardes us in our deliverance and defence, in the wonderfull overthrow and destruction showed by his mightie hand on our malytious enemyes the Spanyardes, whoe had thought to invade and make a conquest of the real me.

"The lyke letter wrytten unto the deane and chapter of the byshoprick of Yorke to take the same order within the Dyocese of that B: as was in all points specyfied in the former letter." [8]

The Queen also directed a public and solemn thanksgiving to be made at the metropolitan church of St. Paul, to which all the trophies taken from the enemy were carried in procession, and deposited in the church; she then applied herself to the distribution of rewards to the Lord High Admiral and to the officers and seamen of the fleet for their gallant behaviour.

Several medals were struck in England in memory of the glorious defeat of the Armada. One in particular was intended solely in honour of the Queen; it represented ships issuing flames, and proceeding towards a fleet making off in great hurry and confusion, with the inscription *Dux faemina facti;* alluding to the circumstance, generally believed at the time, that Elizabeth, on hearing that the Armada had anchored before Calais, threw out the hint to Lord Charles Howard of the expediency of sending a few fire-ships among them. There is no direct acknowledgment in writing from the Lord Admiral, but in a letter alluding to the success of the measure, he says, "the bearer came in good time on board this ship, and brings with him as good knowledge as we could wish." Another medal representing a flying fleet had this inscription, *venit, vidit, fugit.*" The Zealanders had several medals struck: one, the Spanish fleet scattered in confusion, with the motto, "*Impius fugit, nemine sequente.*"

Among the numerous epigrams was the following –

In classem Hispaniam
misere dispersam
Epigramma.
Praeda licet Mundus non sit satis ampla Philippo,
Ampla satis Mundo praeda Philippus erit.

Tho'. Moravius Scotus.

Although the total failure of any assistance from the Duke of Parma, who was not only wholly unprovided, but apparently indisposed to act in concert with Spain; and the dispersion, and flight, and destitute state of the Spanish fleet, might have removed all apprehension of a renewal of hostilities from any quarter; yet it will appear from the several letters of the Lord High Admiral and Sir Francis Drake that they were very desirous of keeping their fleet together. That which follows, being first in date, is of a different character - from Lord Henry Seymour to Sir Francis Walsingham this officer signifying his desire to be superseded, because, he says, he is envied, being a man not suitable to them, and therefore, his actions and services will be in vain; besides that his summer ship will not stand the Irish or Spanish seas.

19th Aug. 1588.

LORD HENRY SEYMOUR TO SIR FRANCIS WALSINGHAM.

SIR,

I SHALL be glade to doe her Majestic all the service I can, which in duty I am bounde as otherwise for my cuntrye. I fynde my Lord Admirall doth repayre to these quarters, as I gather to this ende, to seeke the Spanyards whome when he shall fynde I wyshe him no better advantage then he had uppon our last conflict with them. But I hardly dowbt the metinge of them this yere, and for my owne parte desire to be spared att home for divers respects which hereafter I may unfolde.

I knowe I am envied, beinge a man not sutable with them, and therfore my actions and servises shall be in vayne,besydes my Sommer shippe,always ordeyned for the narowe seas, will never be able to goe thoroughe with the Northern, Irishe, or Spanyshe seas, withowte great harme and spoyle of our own people by sicknes. I have hetherto (*invita Minerva*) mayntayned my honor and creditt in all my servises as best becometh me. I wolde be loath nowe to stande *ad arbitrium Judicis,* and thereafter do praye you to respect your good devoted frynd, who hath many weighty irons of his owne to looke unto, and so do comytt you to God. From aborde the Raynbowe the 19 of August, 1588.

Your very loving,

Assured frend, H. SEYMOUR.

(Postcript.) I shall be enforced to send awaye my cosin Knevet and his company tomorowe to London by cause of their short victualls as other lacks which must be supplyed yf the servyse be any more commanded.

To the ryght Honerable
    Sir Fras. Walsingham. [9]

The next letter from Lord Effingham to the Queen relates to a disease that had broken out in the fleet. And on the same day, 22nd August, he writes to Sir Francis Walsingham, in which he alludes to a report he has received from Sir E. Norris, that the Spanish fleet is said to be returning, and requests that ships and mariners may be sent from London forthwith. A third letter of the same date, addressed to the same, contains a detail of all their wants, and, among others, ships and mariners, and calls out "haste, haste, poaste haste." This letter is dated from Dover.

22 Aug. 1588.

LORD EFFINGHAM TO THE QUEEN.

MY MOST GRASIOUS SOFEREN,

THE graet goodnes of your Majestic towards me, that hathe so lyttell desarved, dowthe make me in case that I know not how to wryght to your Majestic how muche I am bound to you for your infynyte goodueses, nor chann be ancered by any wayse but with the spend of my blud and lyfe in your Majestie's sarvis, wyche I wyll be as redy and as wyllyng to dow as ever cretur that lyved was for ther pry nee.

My most grasious Ladie, with graet gryfe I must wryght unto you in what state I rynd your flyte in heer. The infecsion is growne verry graet, and in many shypse, and now verry dangerous; and those that comme in freshe are sonest infected: they sicken the on day and dy the next: it is a thynge that ever folloethe such graet sarvyses, andjl dowt not but with good care and Godse goodnes, wyche dowthe alwayse bles your Majestic and yourse, it wyll quenche agayne. The course that we heer thynk meet to be kepte, bothe for the sarvis as also for the safte of your Majestie's pepell, we have wryghten at large unto my lords of your Majestie's Pryvy Councell, to informe your Majestic, and hffve also sent this berrer, Mr. Tho. Fenor, who is bothe wyse and chann informe your Majestic how all things standethe heer. And because it requyerethe sped and resolusion of your Majestic, I dow leve to trowble your Majestic any farder. Preyinge to the Almyghtie God to make your Majestic to lyve mor hapyer dayse then ever cretur that lyved on the erthe. From Dover, the 22 of August.

Your Majestie's most bound, most
faythfull and obedient sarvant, C. HOWARD.

Evne as I had wryghten thus muche, Mr. E. Noreys chame, woose advertysment dowth altter the case muche.

To the Queen's most Excelent Majestie. [10]

22nd Aug., 1588.

LORD EFFINGHAM TO SIR FRANCIS WALSINGHAM.

SIR,

159

BEINGE aboute to write unto you of the mortalitie and sicknes in oure fleete, and divers other matters, I receaved intelligence bye this gentleman, Sir Edward Noris, of the returne of the Spanishe fleete; wherefore, neglectinge all things eles, I bend myself wholie unto suche things as cheeflie concearne the service, and refer the particuler relatione of the same advertismente unto himself, prayinge you with all possible speede to send downe all the shippinge and rnaryners from London that you can, and that with all speede. Besides, the Rowebucke is not yet come, wherby we misse that pouder and shot in her; therfore I praie you that we maie have supplie of all such things in that great este quantitie you can, and soe in greateste haste I bid you hartelie farewell. From Dover the 22 of Auguste, 1588.

Your verie lovinge freind, C. HOWARD.

Postscript. Sir, there is here noe provisione of fireworks, nor boats, not anie thinge elles, for they relie so uppon my Lord Cobham, that without his warrant they will doe nothinge, for soe Mr. Barry sent me worde.

To the right honourable, my verie
   lovinge freinde, Sir Francis Walsingham, [11]
     knight, &c. *Haste, haste, haste poaste, haste.*

22nd Aug. 1588.

LORD EFFINGHAM TO SIR FRANCIS WALSINGHAM.

SIR,
THE absence of the Rowebucke dothe hinder us wonderfullie for lacke of the pouder in her. Mr. Barrie is sicke, and there is neather fireworks nor boats readie here againste anie service if the enemy hold anker anywhere; therefore, eather my Lord Cobham muste com downe himself, or send such as hathe authoritie to provide us of such necessarie things for service. We wante pitch and tarr here; it were good that some were sente to Sandwiche. I praie you send me word whether it was not appoynted that a hunderethe saile of ships shold be kep & retained in her Majestie's service by Sir Francis Drake and Mr. Hawkynse when they were sent downe before me; and I bid you moste hartelie farewell. From Dover, the 22 of Auguste, 1588.

Your lovinge and assured freind, C. HOWARD.

SIR,
I DOW assur you I dow not see that we are yet [qy. safe [12]] heer tell they of London come agayne; above 60 saylse, graet and small; and we ar very ill maned. I pray let maryners be sent away with all expedysion. I wold my counsell had taken plase that the forses by land had byne kepte together tell the full of .the mone (moon) had byne paste.

To the right honorable, my verie lovinge freind,
   Sir Francis Walsingham,
     knight, &c, *Haste, haste*
       poaste, haste, haste. [13]

On the 27th August, the Lord High Admiral and Drake sent what may be termed a joint letter to Sir Francis Walsingham, by which it appears he had expressed to them the desire of her Majesty that they should use means of intercepting the King of Spain's treasure coming from the Indies; and they reply that they are unable to select any ship then with them in anywise able to be sent on such a voyage; and as to keeping the matter secret, that they represent as quite impossible. The Lord High Admiral complains most grievously of the state of his finances, and that he has drawn out of Sir Francis Drake's money he had from Don Pedro de Valdez's ship 3000 pistolets out of 25,300 in possession.

27th August, 1588.

LORD EFFINGHAM AND SIR FRANCIS DRAKE TO SIR FRANCIS WALSINGHAM.

SIR,

APONE your letter I sent presentlie for Sir F. Drake, and showed him the desier that heer Majestic had for the interceptyng of the king's tresur from the Indias, and so we considered of it, and nether of us fyndyng any shypse heer in the flyte anywayse able to goo such a voyage, befor they have byne aground, wych chanot be downe in any plase but at Chatham; and now that this spryng is so far past, it wyll be *fourteen dayse* befor they chan be grounded. And wher you wryght that I shuld make nobody aquaynted with it but Sir F. Drake, it is verry strange to me that anny body chan thynk that yf it wer that if the smalest barks weer to be sent out, but that the offysers must know it; for this is not as if a man wold send but over to the cost of France. I dare asure you Sir F. Drake, who is a man of jugment and aquaynted with it, wyll tell you what must be downe for such a journey. Belike it is thowght the ilands be but heer by; it is not thought how the yeer is spent. I thowght it good, therfore, to send with all sped Sir F. D. 3 althowghe he be not very well, to inform you ryghtly of all, and look what shall be then thowght meet. I wyll dow my indevor with all the powr I maye, for I protest before God I would gyve all that I have that it weer met withall, for that bio, after this he hath, wold mak him safe. Sir, for Sir Thos. Morgayne and the dischargyng of shypse I will deell with all when the spryng [14] is past, but befor I dare not venture; for them of London I dow not heer of them it (yet) but those that be with my cosyne Knivet. Sir, I send you heer inclosed *a note of the money* that Sir F. Drake had abourd Don Pedro. I did take now at my comyng downe 3000 pystolets, as I told you I wold, for by Jesus I had not three pounds lefte in the worlde, and had nor anythinge coulde geet mony in London. And I dow assur you my plat has gone befor, but I wyll repay it within ten days after my comyng home. I pray you let her Majestic know so; and by the Lord God of hevne I had not one crown mor, and had it not byne meer nesesite I wold not have touched one; but if I had not sum to have bestoed apon sum pour and myserable men I should have wyshed myselfe out of the worlde. Sir, let me not lyve longer then I shall be most wylling to dow all sarvys, and to take any paynse I chan for her Majestie's sarvis. I thynk Sir F. Drake wyll say I have lyttell rest, day or nyght. The Ark, in Dover Road, the 27 of August (1588).

Your most assured, C. HOWARD.

To my verie lovinge freinde,
    Mr. Secretaire Walsinghame, at the Courte.

(*Inclosure.*)

7,200
10,000
5,600
2,500

_____

25,300

FRA: DRAKE.

This I confess to have caryed abourd to my Lord Admerall, by his Lordship's commaundment, the 23d of August, 1588, three thousande pystolettes.

C. HOWARD.   FRA: DRAKE.

Taken out of the sum above written, by my Lord Admirall's knowledg, three thousande pystolettes. The 27th August, 1588.

FRA: DRAKE. [15]

In the course of the month of September the Queen's ships were paid off, and those of the merchant adventurers returned to their usual pursuits. One nobleman, the Earl of Cumberland, who served as volunteer on the approach of the Armada, an active and resolute man, signified a wish to follow up the recent success, and fit out an expedition against the Spaniard. The Queen was so much pleased with his gallant conduct, that she not only gave him a commission to pursue his intended expedition to the southern ports, which was dated the 4th October, but she also lent him the Golden Lion, of 500 tons, and 250 men, which had been commanded by Lord Thomas Howard. The remainder of his squadron was made up as usual by volunteer adventurers. But it is not intended to pursue the career of the numerous gallant actions of the earl in which he so nobly persevered, but to proceed in the narrative of Drake's public services, in which he was engaged at an early period of the ensuing year.

It is stated in Lediard's "Naval History of England" that ten sail of the Armada were cast away on the coast of Ireland, among which were one of the great galeasses and two Venetian ships, the Batta and Belangara; that those who escaped the shipwreck and reached the shore were all put to the sword, or perished by the hand of the executioner, the Lord Deputy fearing they should join with the rebels. By the following letter in the State Paper Office, this would appear not to be exactly the fact.

14th Sept. 1588.

To THE LORD DEPUTY OF IRELAND.

OUR VERY GOOD LORD,

IMEDATLY after the writing of or last letters to yo. Lp. we went wheare we hard the Spanyarde were, and mett them at St. John O'Dogherty is towne called Illagh. We sent unto them to know who they were, and what their intent was, or why they did invade any pte. of the Queene's Mata domynion, their aunswer was that they did sett foorth to invade England, and were pcell of the fleete wch was overthrown by her Mata navy, and that they were dryven tether by force of wether. Whereupon we (pceiving that they were in nombre above vjc men) did incamp that night wthin muskett shott of them, being in nombre not passing vijxx men [here in the hand-writing of Lord Burleigh is this note: 'A bold attempt of 140 against 600']; and the same nyght about midnyght did skirmish wth them for the space ii houres, and in that skyrmish did slay their lieutenant of the fealde and above xxty more beside the hurting of a great number of their men: so as in the next day (in skyrmishing wth them) they were forced to yeld themselves, and we lost but one soldior: nowe O'Donill and wee are come wth some of them to Dongainne, meaning to go with them wthout companies to yor Lp. And therefore we humbly besech yor honour to graunte warrt for victling of them, as the prysoners are very weake, and unable to travaile, we desire yor Lp. (yf you shall so thinke meete) to gy ve direcon for leveyings of horses and garrans to cary them to Dublin. The best of them seemeth to cary some kinde of maiesty , and hath ben governor of thirty thousand men this xxiiij years past; the rest of the prysoners are men of greate calling, and such as in or oppynion were not amysse to be questioned wthall. So we humbly take our leave. From Dongainne, the xiiij of September, 1588.

Your most humble,
RICH. HOVENDEN, HENRY HOVENDEN. [16]

The Lord Deputy of Ireland.
Haste.

[1] Hakluyt. - Lediard.
[2] Strype.
[3] Stow's Annals.
[4] Lord Somers' Tracts.
[5] Stow.
[6] Stow.
[7] From the Biographia Britannica.
[8] Council Register, H. M. Council Office.
[9] MS. State Paper Office.
[10] MS. State Paper Office.
[11] MS. State Paper Office.
[12] Here in the original a word is omitted.
[13] MS. State paper Office.
[14] Qy. Tides?
[15] MS. State Paper Office.
[16] MS. State Paper Office.

Chapter Nine - Expedition to the Groyne (Corunna), and Lisbon. 1589

Elizabeth was soon convinced that, in the present temper of the Roman Catholics of Spain, no peace was to be looked for with Philip on honourable terms; and that the honour and safety of the nation required the most vigorous measures to be pursued, without waiting for a second visit of another Armada, even though, like the late one, there should be little danger of its proving invincible; threatenings however were still held out, and preparations were understood to be making in her western ports, for the attempt; it was thought, therefore, by the Queen's advisers, that the wisest policy would be to show to Spain that England was as ready prepared to attack as she had been to defend.

But the statement of Camden places affairs at this period in a clear point of view.

"When the Queen had shewn this example of terror (the trial and condemnation of the Earl of Arundel) at home, to make herself equally feared abroad, and pursue the victory which Providence had given her over the Spaniards, conceiving it to be both more safe and honourable to attack the enemy than to stand an assault from them, she suffered a fleet to put to sea upon an expedition against Spain. This Sir John Norris and Sir Francis Drake did generously and frankly undertake, at their own and some other private men's charge, and with very little expense to the Queen's purse, except the fitting out of a few men of war; for, indeed, they were fully convinced that the power of Spain lay rather in common fancy and opinion, than in any real strength they were masters of. The agreement between them was this - that whatever prizes they took should be shared among them by a fair and equal dividend. But it happened that there came not in so many to this expedition as was expected.

"The States added some ships, although they were at present displeased with the English, because Wingfield, governor of Gertruydenburgh, and the English garrison of that place, had betrayed the town to the Spaniard. The present fleet was reckoned to consist of 11,000 soldiers and 1,500 sailors. Don Antonio, the bastard prior of Crato (a natural son of the royal family of Portugal), with a few Portuguese, joined them; for he, it seems, laying claim to the Crown of Portugal by a popular election (for by the laws of that kingdom bastards are not excluded), had made the English mighty promises, hoping, we may suppose, to recover the kingdom by the help of these forces, the revolt of the Portuguese from the Spaniard, and the assistance of Muley Hamet, King of Morocco." [1]

It may be mentioned here, that the petition of Don Antonio was favourably received by the Queen, who saw therein a double object; first, as affording a chance of rescuing Portugal out of the hands of her greatest enemy; and, in the second place, to afford an opportunity of showing to the Spaniard that she was in a condition to invade his territories at home, as well as to harass his dependencies abroad; and, moreover, such an expedition would afford the occasion of destroying any preparation that might be in progress for a second visit to the shores of Great Britain.

Drake was always ready, not only to obey but to anticipate the Queen's wishes; and, as soon as he received her commands to prepare an expedition, in conjunction with General Sir John Norris, for the object of which he was made acquainted, no time was lost in taking the necessary means for fitting out the ships to be employed. Of these the Queen is said to have furnished six, and about sixty thousand pounds in money; but the two Commanders, as already stated, with some other adventurers, proposed to defray the expense of it with little or no charge to her Majesty. The Dutch government, with Don Antonio, were willing to take an active part with the English, promising to bear a proportionate share of the expense; the contingent of the former being four Dutch companies of soldiers and six of their ships of war. The Queen contributed, according to Sir William Monson and others, the following ships of her navy, with their respective commanders:

Ships.	Naval Commanders.	Military Commanders.
The Revenge	Sir Francis Drake	Sir John Norris.
Dreadnought	Capt. Thos. Fenner	Sir Edward Norris.
Aid	Capt. Wm. Fenner	Sir Henry Norris.
Nonpareil	Capt. Sackville	Sir Roger Williams.
Foresight	Capt. Wm. Winter	Capt. Williams.
Swiftsure	Capt. Goring	

These ships, as before stated, were manned with 1,500 seamen; and in the fleet of merchant adventurers, to the amount of 80 sail, or, according to some, 140, including transports, to be engaged to convey the 11,000 soldiers.

No two commanders could have been chosen better qualified to conduct this expedition. Both were accomplished officers; Sir John Norris was a highly distinguished soldier, had seen much service on the continent and in Ireland, and held a chief command on the attempted invasion by the Spaniards; he also served under Coligny in the religious wars of France; and all the other officers were distinguished by their former services. But these mixed expeditions of ships of war and of traffic, so common in those days, how well soever conducted, were rarely successful; and the fitting out of the present one was not auspicious. It was detained a whole month at Plymouth; it was disappointed in its promised forces and equipments; of six hundred English horses; of seven old companies of the Low Countries; of four Dutch companies, besides other matters; and it suffered by the consumption and expense of provisions for a whole month laid wind-bound at Plymouth these were serious losses to the generals and the merchant adventurers; and many grievous complaints were received by the commanders. The following, for instance, is a specimen from some Dutch masters and owners of ships that had engaged as adventurers in the expedition.

1589.

To THE RIGHTE HONORABLE THE LORD NORRIS AND SIR FRANCIS DRAKE, knighte, Generalls in this present Viadge.

In moste humble wise sheweth unto your Honors your poore suppliants, the Maisters and parte owners of the shippes taken and broughte into this porte of Plimouth comming out of Holland, bounde for Rochell, Browadge, and other places in Fraunce. That whereas yt is your Honor's request and speciall commaundement that we togeither with our shippes and companie should voluntarilie and willinglie serve her Majestic and your Honors in this present viadge, wherein we fynde ourselves greatlie hindred and greived - First, that we thinke ourselves to be under the commaundement of the States of Holland, and not of England; and that according to the *entercourse made in the yeare* 1495 by Kinge Henrie the Fifte and the Duke of Burgundy, and si thence maynteyned by her Majestie's predecessors, and the Dukes, Governors of the United Provinces, that we mighte not be disturbed nor molested in anie of her Majestie's ports, but assisted towardes our viadges, according to the 15, 16, and 17 articles of the said entercourse; and, furthermore, we fynde our shippes full of soldiers, and *noe victall to susteyne* them for such a viadge as is pretended, not without other *divers disorders* & *injuries* which be daylie don and offered unto us and companie, not in maner as yf we were *freindes but meere enemies*, contrarie to all our expectacion. and are in continuall *feare to be worse* after our departure to sea. In consideracion whereof we moste humblie praye and beseech your Honors, yf in anie wise yt maye be that wee with our shippes and shippes companie may be releaced to procede our pretended viadge. Yf not that then yt mighte please your Honors that our persons and parte of our companie maye be releaced, for to retorne to our owne contrey, and we wolde praye the Lorde for your Honors prosperouse viadge, for that we will rather loose our shippes, then according to our expectacion and experiences we have of the seas, some theise 20, 30, 40, and some for 50 yeares continuance, - to committ ourselves to *the seas without victualls, or hope of provision, and soe famishe* there, with losse of shipp, goods, and lives, beseeching your Honors to pardon us of this our opynion, and graunte us the premisses, or anie parte thereof, that wee hereafter maye answere our endeavoures before God and the worlde and your Honors, and in so doing we shall be bounde to praye for your Honors prosperouse viadge as aforesaid.

This is the trew original. (Signed)   T. ASHLEY. [2]

This peticion was drawn by Lemon, and exhibited according to his direction.

The next complaint is from the General Sir John Norris (Norreys), calling most earnestly on Lord Burleigh for a supply of victuals, "beseeching that a present and undelayed order may be sent for mayntayninge our vittayls;" and strongly pointing out the fatal consequences if not complied with. It does not appear, however, that Lord Burleigh sent down any supply of money till the 26th April, being 18 days after the General's letter, when the Treasurer sent a messenger with £600, "sealed up in threescore bags," addressed to Mr. Darell, the agent victualler. The following is a copy of the General's somewhat indignant letter:-

8th April, 1589.

SIR J. NORREYS TO LORD BURGHLEY.
RIGHT HONERABLE AND MY VERY GOOD LORD,

ALTHOUGH we never receaved any favorable aunswer of any matter that was moved by us, were yt never so just or reasonable, but contraryly threatninges and chydynges; yet the zeale that we bear to her Majestie's servyce and the good of our cuntry maketh us not leave to importune your Lordship, humbly beesechyng the same that a present and undelayed order may be sent for mayntayninge of our vittayls whylest thys crosse wynd doth hould us in, eyther by letters to the Deputy Lyuetenants and Justices of Peace, or els to Mr. Darell, surveyor of the vittayls, to the end that our sea store may be spared as much as is possible; otherwyse yf the wynd contynewe agaynst us we are utterly unable to supply ourselves, and the viage breakyng we can not thynke what to do wyth the army: for upon faylynge of the viage every man wyll caule for pay from her Majestic, beynge levyed by her Hy: comyssion; and yf they have yt not the cuntry wyll be utterly spoyled, robberyes and outrages commytted in every place, the armes and furniture lost, besydes the dishonor of the matter. Wherfore we infynitely beseech your Lordship to procure us a speedy and convenient dispach for so wayghty a cause; and so restynge redy to doe your Lordship all servyce, I humbly take my leave. Plimouth, thys 8 Aprill, 1589.

Your Lordship's most redy to doe

all humble servyce, J. NORHEYS. [3]

To the Ryght Honerable my very good Lord the
Lord Burghley, Hygh Tresorer of Ingland.

The next is a remonstrance from Drake, and an earnest entreaty that money or a supply of victuals be immediately furnished. He tells the Lord High Treasurer of England that he "never wrote to him with so discontented a minde as he does now."

April, 1589.

SIR FRANCIS DRAKE TO THE LORD HIGH TREASURER.

RIGHTE HONORABLE AND MY VERIE GOOD LORDE,

I DID never write to your Lordship with so discontentede a minde as I doe now. The cause is (as it maie please your Lordship) in that it pleaseth God to staie our forces in harborough by contrarie windes; wherby our victualls have beene and doe dailie consume without doeinge anie service: which (if God favor us not with a tymelie winde) must needes be the onlie meanes that the accion will be dissolvede: We have used our best meanes as longe as we coulde to upuholde the service, as farre as our owne abilities, and the creditte of our freends could anie waie be stretchede to serve our turnes: butt for that the nombers of our men are so manie, and our dailie charge so greate by reason of our staie, we are no further able to continewe the same as we have donne. If this action beinge broughte to that perfection (as we are readie to take the first goode winde that shall blowe) should nowe be dissolved by reason of anie particular wantes, the dishonour therein must needes be great to her Majestic: The losse not a litle to us, and suche as are adventurers, and the clamour of the nombers which must be dischargede most intollerable: who must needes and will be satisfiede of their paie for the tyme of their service, at her Majesties hands, or ours; and ourselves no waie able to accomplishe it: Wherefore I have thought it my duetie to acquaint your Lordship herewith, for the consideracion of the greatnes of the cause: humblie beseechinge your Lordship to move to her Majestic herewith: that present order maie be sente the Leivetenants and Justices of the peace of the Sheires next adioyiiing, or to Mr. Darell: whome your Lordship maie depute as Commissioners in that behalf. That by the countrie adioyning, our presente necessitie maie be suppliede: where we might have sufficiente enoughe, if we had present monies to make satisfaccion accordinglie. Thus I humblie take my leave of your Lordship.

From Plymouthe, this (not dated) of Aprill, 1589.

Your Lordship's allwaies readie

to be commaundede

(signed) FRA: DRAKE. [4]

To the Ryght Honorable
  my verie good Lorde
    the Lord hiegh Treasorer
      of England.

The next letter from Sir Francis Drake conveys his satisfaction "that Her Majestic is pleased to releave us of some vittual;" but it alludes to a grievance which is stated to be "a very great trouble to us;" and that was the intention of the Earl of Essex joining them as a volunteer. This intention being made known to the Queen, she gave orders to the commanders of the expedition to find him out (for no one knew where he was), and to send him to Court. However they did not succeed in getting any intelligence of him previous to their sailing.

19 April, 1589.

SIR F. DRAKE TO THE LORD HIGH CHANCELLOR,

MOST HONORABLE AND MY ESPECIALL GOOD LORD,

FOR that we now understand that her Majestic is pleased to releve us with som vittuall, I thincke yf it shall so please your Lordship that Captayne Crosse will be a very meett man to be sent after us with the sam vittuall, for that we have aqwaynted hym throwghly with the particullers of the statt of our armey, and cann judge well wher to fynd us uppon the cost of Spayne uppon such advertisments as I have geven hym. This cawse of the Erll of Essexe hath been and is a very great truble unto us, for that we hyere contynewally that his Lordships abyding is uncertayne in any one partyculler place. We have sent bothe by sea and land and dow dayly exspecte to hyer from his Lordship.

Yf his Lordship be not gonn for the cost of France, we shall meett with hym very shortly, for that we have great hope of this fayer wether, when we shall dow our best endeavoures for the satisfyeing of her Majesties expresse commaundement in sending his Lordship to the court.

God geve us a good wynd as we hope well; that ther may be som pleasinger matter to writ unto your good Lordship. Humbly takyng my leave, this 19th of Aprell, 1589, from abourd her Majesties ship the Reveng.

Your good Lordships humbly
at commandment
(signed)   FRA: DRAKE. [5]

To the Right Honorable
  & my verye good Lord
    the Lord Hiegh Chauncellour
      of England.

At length the expedition put to sea, but the wind for two days continued cross, and many of the fleet, as might be expected from such a heterogeneous mass, were dispersed, and never again joined, it being supposed that the transports, with twenty-five companies on board, had left them, "either not beingable, or not willing, to double Ushant." [6] The number missing is said to have been nearly 3000, some having got into France, and some to England. The weather, however, soon moderated, and five days brought them into the

Bay of Corunna (corrupted into Groyne), where the ships anchored about a mile below the town.

At the entrance of the haven, Captain Fenner says, they burnt four ships of the King of Spain, one of them being the flag-ship of Don Martin de Recaldé, a Vice-Admiral in the Armada, and in her were taken 68 pieces of brass cannon. [7] This, however, appears to be a mistake. The "True Copy of Discourse" says that the galleon named San Juan, with some others, bent upon them and the companies as they passed to and fro the first night. [8] She was afterwards burnt. The next day they attacked the lower town on three sides, and carried it without much resistance, and found therein an immense quantity of wine and oil; and having preserved a sufficient supply of provisions for the fleet, they burned all the remainder. They took the governor, Don Juan de Luna, prisoner, with some other persons of note, and destroyed a large quantity of ammunition and stores which had been sent thither for the new expedition intended to be sent against England. About five hundred Spaniards are said to have been killed in the heat of the plunder. But several of the English lost their lives, less by the enemy than by their indulgence in the wine-cellars, by which great sickness was caused among the troops, and many died. The quantity of wine consumed, carried away, and destroyed, is said to have amounted to about 2000 pipes, collected for the use of the next Spanish expedition; and not only this, but money and other stores and provisions had been sent from Spain for the same purpose.

The Spaniards themselves set fire to a monstrous large ship which lay in the harbour, and which burnt for two days together, which was done to prevent her from falling into the hands of the invaders, and at the same time not without a malicious purpose; for before firing her, the Spaniards loaded her guns to such a degree that fourand-thirty of them burst. This was the galleon San Juan, one of the few which had escaped the general wreck of the Armada. The night previous, our troops had taken up their lodgings in the neighbouring villages, houses and wind-mills, and this ship, with two galleys and three smaller vessels, had fired upon their lodgings during the night. [9]

Preparations were now made for besieging the upper town. Near one of the gates was a convent of St. Domingo; the general ordered it to be occupied, and from the upper part of the building they fired into the town. On the following night it was intended to get possession of a long munition-house built upon the wall; but the Spaniards, suspecting the intention, set fire to it themselves. In the meantime a large fire broke out in the lower part of the town, which had it not been speedily got under by the General's precaution of pulling down the adjacent houses, all the provision-stores would have been consumed "to our wonderful hindrance." [10] By this time General Norris had taken a survey of the walls, which he found to be in most places based upon rock; one particular point, however, admitted of working a mine. After three days' labour it was deemed ready for springing; it failed. Two days after a second mine was sprung; the explosion brought down half the tower under which the mine had been made. The breach was practicable, and immediately assaulted; but on the men having gained the summit, the other half of the tower fell, and crushed about thirty of the assailants - Captain W. Winter says, the chief-engineer and 300 of his workmen. He also says that Captains Sydenham and Kersey were killed, and not fewer than 250 inferior officers and men. [11]

"Captain Sydenham," says Hakluyt, "was pittifully lost, who, having three or four large stones upon his lower extremities, was so wedged in, that neither he himself could stir, nor were the company about him able to release him, notwithstanding the next day he was still alive, with eight or ten men around him dead. These faithful soldiers had been exposed to the fire of the Spaniards, while performing this act of humanity so honourable to human nature." [12]

"The General having planted his ordnance, summoned the town by a drum, which was shot at; but immediately after a Spaniard was hanged, information being sent that he was the man who had shot at the drum; the Spaniards said they only wanted fair war, with promise on their part to observe it." [13]

A breach had been made in the convent garden wall, and some officers and men entered it with their pikes, but were opposed at the summits by the Spaniards, who had prepared all means of defence, and were encouraged, as Mr. Southey [14] says, by the masculine exertions of Maria Pita, the wife of an alferez, or ensign, who, "with a spirit which women have more often displayed in Spain than in any other country, snatched up sword and buckler, and took her stand among the foremost of the defendants; and so much was ascribed by the people to the effect of her example, that she was rewarded for this service with the full pay of an ensign for life, and the half-pay was settled upon her descendants in perpetuity." [15] And it is moreover stated, on the authority of Faria y Souza, "that this virago lost none of her courage at seeing her husband killed before her eyes, and that she wounded an English standard-bearer mortally with a lance."

So true is it, regarding female spirit in Spain, that Maria Pita, the Matron of Corunna, is but the prototype of Augustina, the Maid of Saragoza, who enspirited her countrymen at the siege of that place with such 'enduring courage, even after her lover was killed before her eyes. How the memory of the heroic deeds of this young maiden may still survive, among her countrymen, is best known to themselves; but her masculine and persevering efforts against the invaders of her country have been recorded in imperishable verse by one of the first English poets of the age: [16]

Ye who shall marvel when you hear her tale,
Oh! had you known her in her softer hour,
Marked her black eye that mocks her coal-black veil,
Heard her light, lively tones in lady's bower,
Seen her long locks that foil the painter's power,

Her fairy form, with more than female grace,
Scarce would you deem that Saragoza's tower
Beheld her smile in Danger's Gorgon-face,
Thin the closed ranks, and lead in Glory's fearful chace.
Her lover sinks - she sheds no ill-timed tear;
Her chief is slain - she fills his fatal post;
Her fellows flee - she checks their base career;
The foe retires - she heads the sallying host:
Who can appease like her a lover's ghost?
Who can avenge so well a leader's fall?
What maid retrieve when man's flush'd hope is lost?
Who hang so fiercely on the flying Gaul,
Foil'd by a woman's hand, before a batter'd wall?

"Yet," - how truly does the poet say -

"Yet are Spain's maids no race of Amazons." [17]

The breach in the wall no longer appearing practicable, the assault was not renewed, and the failure was so complete that the General determined to abandon an enterprise which he now considered hopeless. But to secure his embarkation, without being molested, he deemed it expedient to disperse a very large military force with which the Conde de Antrade was encamped, behind the Puente de Burgos, waiting there to be joined by the Conde de Altamira, in order that, with their united strength, they should advance for the relief of the town, and to cut off their retreat.

The following extract from a joint letter of Sir John Norris and Sir Francis Drake to the Privy Council will best describe their proceedings.

7th May, 1589.

EXTRACTED OUT OF A LETTER FROM SIR JOHN NORRIS AND SIR FRANCIS DRAKE TO THE COUNCIL.

Even as this letter was almost ended, certaine cumpanies of the Flemings being sent abroade on foraging browght in a prisoner whoe upon his lief assured us that theare weare 15,000 soldiers assembled and encamped verie strongelie at *Puente de Burgos* abowt 5 Englishe miles from us, under the conduct and commaundment of the Erles of Altamira and Andrada. Wheareuppon on Tuesday the 6th of this present, wee marched towardes them with 7000 soldiers, leaving the rest for the guard and siege of the towne, and encountringe with them, theie continued fighte the space of three quarters of an hower; and then we forced them to retire to the foote of a bridge, wheareon not above three could martche in ranke, and was abowt ten scoare in length, from whence (althowgh theie weare theare defended by some fortificacions and had the benefitt and succour of certaine howses, and other places adioining) theie weare followed with our shott and pikes, with such courage and fiercenes, as, after some fewe vollies on both sides, theie entred the bridge, wheare in the middest, with the pushe of the pike, forced to make retreate into their trenches to the further foote of the bridge wheare theie encamped which also (being pursued) theie forsooke and betooke themselves to flighte abandonninge their weapons, bagge and baggage, and loste about 1000 in skirmishe and pursuite.

Had wee had either horse on lande, or some companies of Irish kerne to have pursued them, theare had none of them escaped; which cannot be but a notable dishonour to the Kinge, and in our opinions noe small furtherance to the service intended: Wee lost not above 2 common soldiers and one of the corporalls of the feeld. Sir Edward Norris, whoe ledd the vanntgard, grevouslie hurt with a blowe on the head, and Captaine Fulford shott in the arme. Capteine George shott in the left eie. Captaine Hinde wounded in three places of the head, but noe danger of lief in annie of them.

Thus it hath pleased God to geve her Majestic the victorie which wee have great hope to pursue elsewheare with like success if wee maie be succored with such necessaries as are neadefull: if not, wee can but doe our endevours, and leave the rest to the consideracion of your Lordships, whome we humblie leave to the protection of the Almighty. From the Groine the 7th of Maye 1589. [18]

Captain Fenner enters into a few more particulars. "General Norris," he says, "with 1700 men attempted the bridge, but was driven back. A second time he entered with Sir Edward Norris, Colonel Sidney, and Captain Cooper, and succeeded in driving back the Spaniards, beating them out of their entrenchments, and continued slaying them in pursuit for more than a mile, in which affair from 1200 to 1300 Spaniards were supposed to be slain: three English captains were killed, Sir Edward Norris and Colonel Sidney wounded. This service ended, and no hope left of gaining the higher town, for want of powder in the fleet, the General gave orders for the companies to re-embark."

This account of Captain Fenner is a very imperfect one; the letters of General Norris and Admiral Sir F. Drake give more particulars; the "True Discourse" is ample in details, but too long to insert.

The last letter received from this place is from Sir Francis Drake to the Lord High Treasurer of England, dated the 8th May, the day following that of the joint letter.

8 May, 1589.

SIR F. DRAKE TO LORD BURGHLEY.

RIGHT HONORABLE AND MY VERIE GOOD LORDE,

THE 23th of the last monethe we fell with Ortingall in Gallizea, the winde blowinge verie muche easterlie. And the daie followinge we landede at the Groyne 7000 of our men: where we had attemptede the takinge of the Base Towne the same nighte, if extreame raine and verie fowle weather had not lettede us. The 25th we assaultede the Base Towne bothe by sea and lande, and tooke it with the onlie losse of 20 of our men, and 500 of the enemye. The windes have beene allwaies contrarie since our cominge here, blowinge verie muche with a greate sea and continewall showres of raine, which did somewhatt lett the service. We founde at our cominge thither fower greate shippes, makinge readie with all expedicion for a freshe Armado against Englande. Emongest which there

172

was the Gallion St. John, the Vize Admirall of the Kinge's last fleete, which is burnte, and the other three taken: we have taken of the enemies in this place, out of the shippes, and towne, verie neere 150 peices of ordinaunce: and have made spoile of manie great provisions in readines for this newe armye. To deferre the tyme, beinge staiede in by contrarie windes, wee layede batterie to the hiegher towne, findinge it to be stronglie defended, by reason of divers companies of old souldiers which were remayning there readie to goe fourth in this armye. The 5th of this monethe we tooke a souldier in the countrie: by whorae we understood howe the Governors of the countrie had assemblede by rowle 15,000 olde souldiers and men of the countrie which (as we since heare) are but 10,000. Being shortlie advertisede that they had entrenched themselves within 5 miles of us, we thought it meete, uppon consultacion had the next morning, to salley fourth with 7000 of our men: who understanding our forces to come nighe unto them resolved to fighte, where it pleaseth God to allott us the victorie, which is no litle quailing to the enemye. My opinion is that great happines is fallen to our Queene and countrie by our cominge hither, where we staie untill God sende us a fair winde. If there had been good reckoninge made at first of the necessitie of this service, we should not then have needed theise particular wants of victuall, cannon, & powder. The wante of the one maketh us to leave some services halfe donne; and the other to seeke meate to live: whereof if there be no speedie supplie made, it maie be the cause to hinder suche an action as I shall not live to see the like, to performe great matters at so convenient a tyme.

Thus I humblie take my leave of your good Lordship; from the Groine this 8th of Maye, 1539.

Your good Lordships humblie to be comaundede,   (Signed) FRA: DRAKE.
To the Right Honorable
   my verie goode Lorde the Lorde Burgheley
   L: hieghe Treasorer of England. [19]

Having plundered and burnt all the adjacent villages and the lower town, with the enemy's camp, and taken such ammunition, provisions, and plate they fell in with, they re-embarked the troops without any loss of men, and on the 10th made sail down the coast of Portugal, and were joined at sea by the Earl of Essex; with some ships laden with corn, which he brought with him into the fleet. He was accompanied by his brother Walter Devereux, Sir Roger Williams, Sir Philip Butler, and Sir Edward Wingfield.

"This young nobleman," as Camden says, "was supposed to be urged to join the expedition, partly from a thirst after glory, and partly from a hatred he bore to the Spaniards, and also from the generous motive of a compassionate feeling towards the exiled Don Antonio; whatever might have been his motives or ambition that made him quit the pleasures of a court, to try his fortune at sea and on the field of battle, he joined the expedition, without the Queen's leave or approbation." [20]

The Latin pamphlet above noticed, thus speaks of Essex: "Essex is considered by us as the child of Mars, descended from a heroic and warlike family, a youth of lofty and enlightened mind, a great favourite of the people, the nobility, and the Queen, with a resolution to suffer and undergo all dangers, and rather than not be present at so splendid an expedition, he preferred being a private soldier without any command than to remain at home in high favour with every one, surrounded by a herd of courtiers." [21]

Of this nobleman the True Copy of the Discourse says, "The Earle havinge put himself into the journey against the opinion of the world, and, as it seemed, to the hazard of his great fortune, though to the great advancement of his reputation, and as the honorable carriage of himself towards all men doth make him highly esteemed at home, so did his exceeding forwardness in all services make him to be wondered at amongst us. After his coming into the fleet, to the great rejoicing of us all, he demanded of the General, that he might always have the leading of the van-guard, which he readily yielded unto, as being desirous to satisfie him in all things, but especially in matters so much tending to his honour as this did." [22]

The expedition arrived in nine days at Peniche, about forty miles from Lisbon; and here the troops were disembarked with the loss of a boat and above twenty men in the surf. A party of two troops was placed under the command of Essex, one of which he left to protect the landing, and with the other advanced towards the town against some Spanish troops that came out to oppose him; "but not being proof against the push of the pike, they fled, and he entered the open town, without opposition, summoned the castle, which the commandant readily surrendered to Don Antonio, acknowledging him as his King." [23]

The troops being landed, Sir John Norris decided on proceeding at once by land, and Sir Francis Drake promised to meet them at Lisbon. Such a promise could only be conditional. It has been stated that when they were all marshalled and ready to march, Drake, "to make known the honourable desire he had of taking equal part in all fortune with them, stood upon the ascent of a hill by which the battalions marched, and, with a pleasing kindness, took his leave severally of the commanders of every regiment, wishing them happy success, with a constant promise that *if the weather did not hinder him,* he would meet them at Lisbon with the fleet." [24]

In the march to Lisbon, Don Antonio, being there in person, looked for the nobility and chiefs of the country to meet him, and submit themselves with offer of such forces as they might be able to raise for the assistance of their King; but none appeared except a company of poor peasants, without hose or shoes, and one gentleman, who presented him with a basket of cherries and plums. The troops, on their way, took the town of Torres Vedras, with little or no resistance, except a few skirmishes, in all of which the Spaniards had the worst of it; and on the 25th they came before Lisbon. [25]

In the course of the march a party of the enemy's horse hovered about the troops. Captain Yorke, who commanded the General's horse-company, willing to make trial of the valour of the enemy's cavalry, ordered a corporal with eight horses to charge through a party of forty, while himself with forty dashed at another party of about two hundred, who made way, and galloped off in disorder. [26]

"Divers of the men," says Captain Fenner, "fainted by the way with heat, and divers died for want of food, and many, who would otherwise have died, were saved by the Earl of Essex, who commanded all his stuff to be cast out of his carriages, and them to be filled with the sick men and gentlemen who had fainted." [27]

The suburbs of St. Katharine or Bonavista were taken without opposition, but the army was received with coldness and indifference, and not the least inclination was apparent on the part of the people to declare for, or to render any assistance to the Prince, none but some old folks and beggars calling out *Viva el Rey Don Antonio!* nor was there any intelligence whatever of the ships and men of which Antonio had been promised by the Emperor of Morocco. It was found too that the army was from day to day decreasing from sickness, that their provisions were also rapidly decreasing, and that they were wanting in cannon and ammunition; that they had not even a fieldpiece by which they could blow down one of the gates of Lisbon. It was not then known that a bag of gunpowder, attached to the gate, would effect that object.

On one of these occasions, not only did Essex pursue the Spaniards to the very gates of Lisbon, but was with difficulty prevented from rushing through in the thick of them, and would have fearlessly forced himself in, beyond a doubt, had not his friend Sir Roger Williams held him back by main force. On another occasion the Earl of Essex knocked at the gates of the city, wherein it was said there were not above 700 Spaniards to guard it.

But for an army marching into the interior of an enemy's country, and to the very gates of a large fortified city, without the common implements and ammunition of war, without even a field-piece, seems to have been a most extraordinary omission. Captain William Fenner, who calls the whole expedition, from first to last, "a miserable action," thus describes their position before Lisbon:

"The want of a single piece to make a breach or shoot against the gates prevented the English from taking it. - The want of match among the soldiers, and of powder for their muskets, forced them to retire, when the Spaniards would sally out, in the habits of Portuguese, crying *amigos,* and slay the sick in the rear of the army; disregarding their wants, sick and sound together. Three captains, the Provost Marshal and Lieutenant of Ordnance being mortally wounded, were left behind for want of carriage." [28] Sir William Monson ascribes the loss of Lisbon to the want of fieldpieces; for, he says, "the strength consisting in the castle, and we having only an army to countenance us, but no means for battery, we were the loss of the victory ourselves; for it was apparent, by the intelligence we received, if we had presented them with battery, they were resolved to parley, and so, by consequence, to yield, and this was the main and chief reason of the Portuguese excuse for not joining with us." [29]

The army, however, might easily have made themselves complete masters of the suburbs and obtained a rich booty, "rich enough," as Fenner says, "for two armies, if the soldiers might have had the liberty of plundering them. But the entreaty of Don Antonio, and the strict order of the General, on pain of death, and the hope of better pillage, had such effect, that things were left almost untouched, the churches unspoiled, the people unplundered, and the houses unburnt." [30]

It was, in fact, at the earnest request of Antonio that the army refrained from enriching themselves with the spoils of the suburbs; the abundance of pepper, cinnamon, nutmegs, cloves, mace, and every kind of spices were said to be not less in value than 300,000 crowns; household furniture, domestic utensils and plate, as much more. In the public stores were grain of different kinds, biscuits, wine, and all mariner of provisions, more than sufficient to feed the whole army for two or three months. To all these, and the royal and public granaries and military store-houses, with clothing and accoutrements, the Spaniards themselves set fire, lest they should fall into the hands of the English. "Had we marched through the countrie," says the True Discourse, "as enemies, our soldiers had been well supplied in all their wants; had we made enemies of the suburbs of Lisbon, we had been the richest armie that ever went out of England." [31]

Seeing there was nothing further to be done here, the army began its march by land to join Drake at Cascais. They were followed at a distance by a large body of troops, and when they found that the English were in reality on their retreat, it was announced to the General, by one of his scouts, that a certain Peter Henry de Guzman (who bears, in the Latin treatise, the title of Comes de Fontibus, in Spanish or Portuguese, Conde de Fuentes) had pitched his army not more than 2000 paces from the camp; that he had 6000 foot and 500 horse; and it had been ascertained that this great man had caused it, by words, letters, and pamphlets, to be scattered among the people, that the English army had been routed at Lisbon, and put to flight. Norris, highly indignant that such lies should be circulated, sent this person a letter at daylight, under his own hand, by a trumpet, informing him that with his little army he should be with him before noon to confute his falsehoods, not by words, but arms, if he would only wait for his advance at the time proposed, that a trial might be made whether an Englishman or a Spaniard should be the first to run away.

At the same time, arid by the same messenger, the Earl of Essex challenged him to single combat, or any other Spaniard of his rank; or, if he had no taste for it himself, ten Englishmen should try their hands with ten Spaniards. This gallant knight, however, not much relishing the proposals, either of Sir John Norris or the Earl of Essex, disappeared with the whole of his force in the middle of the night. The trumpet followed him nearly to Lisbon, but could get no answer to either of the two letters, except threatening to hang him for daring to bring such a message; but the general had written, on the back of the passport, that if any violence was offered to his messenger, he would hang the best prisoners that he had of theirs. [32]

Drake had, in the first instance, taken possession of the town of Cascais, the inhabitants having abandoned it on his landing; but on giving his assurance of protection and peaceable intentions, they returned, on condition, however, that they would acknowledge Antonio as their sovereign, and supply the fleet with provisions and necessaries; but the castle, held by a Spanish garrison, affected to hold out. Drake, however, soon made them surrender, and blew up a great portion of it. He seized sixty sail of ships belonging to the Hanse towns, which, in defiance of the Queen's prohibition, had arrived there laden with corn and all manner of naval stores, evidently designed towards the preparation of a Spanish fleet, meant to try its fortune a second time against England. In his passage to Cascais he had fallen in with and taken many ships carrying provisions and naval stores for Lisbon; some, of considerable burden, nearly empty, and evidently built as ships of war, so that it could not be doubted they were intended to form a part of the projected expedition.

The army, having reached Cascais, and everything being prepared, lost no time in re-embarking. A captain and his company had been left at Peniche, together with the sick, and certain vessels were sent to receive them on board; but the commandant, on receiving information of what had happened, embarked in such barks as were on the spot, and with such haste, that he neither brought away the artillery nor all his men. [33] Captain Fenner gives a somewhat different account of this affair. "Captain Bertie, being left with 200 soldiers to guard the castle, shipped himself on board a French vessel which happened to be there, with two Scotchmen, and returned in her to England, abandoning his men to the mercy of the Spaniards, by whom they were all afterwards put to the sword." [34] He also says, "died at Cascais, after re-embarking the men, Captain William Fenner, rear-admiral, and Colonel Edward Horton, who were both wounded by a great shot from the castle." This would seem to imply that, after all but a few officers were embarked, the Spaniards fired upon them from the castle of Cascais. The writer of this account is Captain *Thomas* Fenner, there being two of the name in the Expedition.

The fleet was dispersed in a gale, and for seventeen days kept the sea before they could reach Vigo, in which interval they were compelled to cast a great many of the men into the sea, who were dying daily, not only from a fearful sickness raging among them, but many from absolute hunger; and it is said that many more must have perished from lack of sufficient food, had not the dreadful mortality been the means of thinning their ranks, and thus leaving an increased allowance for the survivors. In this afflicting state, it was deemed expedient to land, and obtain provisions by force of arms or otherwise. They found the number of their effective men not to exceed 2000: with these they landed and approached the town on two sides; and though the streets were barricadoed, the inhabitants made no resistance, the greater part having withdrawn, and carried with them everything of value, except a good store of wine. The invaders, therefore, contented themselves with spoiling the country for a few miles round, burning the villages and the standing corn; then, after setting fire to the town, they re-embarked.

It was agreed that Drake should draft the able men into twenty of the best ships, and that he should take them under his orders to the Azores, for the chance of falling in with the Indian return fleet, while Norris, with the rest of the armament, should proceed homewards. They had scarcely separated, when a violent storm arose. One of the detachments of merchant ships, in the midst of this violent storm, having lost the fleet, Captain Fenner says, "being separated from the rest, we wandered as lost sheep in search of the Generals, being chased day by day by the galleys, and often almost taken, but were at last delivered when past hope. He and his company, for want of water, which was their drink, sailed for Porto Santo (near Madeira), when, by good fortune, he took a small pinnace laden with apricots and red plums, which for four clays refreshed his men, when he met with his Admiral (his superior officer, Captain Cross) alone, as himself was, without any one of the fleet or Sir Francis Drake with him. Captains Cross and Fenner, with their seventeen sail, meeting thus, entered the road of Porto Santo, where lying one night in hope by some means to get fresh water, the next morning seven sail more of their company came to them; upon which they landed, and took the island, where they refreshed themselves for two days, and then ransomed the town, saving it and the church for the following contributions:- 24 pipes of fresh fountain water, 16 pipes of water, 68 jars of sweet oil, 2 hogsheads of white vinegar, 2 rundlets of red vinegar, 1120 hens and chickens, 10 fat oxen, 100 fat sheep, and as many muskmelons, grapes, mulberries, and figs as they wanted." [35] With this good stock of provisions and delicacies they sailed for England.

The two squadrons under Drake and Norris were also dispersed; and when Norris, twelve days afterwards, reached Plymouth, he found that Drake had already arrived there with all the Queen's ships and several others; but many had taken the opportunity, which the storm afforded, of going their own way, and carrying the prizes with them, in order to turn them to their own advantage. At Plymouth the army was dissolved; and every soldier received five shillings and his arms, and this, says Hakluyt, "was believed to be more than could by any means be due to them." [36] A rich booty is said to have been brought home, and 150 pieces of great ordnance; but the loss of lives was very great; of 12,000 men little more than 6000 remaining alive.

From this voyage "they returned into England," says Camden, "with 150 pieces of great ordnance and a very rich booty; part of which was divided among the seamen, who began to mutiny, but could not satisfy them.

"Most men were of opinion that the English hereby answered all points, both of revenge and honour, having in so short a compass of time taken one town by storm, made a glorious assault upon another, driven before them a very potent army, landed their forces in four several places, marched seven days together in order of battle, and with colours flying, through the enemy's country, attacked a strong and flourishing city with a small handful of men, and lodged for three nights in the suburbs of it. Besides that, they beat the enemy back to the very gates after they had made a sally; took two castles lying on the sea, and spoiled the enemy of all their stores and ammunition.

"However, there were others who thought all this was no manner of equivalent for the damages sustained in this enterprise; the loss of soldiers and seamen by sickness alone amounting to 6,000.

"But most certain it is that England was so far a gainer by this expedition as from that time to apprehend no incursions from Spain, but rather to grow more warm and animated against that country." [37]

After all, nothing could be worse than the system, then prevailing, of allowing volunteer adventurers to be united in hostile expeditions with the naval and military forces of the nation; and nothing could afford a stronger example of the viciousness of such a system than this expedition to Portugal. In our days the commander of a fleet or squadron would disdain to be hampered with such auxiliaries, who were in fact of real disservice to the state, by abstracting seamen from the regular navy; but in this respect we have not greatly improved, by the encouragement that is given to the privateer system in time of war.

It was said that the two commanders quarrelled; but there does not, in any of the narratives, nor in their correspondence, appear the least grounds for such a conclusion. Blame was attempted to be cast on Sir Francis Drake, for having broken his promise to join the army at Lisbon. His promise, however, was conditional, as all promises of this nature must be so understood but "He did not keep his promise," says Monson, "and therefore he was much blamed by the common consent of all men, imputing the overthrow of the action to him. It will not excuse Sir Francis Drake, in his promise made to Sir John Norris, though I would utterly have accused him of want of discretion, if he had put the fleet to so great an adventure to so little purpose; for his being in the harbour of Lisbon was nothing to the taking of the castle, which was two miles from thence; and had the castle been taken, the town would have been taken of course.

"And, moreover, the ships could not furnish the army with more men or victuals than they had; wherefore I understand not wherein his going up was necessary, and yet the fleet was to endure many hazards to this little purpose. For, betwixt Cascaes and Lisbon there are three castles, St. Julian, St. Francis, and Belem. The first of the three, I hold one of the most impregnable forts, to seaward, in Europe, by which the fleet was to pass, within culliver-shot; though, I confess, the greatest danger was not the passing it, for, with a reasonable gale of wind, any fort is to be passed with small hazard." [38]

We have, however, in our own times, a similar instance of an admiral, as bold and brave as Drake, failing in his promise on an occasion of much greater importance. The expedition that was fitted out and assembled in the Downs for Antwerp, was the most complete, perhaps, that ever left the shores of England, and its destination kept with an extraordinary degree of secrecy. On sailing, the Admiral gave a most solemn pledge that he would at once convey the army up the Scheldt and land them at Sandfleet, from whence they would reach Antwerp before a single French soldier had marched for that garrison. He sailed, and the first despatch contained his gratifying intelligence, "that his fleet had safely anchored in the Room-pot (literally *cream*-pot), and that the head-quarters of the commander in chief were comfortably established in the city of Middleburg." Before the Admiral got out of the cream-pot, Antwerp was strongly garrisoned by a French army, while the only trophy we acquired was a deadly Walcheren fever.

Sir William, however, considers the landing at the Groyne to have been the great mistake, the *origo malorum:* "it was a lingering of the other design, a consuming of victuals, weakening of the armies by the immoderate drinking of the soldiers, which brought a lamentable sickness amongst them, a warning to the Spaniards to strengthen Portugal, and, what was more than all this, a discouragement to proceed farther, being repulsed in the first attempt." [39]

The letters, which the two Commanders wrote from Plymouth, indicate too clearly the ill effects that were likely to ensue from the parsimony of the Government, even in the supply of articles absolutely necessary for the support of life, and without which life is not to be sustained. The Queen was anxious enough to avenge the insults of her enemies, to carry the war into their country; and she contributed as far as her means would allow her. But the history of her reign shows the extreme difficulty of raising the necessary supplies; and the consequence was, that the system of carrying on a war was deplorably defective. The advantage, and the only one, arising out of the admission of private adventurers, was that of bearing a part of the expenses of the war, which they readily did in the hope of sharing in the reprisals; but by these having an ostensible share in the issue of the war, they detracted, if successful, from the honour of the regular army and navy, while any reverse was attributed solely to the regular service. If the country at this time had been blessed with a Wellington, who would have told it of the folly and futility of waging "a little war," such a miserable expedition as that to Portugal, to avenge or avert another attempt of invasion, would not have been cramped and confined like that voluntarily and heartily accepted by two such distinguished officers as Sir Francis Drake and Sir John Norris.

The "True Discourse," however, maintains that one of the great purposes of the expedition was fully answered as a blow against Philip. "In this short time of our adventure, we have wonne a towne by escalade, battered and assaulted another, overthrown a mighty prince's power in the field, landed our army in three several parts of his kingdom, marched seven days in the heart of his country, lyen three nights in the suburbes of his principal citie, beaten his forces into the gates thereof, and possessed two of his frontier forts; spoiled a great part of the provision he had made at the Groyne of all sorts, for a newe voyage into England, burnt three of his ships, whereof one was the second in the last expedition, taken from him 150 pieces of good artillarie, cut off more than 60 hulks, and 20 French ships well manned, fit and ready to serve him as men of warre against us, laden for his store with corn, victuals, masts, cables, and other merchandizes; slain and taken the principal men of warre he had in Galatia; and made Don Pedro de Gusman, Conde de Fuentes, shamefully runne at Peniche." [40]

It cannot be doubted, however, that all the adventurers in this expedition were disappointed and dissatisfied; the destruction, instead of the capture, of ships and property diminished their share of booty, for which alone many of them had volunteered on the enterprise. Among others the Dutchmen made a demand of 5,019*l.* on Drake and Norris for the services of 44 vessels employed in the conveyance of troops; but the Lords of the Council, Burleigh, Hatton, &c. decided, that the most that could be allowed to them was 2,540*l.* if the 44 ships had served without any other recompense or consideration; remarking that 40 of these ships acquitted the two Commanders from all demands, on receiving their discharge and passports; and that they shared in part of the spoils at the Groyne, Peniche, and Cascaes.

But among the most disappointed of the adventurers, for he was strictly such, was the exiled Don Antonio. The case of this poor claimant of a throne was a most distressing one, as we are told, and too truly told by Strype.

"As the Queen had assisted Don Antonio to recover his kingdom of Portugal, according to his claimed right to it, against Philip King of Spain, so his condition now grew very mean, so as he became an object of compassion for his poverty and inability even to pay his servants, which occasioned one Edward Prince, a person near him, to acquaint the Lord Treasurer with his circumstances; especially now, upon the success of a late voyage, undertaken by the Queen's permission; wherein Sir Francis Drake took a very rich ship of Portugal (called the Great Carack), whereupon many merchants and noblemen in France, as Prince writ to the said Treasurer, were of opinion that the Queen would lend that King, his master, out of that rich prize 200,000 crowns, to enable him to levy an army for the voyage of Portugal. I could be large, continues Prince, in shewing the most pitiful estate of the poor King. In honour, my good Lord, her Majesty should take pity of the distressed King, and cause the same sum above-named to be paid unto the poor creditors of this poor King's misery, weighing his poor estate with your true balances, and uses herein your honourable favours. Under which the state of this poor house dependeth, having no other refuge but in your honour." [41] "What favour," continues Strype, "was shewn to Don Antonio and his creditors, out of that rich Carack, I know not." From that source, it may be apprehended, nothing in justice to the captors could be assigned to the poor King; he remained in England, and no doubt received the royal bounty until, at his own request, he was sent out with the expedition under Drake and Norris to Portugal.

His case was now more hopeless than ever, and his fate as to the throne of Portugal pretty well decided. That the Queen afforded him some temporary relief can hardly be doubted, but he had nothing more to expect in England. He therefore repaired to France, where he hoped to find friends, but in this was, probably, disappointed; for it appears that, after wandering as an exile through the various countries of Europe, he died in Paris in the year 1595; at which time his only follower was a Portuguese noble, Don Diego Bothei, who attended his master to the last with unshaken fidelity, and only asked, as the reward of all his services, to be buried at his feet. [42]

As to Essex, who embarked in the enterprise, contrary to the Queen's commands, his fortunes were desperate at the time he embarked in the present undertaking, as appears by the following letter, addressed to the Vice Chamberlain; but by some means or other he succeeded in procuring a ship well-armed and manned, by which he captured several prizes previous to his joining the expedition, in consequence of which he had no cause to be disappointed.

March, 1589.

THE EARL OF ESSEX, BEFORE HIS DEPARTURE ON THE VOYAGE TO PORTUGAL, TO MR. VICE-CHAMBERLAIN.

SIR,

WHAT my courses may have been I need not repeat, for no man knoweth them better than yourself. What my state is now, I will tell you: my revenue no greater than it was when I sued my livery; my debts, at the least, two or three-and-twenty thousand pounds. Her Majesty's goodness hath been so great, as I could not ask more of her. No way left to repair myself but mine own adventure, which I had much rather undertake then to offend Her Majesty, with sutes, as I have done heretofore. If I speed well I will adventure to be rich; if not, I will never leiev to see the end of my poverty. And so wishing that this letter, which I have left for you, may come to your hands, I commit you to God's good protection.

From my study some few days before my departure.

Your assured friend,
ESSEX. [43]

To my honourable friend,
Mr. Vice-Chamberlain.

This young nobleman might be considered as fortune's favourite child, caressed and loved by every one, from the Queen downwards. He possessed all those amiable and great qualities, which are given to him by the writer of the Latin narrative of the present expedition, "Summo omnium applausu et laetitia excipitur; est enim propter virtutes animi, corporisque dotes, generis et familiae nobilitatem, et in re militari scientiam, et industriam, nobilis longè gratissimus." [44] Elizabeth also, who knew well how to reward valorous deeds, was so pleased on his return, that she took the earliest opportunity of showering honours and rewards upon him - made him Commander-in-Chief and Lord Lieutenant of Ireland; created him Earl Marshal of England, and employed him on various important services. But he had the misfortune of displeasing her, by an offensive but probably thoughtless act, for which in return he received from her a blow; and for this indignity, his wounded honour carried his resentment utterly beyond the bounds of prudence; and by his obstinacy, which the earnest endeavours of his most powerful and warmest friends failed to subdue, his mind became so excited, as to hurry him on to treasonable practices, for which he was tried, condemned, and executed, in the thirty-fourth year of his age; a termination which, from an unfortunate circumstance that might have arrested it, was the cause of hastening the death of Queen Elizabeth.

"The Earl of Essex," says Hume, "was but thirty-four years of age when his rashness, imprudence, and violence brought him to this untimely end. We must here, as on many other instances, lament the inconstancy of human nature, that a person endowed with so many noble virtues, generosity, sincerity, friendship, valour, eloquence, and industry, should, in the latter period of his life, have given reins to his ungovernable passions, and involved not only himself, but many of his friends, in utter ruin." [45]

The fate of this noble and unfortunate youth furnishes a melancholy illustration of that part of Bolingbroke's character of Elizabeth which says, "She had private friendships, she had favourites; but she never suffered her friends to forget she was their Queen; and when her favourites did, she made them feel that she was so."

[1] Camden.
[2] MS. State Paper Office.
[3] MS. State Paper Office.
[4] MS. State Paper Office.
[5] MS. State Paper Office.
[6] Hakluyt.
[7] Captain W. Fenner's account in Birch's Memoirs.
[8] The best and fullest account of this expedition, published within the year 1589, bears this title: "A true Coppie of a Discourse, written by a gentleman, employed in the late Voyage of Spain and Portingale." Published at the same time, and by the same publisher, a Latin abstract (not a translation), entitled "Ephemeris Expeditionis Norreysii et Draki in Lusitaniam."
[9] True Copy of Discourse.
[10] True Discourse.
[11] Winter, in Birch's Memoirs.
[12] Hakluyt - True Discourse.
[13] True Discourse.
[14] Southey, on the authority of Gondara.
[15] Gondara, whom Southey considers as good authority,
[16] Need Byron be named?
[17] Childe Harold.
[18] MS. State Paper Office.
[19] MS. State Paper Office.
[20] Camden.
[21] Ephemeris Expeditionis.
[22] True Discourse.
[23] Hakluyt.
[24] True Discourse Hakluyt.
[25] Birch's Memoirs.
[26] The True Discourse.
[27] Birch's Memoirs.
[28] Birch's Memoirs.
[29] Monson's Tracts.

[30] Birch's Memoirs.
[31] True Discourse.
[32] True Discourse.
[33] Hakluyt.
[34] Birch's Memoirs.
[35] Birch's Memoirs.
[36] Hakluyt.
[37] Camden.
[38] Monson.
[39] Monson's Tracts.
[40] True Discourse.
[41] Strype.
[42] Lord Somers's Tracts.
[43] Burley's State Papers.
[44] Ephemeris Expeditionis.
[45] Hume's History.

Chapter Ten - Voyage of Drake and Hawkins to the Spanish Colonies, 1590-1596

It was some years after the return from the last expedition, before Sir Francis Drake had to prepare the one about to be described; but we are not to suppose, that a man of his active and inquisitive mind was likely to remain in a state of idleness, so abhorrent from his character. The first we hear of him is by a letter, in Latin, which he writes to the Prince Henry de Bourbon, dated in November, 1590. It is to be found in Rymer's Foedera; and of which the following is a translation:

TO THE PRINCE HENRY DE BOURBON.

AFTER it was made known here that the common enemy of the two kingdoms had landed forces at Nunnetum (Brittany), Her Most Serene Majesty, my Mistress, by the advice of her Council, commanded a small vessel (celox) to be fitted out as speedily as possible, and that I should repair into the ports of the northern provinces (Armoricae) and discover, by every fit means, what these Spaniards may be contriving; in what places they abide, and what is the state of their affairs.

I have therefore considered that, of all these matters, I should be made more certain from no one so well as from Your Highness, whose authority is omnipotent through the whole country, and may be acted upon safely in such affairs.

For this purpose, as is meet, I earnestly beseech, with all entreaty, that it may not seem troublesome to Your Highness, concerning the councils, the preparations and the designs of those enemies, which are things very necessary you should be made acquainted with: also that you would communicate with me, as early as possible, hoping (as I pray without ceasing to our Lord Jesus Christ, the King of kings) that the ferocity of this common enemy may speedily yield to the benefit of France and England.

FRANCIS DRAKE.
Datae A.D.N. Idus Novembris, 1590.

To which was returned the following reply, also in Latin:

HENRY BOURBON, PRINCE or THE DOMBAE, TO THE MOST RENOWNED FRANCIS DRAKE. - HEALTH.

IT is a royal act (most illustrious Knight), of one's own accord to succour the wretched. Then how much more royal is the mind of your Queen, that so many and such great kindnesses should be manifested towards the Most Christian King, and all France, more especially in these times, in which she hath often sent troops and succour against an invading enemy.

But lest it should seem that one part only of the kingdom of France should be taken care of, and the rest neglected, as soon as it was known that a military force of Spain had landed in this province, and that you, a man celebrated by fame and noble deeds, are desirous of knowing from me what should be done, and where the enemy is posted - this is what you ask me in your letter.

Most willingly and truly I obey the commands of such a Queen, and will satisfy your desire.

Your Lordship therefore may be informed that the common enemy now occupies the city, which, in the country idiom, is called Hennebon; is blockading both it and the port, which is not far from the city, and which we call Blaovet, and is there constructing a strong fortified citadel.

If these enterprises be not, as quickly as possible, provided against, it is to be feared lest this injury, which seems to be destined for us, may end in detriment to your republic.

Now I, relying on your advice, have sent a letter to the Queen, your Mistress, concerning these affairs, by a noble person, the Viscount Turen, who visited England by command of His Most Christian Majesty; and I have earnestly entreated for auxiliary forces; but I also now, in another letter to the Queen, have requested the same thing; and I eagerly entreat you, most Excellent Sir, that you would strengthen my petition before the Queen, as much as possible, by your authority and favour. - Accept the rest from a Nobleman who is wanting in words:

    Tuus ad omnia paratissimus.   HENRY DE BOURBON. [1]

The King of Spain had every facility for these incursions, owing to the proximity of the Duke of Parma, who, by his former remissness, might be glad of an opportunity to re-instate himself in the good graces of Philip. Besides, the confusion into which France was thrown, by the murder of the Duke of Guise, and of Henry III. by a blood-thirsty Dominican friar, gave great encouragement to the Spaniards; but Elizabeth, ever awake to the dangers of the country, employed Drake to ascertain the state of matters in the northern provinces of France, which gave occasion to the foregoing correspondence. She sent a reinforcement to Henry IV. of 4000 men, to join the French at Dieppe, and a further supply under the Earl of Essex. She also, in the same year, sent out a squadron of seven of her ships, under the command of Lord Thomas Howard, with Sir Richard Greenvil his Vice-Admiral, with order to proceed to the Azores to intercept the Plata fleet; but Philip, being apprized of it, despatched a powerful fleet of more than fifty sail; they met and fought, but the superiority of the Spaniards was so great, that the English were compelled to give way, with the exception of Sir Richard Greenvil, who, alone, in the Revenge, fought, with the most determined bravery, the whole fleet for twelve hours, repulsing the enemy, who boarded him fifteen times; was twice wounded, carried down, received a shot in the head, and the surgeon, who was dressing him, killed by his side. In this hopeless state he advised they should sink the ship rather than yield; but most of the crew opposed it, and she was taken. "The only ship of war," says Monson, "that was yet taken by the Spaniards;" and of no avail to them, the Revenge having gone down with 200 Spaniards in her. This noble and heroic commander lived but a few days after; but his death was as noble as his life. "Here," he said, "I, Richard Greenvil, die with a joyful and quiet mind; for that I have ended my life as a true soldier ought to do, fighting for his country, Queen, religion, and honour: my soul willingly departing from this body, leaving behind the lasting fame of having behaved as every valiant soldier is in his duty bound to do." [2]

In the parliament of 1592-3, Drake, who sat for Plymouth, had various duties assigned to him, and his name appears upon all the committees on public business, and the bills from several of them put into his hands. He recommended strong measures to be taken by sea and land, as Philip was powerful on both; and spoke and voted for a grant or aid of three subsidies being given to the Queen, to enable her to meet them. [3] Sir Martin Frobisher was also sent to sea with a fleet to harass the trade of Philip; and when the parliament was dissolved, in 1593, the Queen had given notice, that she intended to place a fleet under Sir Francis Drake, who, in the following year, made his arrangements, and associated with him his old friend and early patron, Sir John Hawkins.

This expedition must be considered as something remarkable in its origin, unfortunate in its progress, and fatal in its termination. It is particularly remarkable that Sir John Hawkins, at his advanced age, between 75 and 80, with the rank of a flag officer and the honour of knighthood conferred on him by the Queen, of wealthy circumstances, partly left by his father, who was an opulent merchant and ship owner, but mostly acquired by himself in the course of forty-eight years' service, chiefly spent at sea, and twenty-two years as Treasurer of the Navy. Why such a man should volunteer, as it is said he did, upon a hazardous and unhealthy voyage to the West Indies, a second time in his old age, is still more remarkable. It was only five years before this that the Queen had appointed him and Sir Martin Frobisher to the command of a squadron of ten of her best ships, to scour the coast of Spain, and destroy any shipping belonging to that country which they should fall in with. For seven months that they were out at sea, they did not take a single ship; they attempted Fayal, and found it too strong for them; the carracks from the Indies, on which their hopes depended, had slipped into Lisbon, unseen; all which, though unavoidable, annoyed Sir John Hawkins to such a degree, that he could not help writing an apology to the Queen for their want of success; reminding Her Majesty that the Scripture says, "Paul planteth and Apollos watereth, but God giveth the increase." This allusion to Scripture nettled Her Majesty so, that it elicited one of her usual bursts, "God's death!" she exclaimed, "this fool went out a soldier, and is come home a divine."

It may be that the desire of increasing his wealth, redeeming his character with the Queen, or serving his country, each or all of them motives sufficiently powerful with an active mind to induce him to hazard his fortune, his reputation, and his person a second time in the dangerous service he was about to undertake. But it has been said, which is probable enough, that he had a more laudable object in view than any of these - the opportunity such an expedition might afford, of redeeming a beloved son, who was at this time a prisoner in the hands of the Spaniards in South America.

The case of his son was this. Captain Richard Hawkins, in the year 1593, fitted out two ships for the South Sea; one deserted him on the coast of Brazil. He, however, alone, in his own single ship, passed through the Strait of Magelhaens, took two prizes on the other side, was attacked on the coast of Peru by Admiral de Castro, with a squadron of eight sail, and 2000 men on board, from which enormous disparity of force Hawkins, by superior seamanship, found means to disengage himself, after doing very considerable damage to the Spaniards; but, by delaying too long in that part of the South Sea, in the hope of taking more prizes, he again fell in with De Castro, now much reinforced; and after a gallant defence for three days and three nights, most of his men being killed, himself dangerously wounded, and his ship in a sinking state, he was prevailed on to surrender on honourable terms - that himself and his surviving crew should have a free passage to England as soon as might be.

He remained, however, a long time in South America as a prisoner, where he was treated with great humanity by Admiral de Castro, and in the end was sent a prisoner to Spain, where he was kept for several years. What were the means to be adopted for his release in America does not appear, whether by threats, or terror, or ransom.

That Drake should cheerfully join his early friend and patron in such a project is not surprising: his warm and affectionate regard for the man who had first brought him forward in his career, with whom he had fought in the Invincible Armada, and with whom he lived in ties of the strictest friendship, were quite sufficient to induce him to enter into the scheme; but he had another inducement of a very urgent nature - the inveterate hatred he bore to the Spaniard, who never ceased his animosity towards, and who was again pretending to invade, England with another Invincible Armada. He had besides another motive still more powerful, that of meeting the wishes of the Queen, which, by the offer of his services, he had every reason to know would be acceptable. Monson, in his usual caustic and consequential manner, says, "These two Generals (Sir Francis Drake and Sir John Hawkins), presuming much upon their own experience and knowledge, used many arguments to persuade the Queen to undertake this voyage to the West Indies, assuring her what great services they should perform, and promising to engage very deeply in the adventure themselves, both with their substance and their persons: and such was the opinion every one had conceived of these two valiant Commanders, that great were the expectations of the success of this voyage."
[4]

187

The squadron which the Queen ordered to be fitted out to act against the Spanish colonies in America, and to be placed under the command of Sir Francis Drake and Sir John Hawkins, consisted of the following ships and commanders –

The Defiance, Admiral Sir Francis Drake.
  Garland, Vice-Admiral Sir John Hawkins.
  Hope, Captain Gilbert York.
  Buonaventure, Captain Troughton.
  The Foresight, Captain Winter.
  Adventure, Captain Thomas Drake.
  Commander by land, Sir Thomas Baskerville.

The names of the above-mentioned ships are all contained in the lists of the Royal Navy; but it is said that about twenty others, furnished by individuals, were included in the squadron, among whom, no doubt, the two Admirals were large contributors of the expense. There were also three other officers, of the name of Baskerville, besides the Commander, two of them captains, and one serjeant-major; also Sir Nicholas Clifford, lieutenant-general, and eight other captains for the land service.

The fitting-out and equipment of this grand expedition were not surpassed by that of 1585 to the West Indies, under Sir F. Drake, Vice-Admiral Frobisher, and Rear-Admiral Knolles. Its destination in the first place was intended for Puerto Rico, where the Queen had received information that a vast treasure had been brought, and intended to be sent home from thence for the use of the King of Spain in completing the third grand armament (the second having been destroyed by Drake), which he had in contemplation for the invasion of England. The object of the present fleet was to intercept the treasure, and thereby cut off the main supply of his navy and army destined for that purpose.

Their first intention, however, had been to land at Nombre de Dios, and proceed direct from thence over the isthmus to Panama, in order to seize the treasure, generally brought thither from the mines of Mexico and Peru; but, a few days before their departure from Plymouth, they received letters sent by order of the Queen, informing them that advices had been received from Spain, announcing the arrival of the West Indian or Plata fleet, but that one of them, a very valuable ship, had lost her mast and put into the island of Puerto Rico; and it was therefore her Majesty's recommendation that they should proceed direct to that island, to secure the ship and treasure which was in her, more especially as it was not much out of their way to Nombre de Dios.

The following is the joint reply of Drake and Hawkins to Lord Burleigh, acknowledging the receipt of Her Majesty's letter, being the last that either of them ever wrote:

1595.

DRAKE AND HAWKINS TO LORD BURLEIGH.

OUR dewty in most humble maner remembryd, yt may please yor Lŏ ship, we have answeryd her Maties letter, we hope to her heighnes contentmente whome we wold nott wetyngly or wyllyngly desplease. We humbly thanke your Lo ship for yor manyfold favours wch we have allwayes fownd never varyable, but wth all favour, loue and constancye for wch we can never be suffycyently thanckfull but wt our prayers to god long to blesse yo. good Lo ship wt honour & healthe.

We thynke yt be trew that some small man of warre be taken upon the cost of spayne but they are of very small moment, they be for the most pt soche small carvells as was before this taken from the Spanyards, some small r.omber of our men are yet in spayne, wch ys the onely losse, but, as we lerne, ther be not above one hundrethe left in spayne of them but many retornyd alreddy into Inglond.

& so lokyng daylye for a good wynd we humbly take our leve from plymothe the 18 of August 1595.

Your ll. ever most bownden

FRA: DRAKE. JOHN HAWKYNS. [5]

(Note in a contemporary hand, at the bottom of the letter.)
The q. sent these two brave sea captaines wth a Fleet to Porto Rico in America, belonging to ye Spanyard, having heard of a great mass of tresure brought thither. But it is proved an unsuccesful attempt. And neither of ym returned ever home again, both dying at sea at different places, in this voyage.
To the Ry' honorable
our syngular good lord the Lo. heigh Tresorer of Inglond, gyve this at the Court.

The expedition left Plymouth on the 28th of August, 1595, but did not get clear of the land till the last of that month. They then repaired to Grand Canary, the principal island of the groupe that bears that name, where they did not arrive sooner than the 27th of September. An attempt to subdue this island, and take possession of it, failed. Hawkins remonstrated against this attempt as losing time, and acting contrary to the Queen's wishes and to their main design. But Drake and Baskerville decided for it, and particularly the latter, who undertook to get possession of it in four days, adding, that it would be very desirable to victual the whole squadron there, which could only be done by having uninterrupted possession of the town. The seamen, it was urged, were already complaining of the scarcity of provisions, and so many reasons were assigned that Hawkins reluctantly submitted. This decision turned out to be the first unfortunate blot in their progress; for they were unable to land the fourteen hundred men in the boats on account of the surf, without incurring too great and manifest a risk. However they succeeded to water the ships on the western side of the island. Here Captain Grimston, with a boat's crew, straggling to some distance from the shore, were set upon by some herdsmen, who with their dogs and staves killed the captain and most of the men, wounded the rest, and took the surgeon of one of the ships prisoner, who told all he knew concerning the object of the voyage; upon which the governor dispatched a caraval to all the places he had named;

but, like the secrecy with which all important matters are conducted, the whole of the present expedition was known in Spain before it sailed from Plymouth.

Leaving this and approaching Martinico, Drake going a-head with four or five ships, was separated from the rest of the fleet by a sudden storm. The body of the fleet made for Dominica, full of the race of cannibals, as Hakluyt has it, and Drake for Mariegalante, but they joined company at Guadaloupe. Here they watered, washed the ships, set up the pinnaces, the materials of which they had carried out, and landed the men, that they might refresh themselves on shore.

On the 30th of September, Captain Wignot in the Francis, abark of 35 tons, being the sternmOst of Sir John Hawkins's division, was chased by five of the King of Spain's frigates or zabras, being ships of 200 tons, which came with three other zabras for the treasure of San Juan de Puerto Rico. The Francis, mistaking them for his companions, was taken in sight of our caraval. The Spaniards, indifferent to human suffering, left the Francis driving in the sea with three or four hurt and sick men, and took the rest of her people into their ships, and returned to Puerto Rico.

The squadron now intended to pass through the Virgin Islands, but "here," says Hakluyt, "Sir John Hawkins was extreme sick; which his sickness began upon newes of the taking of the Francis." Remaining here two days, they tarried two days more in a sound, which Drake in his barge had discovered. They then stood for the eastern end of Puerto Rico, where Sir John Hawkins breathed his last. A story runs through some of the old writers that the death of Hawkins was owing to some difference of opinion between the two Commanders, which preyed on his mind; there does not, however, appear to have been any other difference between them than that of their stay at the Canaries; and that was owing chiefly to the confidence expressed by the military commander. The unfortunate circumstance of their whole plan of operations being anticipated by the authorities of Nombre de Dios and Panama may, no doubt, have given him a considerable degree of annoyance, but his great age, and exposure to a most unhealthy climate, which was carrying off hundreds by disease, appear to be quite sufficient to have occasioned his death.

Sir Thomas Baskerville now took possession of the Garland as second in command. The fleet came to anchor at the distance of two miles or less at the eastern side of the town of San Juan de Puerto Rico, "where," says Hakluyt, "we received from their forts and places, where they planted ordnance, some twenty-eight great shot, the last of which strake the Admiral (ship) through the misen, and the last but one strake through her quarter into the steerage, the General being there at supper, and strake the stool from under him, but hurt him not, but hurt at the same table Sir Nicholas Clifford, Mr. Browne, Captain Stratford, with one or two more. Sir Nicholas Clifford and Master Browne died of their hurts." [6] Drake was certainly imprudent in suffering the squadron to take up an anchorage so near to the means of annoyance;

but his former visits had no doubt taught the enemy the prudence of being better prepared for any future occasion; and it is somewhat remarkable that Drake should not have observed his usual caution. Browne was an old and particular favourite of Drake, who usually went by the name of Brute Browne; and he might have exclaimed on this fatal occasion, "Et tu, Brute!" - He did make some such exclamation, as Fuller tells us, and that he had it from Henry Drake who was then present. "Ah, dear Brute, I could grieve for thee! but now is no time for me to let down my spirits." [7]

The following morning the whole fleet came to anchor before the point of the harbour without the town, a little to the westward, where they remained till night-fall; and then twenty-five pinnaces, boats, and shallops, well manned and furnished with fire-works and small shot, entered the road. The great castle or galleon, the object of the present enterprise, had been completely repaired, and was on the point of sailing, when certain intelligence of the intended attack by Drake had reached the island. Every preparation had been made for the defence of the harbour and town; the whole of the treasure had been landed; the galleon was sunk in the mouth of the harbour; a floating barrier of masts and spars was laid on each side of her, near to the forts and castles, so as to render the entrance impassable; within this breakwater were the five zabras moored, their treasure also taken out; all the women and children and infirm people were removed into the interior, and those only left in the town who were able to act in its defence. A heavy fire was opened on the ships of the English, but the adventurers persisted in their desperate attempt, until they had lost, by their own account, some forty or fifty men killed, and as many wounded; but there was consolation in thinking that by burning, drowning, and killing, the loss of the Spaniards could not be less, in fact a great deal more; for the five zabras and a large ship of four hundred tons were burnt, and their several cargoes of silk, oil, and wine destroyed were, as a prisoner reported, valued at three millions of ducats, or five and thirty tons of silver. Defeated in the main object, but not disheartened, the advanced party of pinnaces and small vessels, that had been engaged, returned to the fleet in the offing, and remained at anchor the next day; and then removed to the south-west point of the island to set up more pinnaces, wash the ships and refresh their crews. Here a Spanish man and his wife took refuge with Drake; he said he would be greatly tormented, if taken, for not having repaired to the town according to the Governor's order. Drake inquired no further of him; he saw his distress, and he was too humane a, man to refuse him his protection. [8]

They now proceeded to the Caribbean shore, and took the town of La Hacha, but were satisfied with a ransom offered by the inhabitants of thirty-four thousand ducats. From hence they proceeded along the coast arid took the town or village of Rancheria, after seizing a quantity of pearls, with other pillage, and a brigantine having on board some pearls and silver. The inhabitants at length consented to pay a ransom for the town of 24,000 ducats, and a prisoner promised to give 4000 ducats for his own ransom. In four days they brought in the town's ransom in pearls, but rating them so dear, the General sent them back, giving them four hours' respite to bring the required treasure.

The Governor now made his appearance, and told the General plainly that he cared not for the town, neither would he ransom it; that the pearls were brought without his consent; that he should have come sooner, but that he had to apprize all the towns on the coast that they might convey all their goods, cattle, and wealth into the woods. The General dismissed him, having given him his promise of safe conduct, allowing him two hours to withdraw himself in safety. "Then the town of Rancheria and of Rio de la Hacha were burnt cleane downe to the ground; the churches and a ladie's house only excepted, which, by her letters written to the General, was preserved." [9]

They afterwards burnt several other small villages on the coast, and then took possession of Santa Martha, which they likewise burnt, as nothing was found therein, not even a single piece of gold or silver. One can scarcely conceive that the crime of poverty should have subjected the inhabitants to a further accumulation of misery, and more especially when inflicted by Drake, a man noted for his benevolence and humanity: but he was at the time labouring under the infliction of a severe disease, of which Captain Hope had died some days previous.

After these operations, they proceeded to the port of Nombre de Dios, which had been originally intended as their first destination; the town was easily taken, after a short resistance from the Spaniards, about 100 in number, the rest having all fled, and those few, after a volley of three or four small pieces of ordnance and musket shot, also fled into the woods; the captors, finding neither booty nor ransom, destroyed the place with all the frigates, barks, and galliots that were in the harbour and on the beach, having houses built over them to keep the pitch from melting. In a watch-house on the top of a hill, near the town, they found "twentie sowes of silver, two bars of gold, some pearl, coined money, and other trifling pillage."

It was here decided that an attempt should be made on Panama, where it was almost certain that a large quantity of treasure would be found, that place being the general repository of all the gold and silver dug out of the mines of Peru. For this purpose seven hundred and fifty soldiers were selected to march over the isthmus to Panama, under the command of Sir Thomas Baskerville. Whether he depended on that cordial assistance that Drake had formerly received from Pedro and his Symerons, or Maroons, does not appear, but if so, he must have experienced a grievous disappointment; for on their passage through some narrow defiles, after a couple of troublesome days' marches, they were sorely galled with showers of small shot from the bordering woods. "The march was so sore," says Hakluyt, "as never Englishmen marched before." Finding, moreover, that further on, the pass was defended by a newly-erected fort, and that by good information there were two more they would have to pass, it was deemed prudent they should make the best of their way back to the fleet, having lost some 80 or 90 men, among whom was the quarter-master-general, an ensign, and two or three other officers. Accordingly they returned, wretchedly harassed, and half-starved, having already marched about half way to the shore of the South Sea. "They had so much of this breakfast," says Fuller in his quaint way, "they thought they should surfeit with a dinner and supper of the same." [10]

This change of circumstances, as connected with the two important stations of Nombre de Dios and Panama, since Drake's celebrated visit, might readily have been expected; but it is evident that the newly-erected forts on the isthmus were, in consequence of the information recently received, and of the time allowed them by the extraordinary delay in the expedition, occasioned by their having visited and alarmed so many different places, all inhabited by Spaniards. The mortification that Sir Francis Drake, now seriously indisposed, must have felt, particularly from this last failure, may better be conceived than expressed.

"On the 15th January, on their way towards Puerto Bello, Captain Plat died of sickness, and then Sir Francis Drake began to keep his cabin and to complain of a scowring or fluxe. On the 23rd they set sail and stood up again for Puerto Bello, which is but three leagues to the westward of Nombre de Dios.

"On the 28th, at 4 of the clock in the morning, our General Sir Francis Drake departed this life, havinge been extremely sicke of a fluxe, which began the night before to stop on him. He used some speeches at, or a little before, his death, rising and apparelling himselfe, but being brought to bed againe, within one hour died." [11]

"They moved on to Puerto Bello, and after coming to anchor in the bay, and the solemn burial of our Generall in the sea, Sir Thomas Baskerville being aboord the Defiance, where Mr. Bride made a sermon, having to his audience all the Captaines in the fleete. Sir Thomas having commanded all aboord the Garland, with whom he held a council, and there showing his commission, was accepted for Generall." [12]

With the usual solemnity of the funeral service at sea, were the remains of this noble specimen of a British seaman consigned to the deep. He received a sailor's funeral very near to the place where his great reputation was first established; his body was committed to the deep in a leaden coffin, with the solemn service of the Church of England, rendered more solemn by volleys of musketry and the firing of guns in all the ships of the fleet.

It will readily be imagined that after the death of these two commanders, and the loss of many other officers and men by sickness, the survivors had nothing further to look for, but to return home under the command of Sir Thomas Baskerville.

Proceeding therefore on their voyage they were encountered near the Isles of Pines, off Cuba, by the Spanish fleet of twenty sail, being a part of the sixty ships sent out from Carthagena to intercept the English fleet, forty of them having parted for the Havana. However, Baskerville in the Defiance and Troughton in the Garland gave them so warm a reception that, after an action of two hours, in which several of their best ships were damaged and one of them set on fire and burnt, they sheered off. The Spaniards, however, as usual, published a lying account, in which it is said the English ran away, and that they in vain pursued them. Monson says, "their General Don Bernardino (with a string of other names, says one of our officers, as long as a cable) was an approved coward, as it appeared when he came to encounter the English fleet; but his fear was compensated by the valour of his Vice-Admiral, Juan de Garay, who behaved himself much to his honour."

This General certainly proved himself to be a poltroon, for when Baskerville saw the scandalous falsehood which he published, he demanded satisfaction, and told him that he was ready to meet him in any spot or in any country, at peace with Spain and England, that he would name; but he thought better not to answer the demand made upon him, but submit to be publicly branded as a coward and liar.

The English expedition reached home in the beginning of May, 1596, with very little booty; the small towns set fire to, and the ships destroyed, were but a poor recompense for the loss of two of the ablest sea-officers in Europe.

That the loss of Drake was severely felt is sufficiently manifest from the numerous testimonials that appeared, in verse and prose, of his services and character.

Instead of an Epitaph (says one), these verses were written:

Where Drake first found, there last he lost his name,
And for a tomb left nothing but his fame.
His body's buried under some great wave,
The sea that was his glory is his grave.
On whom an epitaph none can truly make,
For who can say, 'Here lies Sir Francis Drake?'

"Nor shall I here in silence," Prince says, "omit what another in those days added on the same occasion.

The waves became his winding sheet, the waters were his tomb,
But for his fame, the ocean sea was not sufficient room." [13]

"Having formerly," says Fuller, "in my 'Holy State' written Drake's Life at large. I will forbear any addition; and only present this tetrastic, made on his corpse when cast out of the ship (wherein he died) into the sea.

Religio quamvis *Romana* resurgeret *olim*,
    Effoderet tumulum non pute, Drace, tuum.
Non est quod metuas, ne te combusserit ulla
    Posteritas, in aquâ tutus ab igne manes.

Though *Rome's* religion should in time return,
194

Drake, none thy body will ungrave again.
There is no fear posterity should burn
  Those bones which, free from fire, in sea remain." [14]

The following is from Cracherode's papers:

Our age's Tiphys, valours noble mirrour,
Englishman's glory, the Spaniards terror,
The sailor's starre, sea-taming - sail-wing'd Drake,
Whose fame, though he be dead, lives fresh awake,
Which with his corpse whole oceans cannot drown,
But shall endure as long as world is round
Which he encompas'd; one whose like I fear
England will never see again but here.

His mental and personal qualifications have been set forth by several of the old annalists, particularly by Stow and Fuller. The former says,

"Hee was more skillfull in all poyntes of nauigation then any that ever was before his time, in his time, or since his death; he was also of a perfect memory, great observation, eloquent by nature, skillfull in Artillery, expert and apt to let bloud, and give physick unto his people according to the climate; he was lowe of stature, of strong limbs, broad breasted, round headed, browne hayre, full bearded, his eyes rounde, large and clear, well favoured, fayre and of a charefull countenance. His name was a terror to the French, Spanyard, Portugall and Indians; many Princes of Italy, Germany, and other, as well enemies as friends, in his life time desired his picture. He was the second that euer went through the Straights of Magellanes, and the first that euer wente rounde about the worlde: he was lawfully married unto two wives both young, yet he himself and ten of his bretheren died without issue: he made his younger brother Thomas his heire, who was with him in most and chiefest of his Imploymentes; in briefe hee was as famous in Europe and America as Tamberlayne in Asia and Africa.

In his imperfections he was Ambitious for Honor, Unconstant in Amity, and Greatly affected to popularity.

He was fifty and fiue yeares old when he died." [15]

Prince, in his Worthies of Devon (quoting Fuller) says,

"If any should be desirous to know something of the character of Sir Francis Drake's person, he was of stature low, but set and strong grown: a very religious man towards God and his houses, generally sparing the churches whereever he came: chaste in his life, just in his dealings, true of his word, merciful to those that were under him, and hating nothing so much as idlenesse: in matters (especially) of moment, he was never wont to rely on other men's care, how trusty or skilful soever they might seem to be, but always contemning danger, and refusing no toyl; he was wont himself to be one (who ever was a second) at every turn, where courage, skill, or industry, was to be employed." [16]

Among the multitude of poetical panegyrics, the following three stanzas may be selected, more from curiosity than any merit they possess, as being part of a long poem on "The Life and Death of Sir Francis Drake, by Charles Fitz-Geffry," containing 285 stanzas of his "Life's Commendation and his Death's Lamentation."

Oxford, 1596.

278.

Proud Spain! although our Dragon be bereft us,
  We rampant lions have enow for thee;
  Magnanimous Essex heaven's delight is left us,
  And, O long may the heavens let him be!
  Great Cumberland and Howard yet have we;
    And, O long may we have them, and enjoy
    These worthies to our wealth and thine annoy.

280.

And that dear body held in Neptune's womb,
  By Jove shall be translated to the sky;
  The sea no more, heaven then shall be his tomb,
  Where he a new-made star eternally
  Shall shine transparent to spectator's eye,
    A fearful comet in the sight of Spain,
    But shall to us a radiant light remain.

281.

He who alive to them a dragon was,
  Shall be a dragon unto them again;
  For with his death his terror shall not pass,
  But still amid the air he shall remain
  A dreadful meteor in the eye of Spain:
    And, as a fiery dragon, shall portend
    England's success and Spain's disastrous end. [17]

Drake indeed has had the good fortune to be praised by contemporary writers, and his fame to be celebrated in every age, by historians as well as poets. It was left solely to Spanish hatred to defame the name and falsify the character of Drake, as is infamously done in a poem of Lopez de Vega, called *Dragontea.* Even Lord Holland, the admirer of this man, says that his poem is full of virulent and unpoetical abuse; he might have safely said, it is a tissue of falsehood and blasphemy, the most scandalous and revolting that was ever committed to paper, not only against Drake, but Queen Elizabeth, and all her gallant officers. Indeed his Lordship admits that he gives a false account of the death of Sir Francis Drake. "His own people," he says, "instigated by the furies, gave him poison; that being aware of it he refused all food, but then the poison was concealed in his medicine, and thus worked its effect."

"Mirad la disventura y la ruina
   De aquel hombre atrevido y indomable;
Mirad que triste genero de muerte
   Del cuerpo el alma a los infiernos vierte."

"Behold the desolation and the ruin
   Of this bold and untameable man.
Behold the miserable kind of death
   That has dragged the soul from the body into hell." [18]

It may observed that, as recorded by his biographers, this furious bigot became so idiotical as to hasten his death by the violent flagellations he inflicted upon himself.

Even the traitor Allen appears to have ceased his persecuting slanders of Drake, after his death, and was satisfied with ordering his portrait to be removed from a painter's collection in Rome, where it was fortuitously placed next that of Philip. "At the sight of this," says Strype, "the Cardinal's (Allen) Mace-bearer was enraged with many passionate Italian words, as an insufferable indignity offered to that great Catholic King. And this was not all, but notice was immediately given by him to the Cardinal at the palace; and a messenger despatched back to put Drake's picture down; though the painter himself, out of fear, presently did it, and notwithstanding came to trouble about it. It is well if Drake were not *now* burnt in effigy." [19]

Drake's character, however, does not rest on the abusive falsehoods of the Spaniards, but on the solid foundation of truth recorded by his countrymen, who were his contemporaries, and by succeeding generations.

Among other qualifications, there is one which appears to have escaped his biographers; he was no mean poet, as one solitary example will be sufficient to show. A book was published by Sir Humphrey Gilbert, Knight, in the year 1583, entitled "A True Report of the late discoveries, and possession taken in the righte of the Crowne of Englande, of the *New found Landes*," to which, as was usual in those days, was appended "Commendations by principal persons friendly to the author or the work." Among many others we find,

"Sir Frauncis Drake, Knight, in commendation of the above Treatise.

"Who seekes by worthie deedes to gaine renowne for hire,
Whose hart, whose hand, whose purse is prest to purchase his desire,
If anie such there bee, that thirsteth after fame,
Lo, heare a meane, to winne himself an everlasting name;
Who seekes by gaine and wealth to advance his house and blood,
Whose care is great, whose toile no lesse, whose hope is all for
If anie one there bee that covettes such a trade,
Lo heere the plot for commonwealth, and private gaine is made,
He that for vertue's sake will venture farre and neere,
Whose zeale is strong, whose practize trueth, whose faith is void of feere,

If any such there bee, inflamed with holie care,
Heere may hee finde a readie meane, his purpose to declare.
So that for each degree, this Treatise dooth unfolde,
The path to fame, the proofe of zeale, and way to purchase golde.

"FRAUNCES DRAKE."

Monson seizes every occasion to say something ill-natured of Sir Francis Drake; even his death could not refrain this propensity. He says, "Sir Francis Drake, who was wont to rule fortune, now finding his error, and the difference between the present strength of the Indies, and what it was when he first knew it, grew melancholy upon this disappointment, and suddenly, and *I do hope naturally,* died at Puerto Bello." This insinuation is as gratuitous as it is unfounded and uncharitable. "Upon what," says Dr. Johnson, "this conjecture is grounded, does not appear; and we may be allowed to hope, for the honour of so great a man, that it is without foundation; and that he whom no series of success could ever betray to vanity or negligence would have supported a change of fortune without impatience or dejection." Indeed, the whole course of Drake's life belies such an insinuation. And surely, at a time when death was mowing down hundreds both of officers and men with his relentless scythe, is it surprising that the two commanders should not escape? Captain Henry Savile, who was in the same ship, says, "Sir Francis Drake died of the flux which had growen upon him eight days before his death, and yielded up his spirit, like a Christian, to his Creator, quietly in his cabin." [20] The death of his colleague, his friend and early patron, was but a little before him, in the same climate and from the same disease, and not, as Monson says of him too, "from chagrin." The following parallel of these two great and good men, under the signature R. M., who professes to have sailed with both, is drawn with apparent fairness and truth.

"They were both alike given to travelling in their youth, and in their more mature years. They both attempted many honourable voyages; as that of Sir John Hawkins to Guinea, to the isles of America, and to St. Juan de Ulloa; so likewise Sir Francis Drake, after many discoveries in the West Indies, and other parts, was the first Englishman that ever encompassed the globe, in which, as well as in his great knowledge of sea affairs, he far exceeded, not only Sir John Hawkins, but all others. In their natures and dispositions they differed as much as in their management in war. Sir Francis was of a lively spirit, resolute, quick, and sufficiently valiant; Sir John, slow, jealous, and difficult to be brought to a resolution. In council, Sir John Hawkins did often differ from the judgment of others, making a show in difficult cases of knowing more than he would declare. Sir Francis was a willing hearer of every man's opinion, but commonly a follower of his own. He never attempted any action wherein he was an absolute commander but he performed it with great reputation, and could go through the weightiest concerns with wonderful ease. On the contrary, Sir John Hawkins was an undertaker of great things; but for the most part without fortune or success.

"Sir John Hawkins naturally hated land-soldiers, and though he was very popular, affected to keep company with common people rather than his equals; Sir Francis, on the contrary, loved the land-soldiers, always encouraged and preferred merit wheresoever he found it, and was affable and easy of access.

"They had both many virtues, and agreed in some; as in patience in enduring labours and hardships; observation and remembrance of things past, and great discretion in sudden dangers. In other virtues they differed: Sir John Hawkins was merciful, apt to forgive, and faithful to his word; Sir Francis Drake hard to be reconciled, but constant in friendship; and withal at the same time, severe and courteous, magnanimous and liberal. They were both ambitious to a fault, but one more than the other; for Sir Francis had an insatiable thirst after honour beyond all reason. He was full of promises, and more temperate in adversity than in prosperity. He had likewise some other imperfections, as quickness to auger, bitterness in disgracing, and was too much pleased with sordid flattery. Sir John Hawkins had malice with dissimulation, rudeness in behaviour, and was covetous in the last degree. They were both alike happy in being great commanders, but not equally successful. They both grew great and famous by the same means, that is, by their own virtues, courage, and the fortune of the sea. There was no comparison, however, between their merits, taken in general, for therein Sir Francis far exceeded." [21]

Mr. Prince carries the parallel a little further: "Alike they were also in their deaths; as to the place, for they both died on the sea; as to the time, they both expired on the same voyage, the one a little before the other; and, lastly, as to their funerals, for they were both buried in the ocean, over which they both so often rid in triumph; and yet further alike in this, that they had neither tomb nor epitaph to recommend their memories to posterity but their own immortal virtues." [22]

To the united efforts of these two brave and indefatigable seamen the navy in its infancy was more indebted than to the government, or any other individuals. By their joint efforts that noble institution, long known as the *Chest at Chatham,* was planned and carried into effect for the humane and wise purpose of relieving the wants and rewarding the merits of seamen maimed or worn out in the service of their country. It was founded at Chatham in 1590, removed to Greenwich in 1804, and in 1814 was, by Act of George III., consolidated with Greenwich Hospital. Its income was derived from the small deduction of sixpence per man per month, a certain share of prize-money, and some other sources, with the interest of about 1,350,000*l.*, to which the capital had accumulated in the course of more than 200 years. In the year 1818, after the long revolutionary war, the number of seamen and marines who received pensions from this fund amounted to 32,278, and the sum to 386,564*l.* For the present year the sum is 212,000*l.*

Sir William Monson has given the following full-length portrait of Drake, many parts of which are not drawn with any kind feeling towards the original, for whom he never entertained much affection:-

"I have laboured in all my relations to walk uprightly, and with integrity, neither swaying to the one hand or bending to the other; I have endeavoured to carry my intentions so equally as not to deserve blame for too much commending; nor reproof for detracting more than truth leads me; and as I have begun so indifferently, so will I continue as sincerely, and say somewhat of this noble gentleman Sir Francis Drake, who is to enter into the next rank of my discourse.

"There is no man so perfect but is fit to be amended; nor none so evil but he has something in him to be praised: and comparing the imperfections of Sir Francis Drake with his perfections, the world, and not I, shall truly judge of his merits.

"His detractors lay to his charge the baseness of his birth and education, his ostentation, and vainglorious boasting; his high, haughty, and insolent carriage; and except against his sufficiency for a general, though they allow him to be an able captain.

"His friends and favourers answer in his behalf, that the meanness of his birth was an argument of his worth; for what he attained to was by no other means than merit. They say, that every man is son to his works; and what one has by his ancestors can scarcely be called his own; that virtue is the cause of preferment, and honour but the effect; that a man is more to be esteemed for being virtuous than being called worshipful; the one is a title of honour, the other of desert.

"Marius, being upbraided by Sylla in the like manner for the baseness of his birth and haughtiness of carriage, answered, 'That he was not of so great a family as Sylla, yet Sylla could not deny but that he was the better man; for in Sylla's house were painted the acts of his fore fathers; but in his were hung up the banners that he himself had won from his enemy.'

"In vindication of Sir Francis Drake's ostentation and vain -glory, they say it was not inherent to him alone, but to most men of his profession and rank. It is true he would speak much and arrogantly, but eloquently, which bred a wonder in many, that his education could yield him those helps of nature. Indeed he had four properties to further his gift of speaking, (viz.) his boldness of speech, his understanding in what he spoke, his inclination to speak, and his use in speaking; and, though vain-glory is a vice not to be excused, yet he obtained that same by his actions, that facility in speaking, and that wisdom by his experience, that I can say no more, but that we are all the children of Adam.

"His friends further say, that his haughty and high carriage is somewhat excusable, when it appears not but in his command; for a general ought to be stern towards his soldiers, courageous in his person, valiant in fight, generous in giving, patient in suffering, and merciful in pardoning; and if Sir Francis Drake was to be praised for most of these virtues, let him not be blamed or condemned for one only vice. Many times where a man seeks obedience, it is imputed to his pride and high carriage; but if people's hate grew upon envy (as it is likely) it appeared greater than if it had been grounded upon injury.

"The exceptions against him by those that condemn him as an ill general are, his neglect of furnishing his fleet to the Indies in 1585; his not keeping Santo Domingo and Carthagena when he was possessed of them in that voyage; his weak preparation for such an expedition as that of Portugal; his promise to go up to Lisbon that voyage, and non-performance; the taking of the pinnace in his way to the Indies, which discovered his directions in 1595. All these I formerly handled: and refer the reader to the place where they are treated of; though something I will say of him, as he was a private captain, especially of his renowned voyage about the world, being the first attempt of that nature ever performed by any nation, except the Spaniards themselves; and it was the more honour to him, seeing that the Streight of Magelhaen was counted so terrible in those days, that the very thoughts of attempting it were dreadful. Secondly, that it had been but once passed, and but by one ship that ever returned into Europe, and at a period sixty-nine years before Drake's enterprize. His praise was, that he could carry a voluntary action so discreetly, so patiently, and so resolutely, in so tedious and unknown a navigation, the condition of seamen being apt to repine and murmur. But, lastly, and principally , that after so many miseries and extremities he endured, and almost two years spent in unpractised seas, when reason would have bid him sought home for his rest, he left his known course, and ventured upon an unknown sea, or passage, which we know had been often attempted by our seas, but never discovered.

"This attempt alone must silence all his detractors; for it shewed an extraordinary resolution in his person, a special desire to enrich and benefit his country, and a singular patience to endure the disasters and mishaps that befel them.

"And yet he must not go so clear without stain or blemish; for you must know, that though he deserved well in the direction and carriage of his journey, yet the ground of his enterprize was unjust, wicked, and unlawful, his design being to steal, and thereby to disturb the peace of princes, to rob the poor traveller, to shed the blood of the innocent, and to make wives widows, and children fatherless.

"No man had more experience of the inconstancy of fortune than he; for the nature of fortune is to bite when she flatters, and to strike when she is angry.

"What his birth and other deserts were, needs no reiteration. Fortune did much for him; but at his death she was angry with him: first, in that there was a doubt whether it was natural; secondly, and the best his friends can say, that it was caused by grief, for failing of his expectation in that voyage; thirdly, after his meritorious services, his heir was prosecuted and perplexed for debts and accounts to the Crown; and, lastly, died like Pizarro and Alma-gro, without a 'child to succeed him, and perpetuate his memory.'" [23]

But the people of Plymouth, in particular, can never forget the obligations they owe to Sir Francis Drake; indeed they have daily and hourly been put in mind of them, down to the present moment, by the enjoyment of one of the greatest blessings bestowed on mankind, a plentiful supply of good fresh wa-ter. "Plymouth," says Prince, "before his time was a dry town; and the inhab-itants were enforced to fetch their water and wash their clothes a mile from thence; but by his great skill and industry, he brought a fresh stream many miles unto this place." Its spring is on the side of Dartmoor, seven or eight miles in a direct line; but by leading the stream through valleys, wastes, and bogs, and cutting a passage for it through rocks which prolonged the length of its course three times the distance, he conveyed a clear, pure stream to the head of the town, from whence an abundant supply is afforded to the inhab-itants, and also to the seamen and mariners resorting to the port.

This work could only, at this time, have been conceived and accomplished by a man of his talents and ability, and in the short period of four winter months. The channel from the river Mew to the town is said to be twenty-five miles, but is reduced by the course pursued to eighteen miles. It was not however completed at the sole expense of Sir Francis. It appears from old records that a sum of about 350*l.* was granted by the corporation to pay the damages to the proprietors of the lands. The revenue derived to the town is, at the present time, about 2000*l.* a year, and is applied to public purposes. Sir Francis built several mills and divers conduits on the stream, of which he had a lease for sixty-seven years.

The Invincible Armada drew attention to all the southern ports of England and Ireland that were open to the assaults of the Spaniards, who, though subdued, still threatened to be troublesome. Plymouth was particularly ex-posed to attack, and no fort or works for its defence. Sir Francis Drake, there-fore, taking the mayor to his assistance, addressed a letter, apparently to Lord Burleigh (as appears by his Lordship's marginal minute that it had passed through his hands). In this letter is shown the readiness of Sir Fran-cis, not only to give them money, but also his personal assistance, and to set them the example. They ask in this letter that Lord Burleigh will move Her Majesty to contribute towards the building of a fort; that if 1200*l.* or 1000*l.* were granted, the inhabitants would never ask for more. [Lord B., in his own hand-writing in the margin, says 1200*l.*] That with such a fort they would be able to withstand the enemy, if they were 50,000 strong, for ten or twelve days at the least, till the forces of the country might come to their relief. That Sir Francis Drake would contribute, at the least, 100*l.* towards this object. They further request that Her Majesty would bestow on them eight or ten brass pieces of ordnance, and the rest they would themselves provide; stat-ing that they have thirteen pieces planted on the Hoe, borrowed from sundry

202

persons, and about twenty-three on St. Nicholas' Island, (since called Drake's Island,) the greater part whereof are likewise borrowed.

It further states, that such was the fear of being invaded, that many of the inhabitants conveyed their goods and themselves out of the town, and others would have followed, had they not been stopped by the arrival of Sir Francis Drake, who the more to assure them brought his wife and family thither. It further states the preparations they had already made on St. Nicholas' Island; and that on May-day, as is the custom yearly, 1300 men, well appointed, were mustered upon the Hoe; and from that day, Sir Francis Drake took order there should be watch and ward kept in the town every night, no less than if it were a garrison town; every master, as captain, to have the charge, and to watch with them himself till midnight, and then be relieved by his deputy.   This watch did Sir Francis himself begin on Friday last. [24]

When Sir Francis was at Plymouth, preparing for his last fatal voyage, and just a month before he sailed, he wrote a joint letter with Mr. Carey, to the Lords of the Privy Council, beseeching them to issue their warrant for training the companies, and repairing the bulwarks and trenches on the sea-coast, the Spaniards having the preceding year landed and burnt several places in the neighbourhood of Penzance, and threatened another invasion of England.

Whenever the exertions of Drake could be of use, publicly or individually, he was ever ready to afford his aid. It has been mentioned, that during his mayoralty he caused a compass to be erected on the Hoe-hill. Nothing of the kind is now to be found; and it has puzzled many to divine what this could be. It was there, however, in the year 1720, 137 years after Drake had placed it: this appears from a passage in an old work, [25] which says, "Between this town (Plymouth) and the sea is an hill, called the Haw (Hoe), on the top of which is a delicate level or plain, which affords a very pleasant prospect on all sides, and a curious compasse for the use of mariners." Little doubt then can remain that this compass was neither more nor less than a true fixed meridian line, from the centre of which perhaps were the points of the compass, such an instrument, at that time, being peculiarly *for the use of mariners.*

One more instance may be given of the ready and liberal support to any project of public utility. Hakluyt had in view the establishing a lecture in the lower part of London, on the art of navigation, for the saving of men's lives and property. "For which cause," says he, "I have dealt with the right worshipfull Sir Francis Drake, that seeing God hath blessed him so wonderfully, he woulde do this honour to himselfe and benefite to his countrey, to bee at the cost to erecte such a lecture: whereunto in most bountiful! maner at the verie first he answered, that he liked so well of the motion, that he woulde giue twentie poundes by the yeare standing, and twentie poundes more before hand to a learned man to furnish him with instruments and maps, that woulde take this thing upon him: yea, so readie he was, that he earnestly requested mee to helpe him to the notice of a fitte man for that purpose, which I, for the zeale I bare to this good actio, did presently, and brought him one, who came vnto him and conferred with him thereupon: but in fine he would not vndertake the lecture, vnlesse he might haue fourtie pounde a yeere standing, and so the matter ceased for that time: howbeit the worthie and good knight remaineth still constant, and will be, as he told me very lately, as good as his worde. Howe if God shoulde put into the head of any noble man to contribute other twentie pounde, to make this lecture a competent living for a learned man, the whole realme no doubt might reape no small benefite thereby." [26]

As a native of Devonshire, and by the frequent communications he had with Plymouth, he was so much attached to the neighbourhood, that in 1587 he purchased the house and domain of Buckland Monachorum of Sir Richard Grenvile, it having been the property of a society of Cistertian monks, whose house was suppressed in the reign of Henry VIII. The church of this convent was converted into a dwelling-house, and was the country residence of Sir Francis, and has always continued a residence of the Drake family. His town residence was an old royal palace near the Steel-yard, in Thames street, close by Dowgate Hill, called the Erber. Buckland Abbey is situated on the banks of the Tay, ten miles from Plymouth; and its many buildings show the grandeur and permanency of such edifices, though their uses and designs have long passed away. Here is a full-length original picture of Sir Francis, AN. 1594, aetatis 53, and a framed copy of his patent of arms. There is also a full length of the Admiral, with the sword and an old drum, which he had with him in his voyage round the world.

About a mile from the abbey is the village of *Buckland Monachorum,* which has a handsome church, within the walls of which are deposited the remains of some of the Heathfields and Drakes, to whose memory several elegant marble monuments have been raised. On that to General Elliot, Baron Heathfield, is a long inscription which thus concludes:

"He married Ann Polixen Drake, daughter of
    Sir Francis Drake, Bart.,
   Who lies interred near this spot;
And by her left a daughter, who was married to
    John Trayton Fuller, Esq."

The descendant of this gentleman took the name of Drake, the armorial bearings, and the property, was created a baronet in 1824, and is the present Sir Thomas Trayton Fuller Elliot Drake, of Nutwell Court, Buckland Abbey, Sherford and Sheafhayne house.

Hakluyt says, "Sir Francis Drake made his brother, Thomas Drake, and Captain Jonas Bodenham executors, and Mr. Thomas Drake's son his heir to all his lands except one manor, which he gave to Captain Bodenham." This may be correct as to his last will. In the records of the Prerogative Court of Doctors' Commons there are two wills, one dated (blank) day of August, 1595, apparently made in contemplation of going into action; he sailed from Plymouth on the 28th of that month. The other is dated the 27th January, 1596, the day before he died. In the first will, Anthony Prowse, William Strode, and Christopher Harris, are executors, and his cousins, Master Richard Drake and Thomas Barret, are named rulers and overseers of the will. By the last his brother Thomas was appointed sole executor, and by both, residuary devisee and legatee of real and personal estate.

It appears there was a suit in the Prerogative Court between the said executor and Dame Elizabeth, the relict; and that sentence was given in favour of the former, pronouncing for the validity of both wills.

Sir Francis Drake was twice elected to a seat in parliament; first, as burgess for the town of Bossiney (otherwise Tintagal) in the county of Cornwall, in the 27th parliament held by Queen Elizabeth; and again in 1592-93, as the representative of the borough of Plymouth, where there could not have been a dissentient voice; for to him and his unceasing exertions for the benefit and prosperity of that town, the inhabitants were indebted to a large return of gratitude - thus the poet says,

"Now Plymouth (great in nothing save renown,
    And therein greater far, because of Drake)
Seems to disdain the title of a town,
    And looks that men for city should her take;
    So proud her patron's favour doth her make;
        As those whom Prince's patronage extoll'd
        Forget themselves, and they were of old.

"Her now bright face, once loathsomely defiled,
    He purg'd and cleansed with a wholesome river;
Her whom her sister cities late reviled,
    Upbraiding her with unsavoury savour,
    Drake of this obloquy doth now deliver:
        That if all poets' pens conceal'd his name,
        The water's glide should still record the same." [27]

It does not appear that he took any general lead, or troubled himself much with politics. He did, however, take a leading part in the latter parliament; described, in a short speech, the King of Spain's strength, and cruelties wherever his forces came; and, as we have seen, was strenuous for means to meet them. He was the Queen's friend, and ever ready to exert his best faculties in her service; but he was no courtier, yet highly respected, and his advice sought for by the Queen's servants; among whom, it appears, he thought it right to follow a custom prevalent in the reign of Elizabeth, of presenting to her certain tokens of regard, on New Year's Day, in the shape of devices in gold, silver, or jewellery. It is recorded, that in 1583 was - "Geven by Sir Frauncis Drake, onne sault of golde, like a globe standing upon two naked men, being the historie of Jupiter and Pallas, with a woman on the top thereof, having a trumpet in her hand; the foot enamelled with flowers."

And, in 1586, - "Geven by Sir Frauncis Drake, a frame of fethers, white and redd, the handle of golde inamuled, with a halfe-moone of motherof-perles, within that a halfe-moone garnished with sparks of dy amends, and a few seede perles on thone side, having her majesty's picture within it, and on the backside a device, with a crowe over it." [28]

This silly custom of New Year's gifts was, by general assent of courtiers, laid aside in the early part of the reign of James I.

In the latter part of the life of Drake, from 1590 to his last fatal voyage in 1595, his whole time appears to have been employed in objects of public utility and private benevolence. He was unquestionably, in conjunction with his two friends and colleagues Sir John Hawkins and Sir Martin Frobisher, the principal founder of our naval celebrity. He it was who first introduced the aid of astronomy into practical navigation; who laboured in the establishment of naval discipline, and in the art of preserving the health and efficiency of the crew; it was he who taught our seamen the advantage of smartness, activity, and good seamanship, by which they learned not only to despise, but effectually to attack, the castellated galleons of the Spaniards, in their little barks of not one fourth part their size. In short, to repeat what has been quoted from Fuller, "This our Captain was a religious man towards God and his houses, generally sparing churches where he came; chaste in his life; just in his dealings; true to his word; and merciful to those who were under him; hating nothing so much as idleness." [29]

[1] Rymer's Foedera.
[2] Camden. - Hakluyt. - Lediard.
[3] D'Ewes.
[4] Monson's Tracts.
[5] Harleian MSS. British Museum.
[6] Hakluyt.
[7] Fuller's Holy State.
[8] Hakluyt.
[9] Hakluyt.
[10] Fuller's Worthies.
[11] Hakluyt.
[12] Hakluyt.
[13] Prince's Worthies of Devon.
[14] Fuller's Worthies.
[15] Stow's Chronicle of England.
[16] Fuller's Holy State.
[17] This old poem was reprinted in 1819 at the private press of Lee Priory, price fifteen shillings!
[18] Lopez de Vega.
[19] Strype.
[20] Hakluyt.
[21] Prince's Worthies of Devon.

[22] Purchas and others.
[23] Monson.
[24] Lansdowne MSS. British Museum.
[25] Magna Britannia et Hibernia Antiqua et Nova. Printed in the Savoy, 1720.
[26] "Divers Voyages touching the Discouerie of America, &c." In an epistolary dedication to Master Philip Sydney. By Richd. Hakluyt.
[27] Chs. Fitz-Geffry - Stanzas 133, 134.
[28] Nicholl's Progresses.
[29] Fuller's Holy State.

www.ingramcontent.com/pod-product-compliance
Lightning Source LLC
Chambersburg PA
CBHW030928090426
42737CB00007B/355